SELLING

THE

GREAT WAR

SELLING

THE

GREAT WAR

THE MAKING OF
AMERICAN PROPAGANDA

ALAN AXELROD

palgrave
macmillan

SELLING THE GREAT WAR
Copyright © Alan Axelrod, 2009.

First published in 2009 by PALGRAVE MACMILLAN® in the U.S.–a division
of St. Martin's Press LLC, 175 Fifth Avenue, New York, NY 10010.

Where this book is distributed in the UK, Europe and the rest of the world, this is
by Palgrave Macmillan, a division of Macmillan Publishers Limited, registered in
England, company number 785998, of Houndmills, Basingstoke, Hampshire
RG21 6XS.

Palgrave Macmillan is the global academic imprint of the above companies and
has companies and representatives throughout the world.

Palgrave® and Macmillan® are registered trademarks in the United States, the
United Kingdom, Europe and other countries.

ISBN–13: 978–0–230–60503–9
ISBN–10: 0–230–60503–6

Axelrod, Alan, 1952–
    Selling the Great War : the making of American propaganda / Alan Axelrod.
        p.   cm.
    Includes bibliographical references.
    ISBN 0–230–60503–6
    1. Creel, George, 1876–1953.   2. Politicians—United States—Biography.
3. Journalists—United States—Biography.   4. Political consultants—United
States—Biography.   5. United States. Committee on Public Information.
6. World War, 1914–1918—Propaganda.   7. World War, 1914–1918—United
States.   8. World War, 1914–1918—Public opinion.   9. Propaganda,
American—History—20th century.   10. Public opinion—United States—
History—20th century.   I. Title.
E748.C937A98   2009
324.2092—dc22

                                                                    2008029565

A catalogue record of the book is available from the British Library.

Design by Letra Libre

First edition: March 2009
10 9 8 7 6 5 4 3 2 1
Printed in the United States of America.

For Ian, on his way
And for Anita, still with me

CONTENTS

PREFACE

My mother and father were children in Chicago, five and seven years old, when President Woodrow Wilson took the United States into Europe's "Great War." They were adults when, twenty-four years later, the Japanese attacked Pearl Harbor and thrust the nation into World War II. To me, they always spoke of both wars in much the same way, as wars against ruthless dictators, to defend the United States, to save the world. They would certainly not have agreed with—perhaps not even have understood—the argument of many recent historians, that Woodrow Wilson made a grave error in committing America to World War I, that whereas World War II was a war of necessity, the earlier conflict had been, at least for the United States, a war of choice, and a bad choice at that.

Except for a small but vocal coterie of intellectuals, most of the generation of Americans who lived through World War I believed it was a righteous and necessary cause and were proud of the victory in which the United States, although a latecomer to the battle, was instrumental. They believed President Wilson when he explained that Americans were being asked to fight and die in a "war to end all wars" and a war to "make the world safe for democracy." Typical of that generation, my mother and father continued to believe this concept even though they also lived through World War II, which proved that the earlier conflict had neither ended war nor made the world safe for democracy. Although they were intelligent, rational people, this cognitive dissonance did not disturb them in the least. That is remarkable in itself, but what is astounding is the fact that their fathers, my grandfathers, had been moved to vote for the reelection of Woodrow Wilson in 1916 largely on the strength of his campaign slogan: *He kept us out of war.* Within less than half a year, those very same antiwar voters became enthusiastic (in many cases fanatical) supporters of war.

Ever since I studied World War I as an undergraduate—the draft card in my wallet bearing a II-S student deferment during those years of the Vietnam War—I wondered how so many Americans, determined to avoid war, could practically overnight become champions of a foreign war fought not in response to any attack but for the sake of a mere theory concerning the future of democracy and the future elimination of armed conflict. Vietnam was different, I thought. We had backed into it. No one was ever really enthusiastic about it. It was a mistake, and everyone knew it, even, deep down, those who still supported it. One thing seemed certain to me: The situation of World War I would never happen again—and certainly not once we were finally out of Vietnam. Unless national survival was clearly at stake, Americans would never again simply be talked into a war.

Then, deep into my middle age, on March 19, 2003, President George W. Bush took the United States to war against Iraq. Most of the country supported him enthusiastically as well.

In 1928, Edward L. Bernays published a little book he called *Propaganda.* "We are governed," he wrote, "our minds are molded, our tastes formed, our ideas suggested, largely by men we have never heard of." As he saw it, these men were, in fact, an "invisible government."[1] Bernays was in a position to know; widely regarded as the father of the American public relations industry, he was one of those men.

Bernays had honed his expertise in mind molding, taste forming, and idea suggesting during World War I, as a member of something called the Committee on Public Information. America's first dedicated ministry of propaganda, it was an agency brought into existence in April 1917 almost single-handedly by George Creel, a mostly self-educated newspaperman of whom not many in the nation had ever heard. One week after the United States entered the Great War, President Woodrow Wilson hired Creel to create a brand-new bureaucracy of thousands of men and women dedicated to selling their fellow citizens on what many Americans still called the "European struggle."

Just about everyone referred to the Committee on Public Information as the Creel Committee, and it controlled virtually every scrap of information America and much of the rest of the world received concerning the war. It did not rely on the censorship so much as the total monopolization of information, shaping news, shaping images, shaping emotions to create a reality in which President Wilson's war emerged as not merely desirable but inevitable. "The astounding success of propaganda during the war," Bernays wrote, "opened the eyes of the intelligent few in all departments of life to the possibilities of regimenting the public mind."[2]

Nazi Germany, Stalinist Russia, the totalitarian states in the interwar "Age of Dictators"—we think of them as the twentieth century's great factories of propaganda. In reality, working within the world's largest democracy to promote a war to "make the world safe for democracy," it was George Creel who carried out the century's first, most ambitious, and most successful experiment in propaganda. Putting a peculiarly American spin on the work, Creel candidly characterized it as a "vast enterprise in salesmanship."[3] By the end of the war, his name and that of his committee were on the lips of many. Some, including President Wilson, spoke the name in admiration and gratitude; others, including a host of congressmen and senators, pronounced it as a curse.

Today, Creel is little remembered outside of academic circles of historians and students of culture and media, but he and the work of his committee were apparently very familiar to such earnest students of propaganda as Adolf Hitler and Joseph Goebbels, both of whom looked to the American government's World War I "information" program as a model on which to build the propaganda industry by which, when the time came, they sold their own war to the people of Germany. Indeed, George Creel had built a machine whose effects were beyond his control or that of anyone else. Congress unceremoniously dissolved the Committee on Public Information on June 30, 1919, but the alumni of the enterprise, men like Bernays and his fellow public relations pioneer Carl Byoir, as well as the advertising giant James Webb Young of the J. Walter Thompson agency, went on to make their professions central to modern American life. Nor were the lessons of "invisible government" lost on those who were actually elected to govern. In World War II, during the cold war, and through the Vietnam era, the propaganda machine set into motion by George Creel in 1917–1918 continued to grind.

Dismayed and puzzled, like a growing number of Americans, over how Congress and the people could have allowed another president to talk the nation into another war to promote democracy, I began to see that, deep into the long shadow cast by the events of September 11, 2001, the ghost of what George Creel had wrought nearly a century earlier continued to haunt the national life. It will be a long time before we emerge from that shadow, and, until we do, it will be difficult, perhaps impossible, to write the history of the propaganda campaign that led inexorably to the American war in Iraq. Enough time, however, has passed to permit an understanding of the propaganda program that defined that European war of my parents' childhood.

Reaching this understanding is the purpose of my book. It may serve as a prelude to sorting out the bewildering and disordered turn our collective lives took in March 2003, setting us on a course without discernible direction or perceptible end. Even more, perhaps it will forestall, in some future year, by some other president, some other Congress, some other electorate, another such tragic detour.

Alan Axelrod
Atlanta, Georgia
July 2008

CHAPTER 1

MAKING OF A MUCKRAKER

When George Creel was born, on December 1, 1876, in Missouri, the Civil War had been over for more than a decade. No matter. The counties of Lafayette and Jackson—the western Missouri world into which Creel emerged—remained an unreconstructed bastion of the Confederacy. Creel was ten years old before he "knew any adult males except 'Southern colonels,'" and when he came home from school, his mother would quiz him on the day's history lesson only to indignantly correct his teacher: "The battle of Antietam, indeed! Why, honey, it was the battle of Sharpsburg, and we *whipped* them."[1]

As Creel felt obliged to confess, he "took in prejudices with mother's milk," prejudices that would exercise an enduring influence on his varied career lifelong—an influence far more profound than a regionally idiosyncratic interpretation of the Civil War. George Creel grew up with the conviction that history was first and last a particular version of a set of facts in time, and, to most people most of the time, it was the version that mattered more than the facts. To create a persuasive version of the facts was, therefore, to create history, and history, Creel believed, exerted a powerful hold on people, shaping their sentiments, forming their loyalties, and prompting their actions.

All around young Creel, the "Southern colonels" relived the Civil War as it *should* have been. The characters Creel recalled were braggarts and ring-tailed roarers seemingly torn from the pages of Missouri's own Mark Twain. The most eccentric of them were truly accomplished fabulists, creators of an egocentric reality they were skilled at weaving and unashamed in sharing. Young George loved to listen to Colonel John recount how he and "a young band of Southrons . . . beat back the iron heel of the invadah, armed only with squirrel guns, hoe handles, pitchforks, and other rude agricultural implements," falling "upon the blue-bellied hordes" and beating "them into dastardly flight." Another veteran piped in: "I was in that fight, and the Yankees whipped hell out of us." At which Colonel John groaned: "Oh, Lord! Another great story ruined by a goddam eyewitness."[2]

To anyone who might have looked in from the outside on Lafayette County (where Creel was born) and Jackson County (where he spent most of his early childhood), the reality of the hardscrabble region would have appeared dull and squalid. Poverty was the rule rather than the exception. Creel's father, Henry Clay Creel, had himself come to Missouri from the outside, having been raised near a tributary of the Ohio River, the Little Kanawha, in what was at the time the western fringe of Virginia (today West Virginia). The son of a Catholic, he had received a solid and urbane education in Cincinnati, at St. Xavier's, which helped earn him, on his return to Virginia, election to the House of Delegates. But he soon fell in with a fast crowd, and his father, Alexander Herbert Creel, sought to stave off his son's complete dissipation by packing him off to Missouri in 1860, with a pair of slaves, to start a farm in Osage County. He did not remain there long, however. When Virginia seceded from the Union, the young man rushed back to his home state and enlisted in a regiment as a captain. After Appomattox, he left Virginia, Missouri-bound once more.

The Creels were luckier than most other ex-Confederates. Alexander Herbert had managed to preserve a significant portion of his wealth and was able to give his son $10,000 in working capital to buy a large farm in Lafayette County, close to the home of the Facklers, among whose daughters was a girl named Virginia, as "slim and lovely" as Henry Creel was "romantically handsome."[3] The veteran captain and brand-new farmer married her in 1868 and, on the farm, in quick succession, three sons were born to them: Wylie, George, and Richard Henry, who would always be called Hal.

The $10,000 his father had given Henry Clay Creel should have gone a long way in Missouri. But it did not. Absent slaves and an overseer to work them, the farm in due course faltered and failed, sending Captain Creel on a headlong retreat into the bottle. By the time son George was born, the senior Creel was a confirmed alcoholic and the family was well on its way to bankruptcy.

That was when the revisionist visions of romantic glory should have ended. Henry Creel sold out at a loss and, because someone—George Creel never knew who—told him there was money to be made raising cattle, he impulsively moved his family southeast, to Hickory County. Predictably, the cattle-raising experiment soon went the way of the farm, taking with it what was left of the family's funds. The next move was back to western Missouri, to the town of Independence, in Jackson County, just west of George's native Lafayette County. Here, Virginia Creel assumed the full burden of supporting the family by taking in boarders. She struggled to shelter George and his two brothers, as well as her "guests," from the bibulous spectacle of Captain Creel. The boys were frequently awakened late at night by the noise of their father's saloon friends dragging him home. Mother would hurry George and his brothers back to bed "with the whisper that Papa was 'sick.' But how could he be sick, I wondered, when he was yelling and laughing?"[4]

Although George would learn to love the tall tales of the Southern colonels of Independence, in the process taking away valuable lessons about the malleability of "history," he also possessed from a very early age an unwillingness or inability to shut his eyes to ugly truths: *If his father was "sick," why was he laughing?*

Mrs. Creel had visions of her own—romantic, to be sure, but with a much harder edge than those of the "colonels" and her own besotted husband. Her grandfather had left Virginia for Missouri in 1842 and settled with nine of his ten children in Saline County, just east of Lafayette County. There, on a large tract of land, he replicated a piece of antebellum Virginia, building a white-columned plantation house, complete with slave quarters adjacent. But he did not idle in nostalgia for the bygone. Instead, he made a go of the farm, amassing sufficient wealth to send one of his sons to St. Louis to study medicine. The young man, George Creel's maternal grandfather, returned to Saline County to practice, but when his bride died, leaving him with a son and two daughters, he deposited the children into the care of his sisters, took down his shingle, and devoted himself ruthlessly to speculation in land.

In the meantime, his progeny were raised in female-dominated Southern gentility. Virginia Fackler, the girl who would become George Creel's mother, was given a classical education and, remembered to the end of her days her languages as well as her lessons in both ancient and modern history. She came into possession of a surprisingly wide range of experience. Whereas George's feckless father had nothing hard about him (save his drinking) and failed to outgrow the parochial fantasies of his antebellum upbringing, young Virginia came to know the Civil War at its most brutal in the guerrilla warfare of Missouri. When her father decided that life under Yankee occupation had become intolerable, he took his children and, with about twenty other disgruntled Missourians, set off in search of a new life in California. They settled in San Francisco, only to return to Missouri after the war.

Her early exposure to war and the world beyond her home made Virginia Creel a strong woman. Living with an impecunious drunk, she needed all her strength. After the Independence boardinghouse, like the Lafayette County farm and the Hickory County cattle ranch, failed, Virginia Creel decided to move from the cozy if poor community of Independence to the big, cold metropolis of Kansas City, which offered nothing more promising than the prospect of a larger and more profitable boardinghouse as well as the possibility of employment for her oldest son, Wylie, and even the middle son, George, neither of whom was yet out of grade school. For George Creel, his Missouri boyhood blended the turbulent streams of several narratives, each bearing a different life-shaping mythology. There were antebellum romance, chivalry, and a passionate attachment to lost causes. These streams washed up a feckless father and watered the charmingly confabulatory fertility of any number of "Southern colonels" living in Independence. Those same streams also nurtured a mother in whom heritage combined with hard and varied experience. When George Creel came to voting age, it was "with a passionate belief in equal suffrage," a belief informed not by any abstract theory of social justice but by the vivid example of his mother.[5]

If George Creel's experience taught him the force of personal mythology, he also learned from a young age something of what a more collective mythology could produce. He was deeply moved by Missouri history, including the story of Father Pierre-Jean De Smet, the nineteenth-century Jesuit missionary who set out from newly founded Independence for the Oregon Country. Creel learned about De Smet when he was a boy, and, many years later, in 1927, when he was making his living as a freelance writer, he included De Smet in a book called *Sons of the Eagle: Soaring Figures from America's Past.* Creel wrote that De Smet was the first white man to find gold in the West. "Crossing the Bitterroot Range, he stopped to drink at a mountain stream and looked down through the clear water to see a golden glitter among the pebbles." At first, "he knew a singing of the heart," believing he had found "wealth more than ample for all of his missionary labors," but then, "as though a shadow blotted the sun, he remembered his days among the Osages, the Potawatomi, and other Missouri River tribes and saw again the drunkenness and degradation worked by the greed of white men." He instantly understood that a single word of his discovery would fill the mountains with "adventurers drawn from every quarter of the globe, debauching the Indians and ending forever his dream of conversion." With this, De Smet dropped the nuggets back into the stream, then "wiped his hands as though they had been soiled, and ran as from an imminent peril."[6]

The story of Father De Smet, an icon of selflessness and self-sacrifice, added another stream to the Missouri narrative from which the career of George Creel would flow, this one the most abundant and powerful of all: idealism. Mingled with romance, realism, and the lure of a good story, idealism would drive a zeal for muckraking journalism and political and social reform, eventually sending George Creel into the arms of Woodrow Wilson, the ultimate American idealist, for whom war, even on a global scale, was the great test of national commitment to the noblest of ideals.

When George was twelve years old, the Kansas City boardinghouse, like the one in Independence, finally failed, and his family moved yet again, this time forty miles east, to the dusty little town of Odessa, where his maternal grandfather owned some land. George looked upon the old man with an intensity of mixed emotions. On one hand, John Fackler presented an example of achievement that stood in stark contrast to the utter failure of his father. He was a pioneering physician, dentist, nutritionist, and what today would be called an exercise guru; yet he quit his medical practice to speculate in land, and he made a fortune doing so. Despite his success, he withheld any financial aid to his daughter, always conditioning it on her separating from a husband he considered (not without good reason) worthless. Virginia Creel would not leave her man, however, and so neither she nor her children received a single dollar until they all moved to Odessa. At last, grandfather allowed the family "the grudging grant of a monthly pittance" and a tiny house on a small property he owned.[7]

On their patch of ground and with their pittance, George, his brothers, and his mother made do. The oldest, Wylie, stayed in Kansas City, where he found work and sent a portion of his salary to his mother. Mrs. Creel busied herself taking in sewing while George and Hal scratched away at truck farming on their small plot, peddling milk from Bess, a diminutive Alderney cow. During the summer, the boys hired themselves out for labor in the fields of neighboring farms, George shucking wheat alongside the adults and Hal riding lead horse to the binder, though his legs were hardly long enough for his feet to find the stirrups.

As always, it was George's mother who made even so hard an existence tolerable. Every night, "when she must have been ready to drop," she drew on her early classical education to tell George and Hal "stories that made dead heroes live again." She supplemented her own tales with books, including the novels of Sir Walter Scott, the poems of Henry Wadsworth Longfellow, Charles Dickens's *Child's History of England,* and juvenile versions of the *Iliad*. Even as an adult, Creel wrote, the Greek heroes Achilles and Ulysses, and the semilegendary Kentish brothers Hengist and Horsa, as well as other figures of myth and history were intensely real to him. He developed what he admitted was an unshakable faith in the printed word. When he encountered a handbill advertising a traveling show and promising "valuable presents" for every boy and girl who bought a ticket, he eagerly handed over the 15 cents he had earned shoveling snow. George brought home a list of the promised "valuable presents," pointing to a rocking chair, which he offered to get for his mother. Virginia Creel gently explained that "such costly articles could not possibly be given away for so small a price," but the boy persisted in pointing to the clear black type on the handbill page. In the end, she told her son to choose a pair of roller skates for himself rather than the rocking chair for her. Elated, he awaited the day appointed for the collection of his present. Yet when that day came, all the promoter had to give him was a tiny tin badge. "I burst into tears and made quite a scene, but when I reached home, still sobbing, there was Mother with the roller skates she had pinched herself to buy."[8]

It was but a tangible emblem of the gifts George Creel received from his mother's hands. To a love of literature, of narrative, of the printed word, she added compassion, understanding, and absolute loyalty. One day, while in school in Odessa, George passed a note to a girl in class. Intercepted by the teacher, the note was presented to the principal, who "came down to our room with a wolfish leer I still remember. First he read it aloud, not once, but twice, rolling his eyes and mincing his tone, and then gave me a brutal switching that raised welts. I told Mother all about it." The next day Virginia Creel accompanied her son to school and confronted the principal: "Georgie deserved punishment for breaking the rule, but discipline does not involve humiliation. If you knew anything about children, you would know that what you did to him was cruel and unforgivable."[9] With that, she took her son out of public school, put him in a private one, then pulled him out altogether and administered the rest of his education at home.

The childhood of George Creel was contradictory: harsh yet sheltered. Alive to everything about him, he nevertheless grew up an outsider, the son of a drunken, shiftless father yet also of a doting, industrious, ever-protective mother, a crusading woman willing to take on the world (or, at least, a school principal) for his sake.

Whatever else childhood taught George Creel, it impressed upon him the contradictory nature of reality itself—that you could be both scorned and loved and that you could be an outsider yet possess the keen awareness of an insider. Most of all he seemed to acquire a sense of the ambiguous, infinitely flexible connection between words and reality.

Apparent confirmation of his youthful world vision came in 1896, when the twenty-year-old Creel managed to get himself hired by the struggling Kansas City *World* as a $4-a-week reporter. Of this, his debut in journalism, he wrote years later, "I still wonder why the city editor . . . ever hired me, for my qualifications would not have gained admission to the kindergarten class in a modern school of journalism." Creel's first assignments included writing book reviews, which made sense, considering that he was an avid reader, but he was also assigned to churn out the paper's society/gossip column. Doubtless due to the desperation engendered by this assignment, impoverished social outsider that he was, he discovered in himself a fount of "ambition . . . backed up by demoniac energy, not to mention the conceit of ignorance."[10]

Yet desperation, ambition, and ignorance could carry Creel only so far. He executed his society column assignments by simply barging in on every Kansas City social event he caught wind of until, one fateful day, his editor commented to him that he wished he had his "cast-iron nerve," the "gall . . . to butt in on parties as if he were an invited guest and not just a reporter." At this, something snapped, and Creel suddenly found that he could not venture into the street "without thinking that fingers of scorn were being pointed at me."[11]

When he was assigned to get the dirt on an especially lurid local scandal, Creel quit, deciding on the instant to leave Kansas City for New York. A sympathetic passenger agent for the Wabash Railroad gave him a pass as far as Chicago, from where he obtained passage to New York in exchange for tending a shipment of cattle. It was a journey that might have been drawn from one of his mother's Homeric bedtime stories. The slow freight rolled for six days and five nights. Because the train stopped in no towns along the way, Creel could buy nothing to eat and subsisted on scraps tossed to him by marginally generous trainmen. After landing in Jersey City at four o'clock on a bitter February morning, he took the ferry to Manhattan and awaited daybreak on bench in City Hall Park. There he found a copy of the *Tribune* with an ad for a boardinghouse on the Lower East Side. By eight in the morning, he had negotiated a room and meals for $3 a week.

Creel gleaned the names and addresses of all the magazines headquartered in Manhattan and, a bundle of manuscripts under his arm, he made the rounds. Rejected everywhere he went, he burned his manuscripts in disgust and took refuge in a saloon offering a free lunch for the price of a beer. In conversation with the man on the stool beside him, he discovered his fellow imbiber was a joke writer, who let him know that Hearst and Pulitzer were inaugurating comic supplements and were paying a buck apiece for funny squibs and a quarter a line for comic verse.

With that, Creel betook himself to the public library in search of base metal he could transform into comic gold. He offered his first fruits to the joke editors at the *World* and the *American*. They passed, and when Creel submitted more, they passed again—and again, day after day. Just as the prospect of having to leave his Lower East Side flop loomed, a heavy snowfall blanketed the city, providing the providential opportunity of earning six blessed dollars shoveling: enough to pay for two more weeks of room and board, which coincided with two more weeks of rejection. Just when all seemed lost, the joke editor at the *Evening Journal* bought four squibs. It was as if the floodgates had opened. Creel began to sell pieces to all the major humor and general-interest magazines as well as the comic supplements of the *Evening Journal* and *Evening World*. By the end of 1897, he was earning $25 a week at a time when a factory employee earned $1.50 for a ten-hour day. Then the *American* put him on the full-time staff of its comic supplement, and, together with his ongoing freelance work, this brought his weekly wage to a lordly $40.

Creel came face to face with yellow journalism—at least through the rear door of the comics, writing copy for *The Katzenjammer Kids*, *Foxy Grandpa*, and *Buster Brown*, a job that gave him a glimpse of William

Randolph Hearst and brought him "into association with Morrill Goddard, head of whole Sunday supplement and the real father of yellow journalism." Gaunt and nerve-racked, "with a pair of mad eyes," Goddard confessed to Creel that his idea of a good paper "was to have the reader reel back after one look at the first page, screaming, 'My God! Oh, my God!'" Goddard suggested to Creel that he quit the comics and start writing "page thrillers," but, beholding the bundle of nerves to which such a career had reduced Goddard, he politely declined.[12]

With the outbreak of the Spanish-American War late in April 1898, Creel impulsively sought escape in combat and enlisted in a volunteer regiment, which, however, failed to be deployed. Unable to find an exit into war, Creel again came to hate what he was doing. In deep discontent, he struck up a relationship with a young New York poet named Arthur Grissom, who had just married the daughter of a rich Kansas City banker. The girl's parents were none too happy with the match, and, to appease them, the newlyweds decided to move to Kansas City—but not before Arthur had persuaded Creel to join him in a new venture, as associate editor of a brand-new weekly journal of opinion to be called *The Independent,* headquartered in Kansas City and to be financed by Grissom's father-in-law.

Homesick for Missouri and heartily sick of New York City, Creel agreed instantly, fled Park Row, entrained for Kansas City, alighted on the passenger platform of the Wabash Railroad station, and was met by Arthur Grissom, who bore the gloomy news that his miserly father-in-law had reneged on his pledge of support. No sooner did he hit Creel with this bombshell, however, than he dismissed it as a minor setback, claiming that, together, the two of them could canvass local merchants for all the start-up cash they needed. In the meantime, Grissom invited Creel to save living expenses by taking up residence with him and his new bride.

To Creel's astonishment, the plan worked. The pair trotted a sixteen-page dummy of *The Independent* from one store and office building to another, raising enough capital to bring out a full debut issue on March 11, 1899. Greeted warmly by the daily press, the journal looked as if it would certainly take off. Closer to home, however, there was deepening trouble. Mrs. Grissom walked out of the house her banker father had given to her and her husband. In December, the banker finally announced that his daughter had consented to seek a divorce. Grissom responded by suing the old man for breaking up the marriage. The banker offered $40,000 by way of settlement, on condition that Arthur consent to the divorce and leave Kansas City immediately. Agreeing to both of these terms, Grissom took off for New York and used a chunk of his settlement to begin publication of what turned out to be the highly successful *Smart Set.* As for Creel, at twenty-three, the former snow shoveler and joke writer found himself sole proprietor and editor-in-chief of *The Independent.* "Out of a naive respect for the printed word, I believed that every editor, even the humblest, had it in his power to be a Molder of Public Opinion, a Light for the Feet of the People. . . . I knew that I wanted to fight for the underdogs of life, but had no very clear idea how to go about it. What was the right gospel for me to preach in order to be a true guide?"[13]

He briefly flirted with the idea of wedding *The Independent* to the Communist Party but turned to softer socialism instead. Finding socialist theory heavy going, he switched to the Fabianism of H. G. Wells and George Bernard Shaw, only, at last, to be "repelled" by what he saw as a "dogmatism and an unwillingness to appreciate the value of intelligent opportunism."[14]

Driven, it would seem, less by a genuinely philosophical craving than by an urgent need to give his weekly some—*any*—editorial direction, Creel next embraced the radical economics of Henry George, the Philadelphian who advocated abolishing all taxes except those on the value of unimproved land. The "single-tax" bandwagon was crowded indeed, Henry George's 1879 book *Progress and Poverty* having sold more than 3 million copies. Much of the wealth created by social and technological advances in a free market economy, George argued, was effectively preempted—stolen—by landowners and monopolists through economic rents, which unjustly restricted access to natural resources, even as the government burdened productive activity with heavy taxes. Thus government policy promoted a kind of slavery. However, if land were taxed for its natural, as opposed to its improved, value, the state would not be obliged to tax any other kind of wealth or enterprise. In effect, only un-earned value would be taxed, whereas productive activity and progress would be freed from the burden of taxation.

Creel later confessed that his thinking at the time was "jumbled," but, amid this jumble, what he saw in Henry George was passionate re-form coupled to brilliantly persuasive clarity of expression. It was this combination that would always serve to attract Creel to any particular political figure, most fatefully, in years to come, to Woodrow Wilson. Discarding both communism and socialism, the young editor of *The Independent* decided that "the American form of government [was] the best system ever devised by man." What evils persisted in it could be corrected by the ballot, and what he now wanted people to vote for was the single tax in order to bring about an end to "the monstrous injustice of having individuals appropriate the wealth created by the community." To achieve this end, it seemed to him far preferable to use existing political parties rather than attempt to organize new ones from scratch. The choice of what party to use was simple. Creel was a Democrat by inheri-tance, and he believed that the Democratic Party was closer to the people than the Republican Party. Missouri had been overwhelmingly Demo-cratic since the end of the Civil War, but, lacking Republicans to fight against, Missouri Democrats fought each other, dividing into bitter fac-tions. In Kansas City, which dominated the state's politics, the two op-posed Democratic sects were denominated the Rabbits and the Goats.

From its inception, even before Grissom jumped ship, *The Independ-ent* had leaned toward the Rabbits, the Populist faction headed by the rough-and-tumble but basically honest Joe Shannon, as opposed to the Goats, whose dictator was Jim Pendergast, a city boss already infamous for being in the pay of big business, primarily the local brewers and "pub-lic service" corporations. In short order, Creel transformed *The Independ-ent* into the semiofficial organ of the Rabbits and rode the crest of reform that would soon be identified nationally with Theodore Roosevelt and the social activist authors Roosevelt would dub the "muckrakers." By aligning *The Independent* with the Rabbits, Creel made an instant transi-tion from theoretical reformer groping for a theory to a down-in-the-dirt crusader against all manner of political corruption in Kansas City. He became a muckraking knight-errant, doing battle against vest-pocket federal judges and crooked cops while also linking his weekly to the burgeoning national reform movement led by Theodore Roosevelt, Lincoln Steffens, and others.

George Creel, born outsider, had found a way in. Infinitely curious if woefully uneducated, and all but drowning in a roiling whirlpool of political theory, he grabbed on to the Rabbits, tied his brand-new weekly to them, and had reason to believe he had found his calling after all. *The Independent* and its editor prospered—for a time.

CHAPTER 2

MUCKRAKER ON THE MAKE

As editor of *The Independent,* George Creel became a prominent figure in Kansas City politics. He was in the forefront of protest against police corruption and voter fraud. In part, he was a roll-up-your-sleeves activist, tackling individual issues and individual politicians and officials one at a time, even if this meant risking a beating—or worse—at the hands of Pendergast goons. Yet Creel never seems to have greatly relished the rough-and-tumble aspects of the political process, and the pleasure he took in raising *The Independent* to at least local prominence would prove fragile and short-lived. In the very thick of heated political campaigning and crusading against corruption, his "pet proposal"—what he characterized as one of his most "ardent enthusiasms"—seems, at this remove in time, far more benign and certainly far less sensational than the role of a crusading journalist. Creel was passionate about his plan to use public schools as social and political centers for adults. "Even as each school is the center of a neighborhood, with attendance taking no account of politics, race, or creed, so would the gathering of adults in the buildings at night be a nonpartisan, nonexclusive meeting of the citizens of the neighborhood." Creel's hope was that providing neighborhood social centers in public schools would mean that discussion and debate of "public business" would no longer be confined to "the heat of a campaign" but would be continuous and ongoing.[1] He proposed nothing less than a modern incarnation of the acropolis of classical Greek democracy, a forum in which government really could be of the people and by the people.

From our own perspective, the idea may seem naive or quixotic, as, doubtless, it seemed to many of his contemporaries. Almost certainly, the system would have proved unwieldy, unworkable, and not truly representative of the people. But Creel never had the opportunity to test the proposal, since the Kansas City Board of Education considered the idea too controversial and turned him down flat. Despite its having been a nonstarter, the proposal was predictive of Creel's future role as the architect and czar of a great propaganda campaign. Having grown up on the margins of American society, George Creel embarked on careers that were all directed at penetrating to the innermost circles of influence and power. His career, varied as it was, was always about only one thing: moving the masses. He began with yellow journalism, which proved hollow. He moved on to political journalism, an effort—we are about to see—that was also fleeting. He then entered direct political action, as a publicist for Woodrow Wilson and, in the Great War, made his deepest inroads into the collective sentiment and will of the American people. His community center proposal was an early essay in creating an American community of ideas, from the bottom up, starting with the people. In 1917–1918, his wartime Committee on Public Information would also have as its object the creation of an American community of ideas, but, this time, it would be organized from the top down, starting with the chief executive of the United States.

The path to that wartime achievement was strewn with discontent. Creel had struggled to break into journalism in New York, only to find himself overcome with self-contempt when he finally achieved a measure of success. This made him an easy mark for Arthur Grissom, who hardly had to push to get him from New York back to Kansas City to serve as associate editor of *The Independent*. When Grissom left him holding the bag, Creel quickly groped for intellectual, philosophical, and political direction, hitched *The Independent* to the Rabbits, and made an unlikely success of the upstart weekly. He did not entirely subordinate the weekly to the cause of the Rabbits, but also used its pages for a variety of crusades, including on behalf of woman suffrage and women's rights and against social prudery and moral censorship. Another favorite target was quacks and quackery, pseudomedical practitioners and promoters of snake-oil patent medicines. In his campaigns against medical hucksters, Creel did more than merely crusade. He operated in the best muckraking mode, engaging in genuine investigative journalism to expose dangerous frauds and con artists on a case-by-case basis.

Impressive though much of the muckraking journalism of *The Independent* was—especially in the campaign against medical frauds—even this failed to sustain Creel's enthusiasm for very long. And whenever his enthusiasm flagged, he was rendered ripe for conversion by some "character." That was the word he himself used. His childhood had been rife with characters in the form of all those Southern colonels. In New York, too, he had met one after another, ranging from the joke writer encountered in a saloon—the man who got him started in yellow journalism—to Arthur Grissom. Now, growing bored with his weekly, despite its success, George Creel encountered the "prize specimen" of all the "characters" who had come his way.[2]

When Creel met him in 1906, Charles Ferguson was the pastor of a small Unitarian church on the outskirts of Kansas City. But he had also been a lawyer and a journalist and claimed that he used "the three sociological professions—the Law, the Church, and the News" to "diagnose the ills of the world" by means, as it were, of "triangulation." Perhaps it was the very scope of Ferguson's triangulated career that most appealed to Creel, who had himself donned and doffed one political-philosophical hat after another. In truth, however, Ferguson bore a resemblance to those medical quacks Creel had so recently exposed. He spoke little of the past, except to note that he had studied at a variety of universities, including Oxford and Heidelberg, and had apprenticed in law under James Coolidge Carter, a noted constitutionalist. Later he served as rector of Boston's Church of the Carpenter alongside the popular orator, writer, and moralist Edward Everett Hale. Then he moved to Toledo, Ohio, where he entered the orbit of the city's Progressive mayor Samuel Milton Jones (nicknamed "Golden Rule" Jones for his outspoken advocacy of the do-unto-others precept) and municipal reformer-journalist Brand

Whitlock as well as Newton Baker, another Ohio Progressive, who would serve as mayor of Cleveland from 1912 to 1915, before accepting, in 1916, appointment as President Woodrow Wilson's secretary of war.[3]

The chameleon qualities that would have made anyone else suspicious of Charles Ferguson seem only to have attracted Creel. He listened enrapt as Ferguson grandly dismissed the legislative reform program Creel, the Rabbits, and the entire Progressive movement advocated, calling it a false approach to the problems of democracy. Instead, he advocated what he described as a "university militant, a new intellectual and spiritual establishment strong enough to withstand both the seductions of the money power and the assaults of the mob." For Ferguson, this was no impulsive notion but the realization of an age-old dream. He explained to Creel that the Old World had been dominated, in succession, by three great visions of order: imperial Rome, followed by the earliest fathers of the Catholic Church, and then the medieval university, which promised to usher in "a world-wide republic of the arts and sciences." The promise failed in the realization, however, because it was overwhelmed during the Middle Ages by "all the morbid traditions of the past." Only a "rough-sketch" remained of the visionary medieval university, and Ferguson told Creel that transforming it into a "true civic order" was now "*our* job."[4]

Ferguson proposed petitioning the federal government to establish a university in the western American desert, "free from the greeds of private initiative and the raids of the freebooting money-maker." He talked Creel into transforming *The Independent* into *The Newsbook,* which would serve as the mouthpiece of a national movement to found a new civic order on the basis of the "university militant."

Ferguson explained that what "people wanted was a higher standard of living and a public organ to articulate that demand" instead of what they had, which was nothing more than a motley assortment of monthly and weekly magazines offering mere "mental lunches and literary vaudeville . . . an infinite outpour of anodynes, a million inducements to spend their time and money, and to relax and scatter their wills."[5]

He wanted *The Newsbook* to serve as a high-level news digest, its editors and writers—the digesters, as it were—constituting "an association created in the spirit that exulted in artistic and scientific achievement," a group utterly "divorced from the profit motive," the "National Fellowship of the University Militant." Creel later claimed that he repeatedly endeavored to hold Ferguson off, but by the end of 1907, he found himself, over the protest of Rabbit leaders and others who had an interest in *The Independent,* helping the charismatic zealot recruit members for the organization. Astoundingly enough, a galaxy of muckrakers, Progressives, and others, mostly prominent writers and journalists, readily signed on, including the popular philosopher-moralist-publisher Elbert Hubbard; the muckraking Chicago journalist Ray Stannard Baker; Charles Zueblin, pioneering professor of sociology at the University of Chicago; Henry M. Alden, editor of *Harper's Monthly;* Julian Hawthorne, the journalist-novelist son of Nathaniel Hawthorne; Ida Tarbell, whose 1904 *History of the Standard Oil Company* was the archetypal work of muckraking journalism; iconoclastic Chicago architect Louis Sullivan; and Edward Everett Hale.

Ten of the members of the National Fellowship convened in New York at the National Arts Club on January 11, 1908, and there approved Ferguson's nomination of Creel as leader of the "journalistic branch" of the organization. Creel's opening mission was to bring out *The Newsbook* as the first link in a chain of weekly newspapers that would be published in all of the nation's major cities. This chain, to be called the Municipal University Press, would serve to create and disseminate what Creel later called the National Fellowship's "propaganda," which was aimed (as Ferguson put it) at winning and holding "the balance of power in American communities" by creating a "university of the people," which would "subordinate all sects, parties, and special interests to the paramount interest of civilization, to wit, the raising of the general standard of living through the practical achievement of science and the humanities."[6]

In the highest of hopes, Creel launched *The Newsbook* on March 7, 1908. He was forced to kill it on June 27 of the same year. It was, he admitted, "a monumental flop. Not only did we fail to make the diggers think and thinkers dig, but we confused readers to a point where they canceled subscriptions in droves. As for advertisers, they wanted to know

what in hell I thought I was doing, and turned away coldly from my ex-
planations."[7]

Charles Ferguson's response to the demise of *The Newsbook* and the
end of the National Fellowship of the University Militant was uncharac-
teristically laconic: "George! Oh, George! What a mess you've made of
it."[8] With that, he left for New York, published a small book titled *The
University Militant* in 1911, later cadged an appointment by Woodrow
Wilson to make some economic studies overseas, then—according to
Creel—effectively dropped off the edge of the earth.

Creel set about reviving *The Independent* by mounting a door-to-door
campaign in Kansas City to win back his alienated subscribers and advertisers. Remarkably, by New Year 1909, he had clawed his way out of
insolvency.

Not only had Creel rescued his weekly, but, by this time, all of the
laws for which *The Independent* and the Rabbits had fought were on the
books and Kansas City had elected an anti-machine mayor. With all local
problems apparently solved, Creel was left to ask himself: "Where was
the point of staying put?" Unable to answer his own question, he offered
The Independent for sale. Several likely purchasers made inquiries, but
when no deal finally crystallized, Creel confessed that he "broke out in
one of my usual sweats."[9]

Of all unpleasant sensations, there was one Creel was powerless to
endure: the complete panic brought on not by failure but by success.

To strive was exciting; to achieve—apparently, that was intolerable.
He therefore called in Clara Kellogg and Katherine Baxter, two women,
quite apolitical, whose public interest was confined solely to running the
local job-printing shop that produced *The Independent.* George Creel
summarily turned *The Independent* over to them. He later confessed that
giving away the journal had been a "headlong business," especially inas-
much as he had "not even thought about where I would go or what I
would do." Objectively regarded, this was crazy, dangerous, crazy behavior—and would have been such in anyone. In George Creel, however, it
was also part of a pattern, an evident compulsion to involve himself

deeply only to cut loose and, once he was entirely at loose ends, to render himself receptive and vulnerable to whatever new "character" happened to come his way. True to form, no sooner had he shed *The Independent* than he was assaulted by one Arthur Stillwell. [10]

In later years, Creel admitted that his experience with Charles Ferguson (let alone with Arthur Grissom just before him) should have given him "sense enough to break and run," but, instead, "I found myself agreeing to go with [Stillwell] to Mexico."[11]

The phrase is most telling: *I found myself agreeing.* As a reform-minded journalist, George Creel was all about leading change, shaping opinion, creating public sentiment, mobilizing the collective will, and yet he repeatedly demonstrated a remarkable paucity of self-direction. At times, it seemed as if he possessed no core controlling sentiment, perhaps no core at all, but instead a passive receptivity to whatever powerful personality happened along to move him.

When Creel encountered him, Stillwell was middle aged, having lived through a "succession of minor failures" that culminated in a sudden decision to become an empire builder—not an empire of mind, as was the case with Charles Ferguson, but a physical empire in the form of a railroad running from Kansas City to the Gulf of Mexico. Despite a total absence of experience in railroading, Stilwell persuaded Dutch investors to fund the project.

As Creel portrayed them, both Ferguson and Stillwell were prey to delusions of grandeur, each man animated by a spectacularly inflated self-assessment. Nevertheless—and this is the most telling feature of these "characters"—they possessed an ability to persuade not just George Creel but the likes of Woodrow Wilson (in the case of Ferguson) and various investors (in the instance of Stillwell). We cannot, therefore, simply dismiss Creel as impulsive or even gullible—although he was, to significant degree, both of these things. The point of Creel's encounters with Ferguson and Stillwell was not that he was easily misguided but that he embraced almost anyone capable of effectively motivating perception, sentiment, desire, will, and action. Whatever else he took away from his encounters with these two men, Creel was exposed through them to the limitless potential of persuasion. It was, Creel learned, a force sufficiently powerful to move him, to shape his actions, his very life, time and again, even when he should have known better.

Stillwell's scheme to build the Kansas City Southern Railway was soon hijacked by some Wall Street sharks, but this only led him to a far grander railroad project. The "Kansas City, Mexico, and Orient Railway" came to Arthur Stilwell in a dream, which revealed to him a map of the United States and Mexico. Out of the surrounding darkness, an angel shape materialized with fingers of fire that traced a line from Kansas City to the obscure Mexican port town of Topolobampo, on the Gulf of California in northwestern Sinaloa, a port of embarkation to points east, including Asia. The angel shape had a godlike voice as well as fingers of flame. "Build a railroad!" it commanded.[12] With this, Stillwell awoke, embarked on another succession of European prospecting journeys, recruited more investors, brought them to the States, then transported the capitalists in luxurious private rail cars to the presidential palace in Mexico City, where the dictator Porfirio Díaz feted them, sang the praises of Stillwell's visionary genius, and persuaded them to invest in Mexican government bonds for the construction of the railroad.

Creel accompanied Stillwell on one of these Mexican train rides and was appalled by the scenes of poverty that materialized through the windows at every stop. Díaz was pliable to the will of the United States government and thus had been touted by the administration of President William Howard Taft as an enlightened leader. Creel had not questioned this assessment until he saw Mexican living conditions with his own eyes, especially in the state of Chihuahua. The governor of that state was one Enrique Clay Creel, a cousin whose father, a Virginian, had fought in the U.S.–Mexican War of 1846 to 1848 and who had remained in Mexico after the Treaty of Guadalupe Hidalgo ended that conflict. Don Enrique, an intimate of Díaz, was affable and courteous, and, because he was family, George Creel spoke frankly with him about the obscene injustice of a society in which the grinding poverty of the many supported the extravagant wealth of the few.

Whatever George Creel may have hoped to achieve by this shoot-from-the-hip talk, all he got was a predictably bitter argument from Cousin Enrique. George Creel returned to Stillwell's train, persuaded that Mexico would be swept by revolution again soon—and that it would be a most welcome event. When, on the return trip to the States, Creel shared these sentiments with Stillwell, the entrepreneur hurriedly ushered him into the baggage car and confined him there so that his investors would not be discouraged. And in this way, Creel's relationship with "Don Arturo" came to an abrupt end.

Back in Kansas City, paperless—indeed, jobless—George Creel confronted the issue of what to do next. He thought of going to Europe, but when his mother objected, he resolved to return to New York for a fresh assault on magazine work. While packing and attending a round of farewell parties, "who should bob up with the offer of a job but Fred Bonfils and Harry Tammen. Two more characters!"[13]

In 1895, Bonfils and Tammen bought the bankrupt Denver *Post* for $12,500 and by 1909 had built it into a $10 million publishing enterprise. The partners could not have been more different from one another. A West Point graduate of Corsican lineage, Frederick Bonfils was darkly handsome, dynamic, yet possessed of a dignified and even reticent manner that belied what Creel described as his "feral eye," a feature calling to mind "a man-eating tiger." Detractors—and their numbers were legion—accused him of having founded his fortune on shady deals in Oklahoma land and oil. Shady deals there were, to be sure, but, in fact, he had made his first real money mainly from running the notorious "Little Louisiana" lottery in Kansas City, Kansas. Whereas Bonfils was dark, tiger-eyed, and quietly dignified, Harry Tammen was blond, short, and pudgy, with kewpie-doll blue eyes set into a round, pink, infantile face that was frequently contorted into the grotesquely hilarious expressions of a born clown. Unlike Bonfils, who sought to cloak the unsavory origins of his wealth in the refined garments and guise of a gentleman, Tammen made no secret of where he had come from and how he had risen. He began life, he boasted, as a journeyman bartender, with no capital other than a "Dutch haircut and white watch." He told anyone who would listen that, when tending bar, his practice was to toss "up the dollars as they rolled in. If they stuck to the ceiling, the house got 'em."[14]

Under the ownership of Bon and Tam, as they were popularly known, the Denver *Post* rapidly acquired a reputation as "the Coney Island of journalism," yellower than anything Hearst or Pulitzer had dared to dream of. This was not to be marveled at, since Bon and Tam's other major enterprise was a circus, and this fact, combined with the reputation of the partners and their paper, prompted Creel to spurn their offer of a job. That is when Bonfils turned on the charm, explaining that he and his partner wanted to hire Creel precisely because they intended to dedicate the *Post* "to the public service without favor, fear, or faltering" And, toward this end, they would give Creel virtually unlimited editorial control.[15]

Could he believe any of this? Two things persuaded Creel that he could. First, as Bonfils spoke, his dark visage "glowed with the zeal of Peter the Hermit," and, second, "It may be an essential weakness, but I have never been able to resist characters."[16]

Thus George Creel took his packed bags and headed for Denver instead of New York. The new employee was never quite sure whether he was working for the newspaper Bon and Tam owned or for their circus, since the *Post* building was daily overrun by brass bands, fully costumed Indians, baby llamas, bearded ladies, and pygmy elephants. On occasion, a "human fly" crawled across the facade, "and when the balcony was not occupied by singers, evangelists, or acrobats, Bonfils would rush out with a canvas bag and scatter pennies to the populace."[17]

Despite what Creel himself characterized as bedlam, he managed to turn out a signed article every day. For the Sunday edition, he was given an entire page to do with as he pleased. It was sufficient to mollify, if not satisfy, Creel for some six months, but, as with Kansas City in the reign of the Goats, Denver was dominated by corrupt urban machine politics, and Creel was eager to begin the kind of journalistic crusade he had carried out in *The Independent.* When he would bring up the subject with Bon and Tam, however, they would invariably put him off until, at length, worn down by Creel's insistence, they gave him license to conduct a series of Progressive crusades. Creel embarked on editorials promoting public initiative, referendum, and the right of recall; a direct primary to elect senators; the installation of a commission form of city government in Denver to replace the corrupt mayoral system; the creation of a railway commission with genuine regulatory authority; endorsement of a constitutional amendment to create a graduated income tax; and the municipal ownership of public utilities.

He then proposed to Bon and Tam that the *Post* back the organization of a new Citizen's Party, which would field its own handpicked slate of candidates for all state and county offices. The partners agreed, and, on the Friday before the election, Creel poured forth an editorial lead fulsome in its starry-eyed enthusiasm: "On Tuesday every man and woman will have opportunity to strike a blow for a free state, a free city. . . . The ballot becomes a gleaming sword and the shabbiest jacket a gift of splendid armor. It is an adventure . . . . For the People! Say that word over. People! *People!* Why, it grows electric! It thrills!"[18]

Creel could hardly wait for Saturday's edition, which was to print the *Post*'s endorsements. But when he saw it, he noted that the key nominees for sheriff, county clerk, and coroner were missing and three "machine" men, including one notorious for election fraud, were in their place. Leaving behind a hastily composed letter of resignation, Creel set off for New York City.

Impulsive, even mercurial, George Creel sought stability not in the socioeconomic status quo but in a perpetual crusade against that condition. Always looking for a "character" with whom to identify, Creel believed he had found in Theodore Roosevelt not only the archetypal character of the great crusader but, through him, a bridge between the profession of journalism and the cause of social justice. Because TR had supported the efforts of such reform crusaders as Lincoln Steffens, Ray Stannard Baker, David Graham Phillips (the muckraking journalist whose articles helped achieve ratification of the 17th Amendment, providing for direct popular election of senators), and Ida Tarbell, Creel returned to New York in the spring of 1911, hopeful of carrying on his portion of the crusade through the pages of the many national magazines headquartered in the city.

But something had changed. Five years earlier, on March 17, 1906, speaking to an audience in Washington, D.C.'s Gridiron Club, President

Theodore Roosevelt had given the speech in which he inspired coinage of the term "muckraker" to apply to the investigative journalists of whom he had so long apparently approved. What he said that evening was not quite a condemnation, but it was no shining compliment either. He compared the journalists to the "Man with the Muck-rake," in John Bunyan's allegorical *Pilgrim's Progress,* "the man who could look no way but downward, with the muck-rake in his hand; who was offered a celestial crown for his muck-rake, but who would neither look up nor regard the crown he was offered, but continued to rake to himself the filth of the floor." Roosevelt conceded that the "filth on the floor . . . must be scraped up with the muck-rake; and there are times and places where this service is the most needed of all the services that can be performed. But the man who never does anything else, who never thinks or speaks or writes, save of his feats with the muck-rake, speedily becomes, not a help to society, not an incitement to good, but one of the most potent forces for evil."[19]

Creel later came to regard this speech as the beginning of Roosevelt's renunciation of Progressivism; however, he journeyed to New York in 1911 apparently believing that the old Rooseveltian spirit still prevailed. Once he began making the rounds of the editors, however, he perceived that this spirit had vanished from every office save that of William Randolph Hearst's *Cosmopolitan,* whose banner writer, Charles Edward Russell, championed Creel with the magazine's editors.

Cosmopolitan sent Creel to cover such powerful political demagogues of the day as the Mississippi senator James K. Vardaman, known as the Great White Chief because his advocacy of white supremacy had led him, when he was governor of the state from 1904 to 1908, to openly sanction the lynching of African Americans as a necessary means to what he deemed a desirable end. Creel was also dispatched to Cincinnati to interview George B. Cox, dean of America's big city bosses. When Creel mentioned to him "the great names in Ohio politics and referred to them as his lieutenants, he grunted contemptuously. 'Lieutenants! That's a laugh. They're my *dogs.*'"[20] Clearly, with or without the driving force of Teddy Roosevelt, there was still plenty of need for national social and political reform.

Creel had the savvy to see through the likes of Vardaman and Cox, but he also shared their rural Populist roots. He never really became a New York sophisticate. True, he made his home in Greenwich Village, because he understood that it was the neighborhood of the liberal intelligentsia, but the most prominent of his Village neighbors—anarchist Emma Goldman, IWW leader "Big Bill" Haywood, and those with a passion for the works of Freud and Jung—seemed "cheap and frowsy" by comparison to the generation of mostly midwestern and western reformers he had worked with in the preceding decade.[21] Thus when *Cosmopolitan* sent him west on a story in September 1911, he was highly receptive to an offer to join the *Rocky Mountain News* as an editorial writer.

Highly receptive, but not nearly as headlong as he had been in the past. The paper was published by former Democratic senator Thomas M. Patterson, whom Creel considered a political kindred spirit. This notwithstanding, he withheld his acceptance of the job offer until he had sat down with Patterson and thoroughly outlined what he wanted to do at the *News,* which was to carry out "a finish fight" against the utility corporations that controlled Colorado and its cities. Virtually every public official, including those in the courts, were in the pay of the utilities, which were collectively known as the Big Mitt, the controlling corporate trusts. Patterson agreed, and thus George Creel left New York yet again and set up in Denver.

As a result of his unrelenting campaign in the pages of the *News,* Creel had, by early December 1911, collected thirty thousand signatures on a petition to call a special election to vote on instituting a commission government for Denver and managed to end the reign of the Big Mitt.

George Creel's journalistic campaign in the *Rocky Mountain News* transformed him from writer to office holder. While his employees wildly celebrated the electoral victory, Senator Patterson refused to be dazzled. He predicted that neither the new mayor, Henry Arnold, nor the others who had been ushered into office as reformers would act in accordance with their pledges to bring about a commission government for Denver. The lure of elective office was simply too strong. Patterson insisted on putting one of his own people in a strategic position to enforce the pledges, and the most strategic position, he declared, was the office of police commissioner. Creel was tapped to serve.

He was reluctant, yet, once in office, Creel went far beyond his ostensible brief, which was merely to keep the new city government honest. In effect, he emulated his former Progressive hero, Theodore Roosevelt, who had served as president of the board of New York City Police Commissioners from 1895 to 1897, a period during which he radically reformed the notoriously corrupt department. Creel set about smashing the police machine that aided and abetted Big Mitt vote fraud, then instituted a new system of traffic control and made a move against illegal gambling. Both of these initiatives met with widespread public approval, but when, as a means of ending police brutality, he issued a directive that deprived police officers of their billy clubs, there was a general outcry and predictions of a reign of criminal terror. This wail of protest, however, was practically drowned out by the one that followed his next order, which permitted the radical IWW labor union—the International Workers of the World—to meet in Denver. Creel did not like the Wobblies, as they were known, but he believed in free speech and was confident that, provided the IWW was confronted by none of the official resistance its leader, Big Bill Haywood, actually craved, the organization would descend upon Denver then leave, not with a bang but a whimper.

That this proved to be the case did not stop the conservative Denver press, the *Post, Times,* and *Republican,* from attacking Creel as a crackpot. One anonymous versifier dubbed him "George Lochinvar Creel," a knight-errant who "came out of the West":

> His ideas were naked, his reforms undressed,
> And save his good nerve, he weapons had none,
> But he boomed into office like a 13 inch gun.
> So erratic in politics, abnormal by far,
> There ne'er was reformer like Creel Lochinvar.
> He stayed not for horse sense, and stopped not for reason,
> He flew into air at most any old season . . .
> A reformer in peace and the real thing in war,
> No one could rave on like Creel Lochinvar.[22]

In true knightly fashion, Creel launched his most ambitious crusade of all, this time against prostitution. In Denver, the flesh trade took the form of the infamous "crib system," in which a kind of improvised street was fashioned between a shantytown row of cubicles, each cubicle ("crib") harboring a half-naked woman beside a soiled bed and a dirty washbowl. The city had long winked at prostitution, but Creel decided to clean it up. Instead of simply cracking down and making arrests, however, he proposed taking over a 266-acre farm owned by the city and building public hospitals and dormitories on it to rehabilitate the prostitutes as well as drug addicts, drunkards, and other social outcasts. As a stopgap, until the facilities could be built, he issued orders closing the usual fronts for prostitution, barring minors from the crib district, and forbidding the sale of alcohol there. Also reasoning that certain amusement establishments were connected with prostitution, Creel hired Josephine Roche as inspector of public amusements—in effect, the first woman police officer in Denver. The daughter of a wealthy Colorado mine owner, the Vassar- and Columbia-educated Roche had already proven herself as a dynamic social worker in the slums of New York. She approached her job with great sympathetic imagination. Instead of rounding up the owners of prostitution-fronting amusement facilities and throwing them in jail, she "talked heart to heart with every proprietor, showing him the evil effects on children and appealing to his own love of family." As Creel judged, "her approach made a friend and supporter of every dance-hall man and rink owner." [23] As Denver police commissioner, Creel, like Roche, sought to do his job by influencing, coaxing, and molding public behavior rather than coercing change. Persuasion, both individual and collective, seemed to him far more compelling than any attempt at forced compliance or conversion under duress.

Creel's use of moral suasion to curb prostitution in Denver also developed into a crusade against the spread of sexually transmitted diseases. That venereal disease was a socially taboo subject appealed to the maverick in Creel. He was always ready to challenge social norms and social complacency. But, again, his aim was to change rather than to punish behavior. He dispatched police patrols to arrest prostitutes, who were subsequently arraigned in court, the judge automatically continuing each case for ten days, so that blood tests could be made. By the time each woman was rearraigned, the results of the tests would be in, and those who were found to be infected were committed to the county hospital for treatment. In all of this, Creel believed that nothing "was more necessary than to gain the co-operation of the sullen, resentful women by convincing them that it was not a mere 'moral crusade,' but a reclamatory movement largely in their own interest." This was not a ploy, but the application of another basic principle of social engineering. Assuming that people naturally want to act in ways that further their own self-interest, Creel sought the means of demonstrating that the social good and the individual good were one and the same. In this, he discovered the core principle behind all truly effective propaganda: the conflation of self-interest with social purpose. Once again Creel worked closely with Josephine Roche, whose "sympathy and understanding won the great majority [of arrested prostitutes] to the hope of a new and better life, many coming in voluntarily."[24]

Creel's crusade against the spread of venereal disease was not cheap, but, convinced that "people, put in the possession of the facts," typically make the "right" decisions (by which Creel meant the decisions that responsible leaders want them to make), he carefully compiled relevant statistics on arrests, voluntary surrenders, diagnoses, and treatments, then published them.[25]

People in possession of the facts did indeed make the right decisions, but Police Commissioner Creel kept pushing, and when he proposed a resolution before the Denver Board of Commissioners that police officers and fire fighters be forbidden to drink at any public bar while in uniform and that, furthermore, all members of the board "submit themselves to the same discipline," his colleagues pushed back, hard.[26] Mayor Henry Arnold called for his resignation, and when Creel refused, the mayor suspended him—whereupon he demanded a public trial. The result was the exposure of corruption within the administration, and although Creel's suspension was upheld, the people of Denver took note and voted in favor of the commission form of government for which Senator Patterson and Creel had crusaded.

George Creel's victory left him with a familiar problem. His enemies all vanquished, what was he to do next? He did not want to continue in city politics or embark on the larger political career Patterson urged on him, "for I had returned to my old belief that a writer with convictions was far more valuable outside office than in." Complicating the decisions that now faced him was a personal matter. In November 1911, he had married Blanche Bates, who had earned national fame as one of producer-playwright David Belasco's biggest stars in such Broadway sensations as *The Darling of the Gods* (1902) and *The Girl of the Golden West* (1905). She gave up—or at least suspended—a brilliant stage career to accompany her husband to Denver. Although he made a name for himself there, his various campaigns had left him almost penniless, and he entertained no illusions that a $60-a-week Denver newspaperman's salary would suffice to support both him and his glamorous wife. Even more urgent than financial considerations was Blanche Creel's intense unhappiness at the social ostracism that Big Mitt continued to wield against Creel and his circle; the Creels were barred from the city's fashionable clubs and even from most of its prominent homes. Yet worse was the unending stream of lies and attacks, both public and personal, some coming in the press, others in obscene, anonymous letters. Pressed by financial need, by the discontent of his bride, and perhaps most of all by his own footloose impulsiveness, George Creel resolved to leave Colorado and try his fortunes, yet again, in New York City.

CHAPTER 3

TOO PROUD TO FIGHT

George Creel left the Mile-High City early in 1913 and watched the rapid unraveling of reform in Denver from a distance of some eighteen hundred miles. Senator Thomas M. Patterson retired in October 1913, shortly after Creel left, selling the *Rocky Mountain News* to Chicago publishing mogul John G. Shaffer, who, one by one, backed off from the paper's many crusades for reform. With the mainstreaming of what had been the city's maverick daily, Denver inexorably returned to the ways of machine politics.

As for Creel, he tried to devote his full attention to making some real money for a change, but he could not bring himself to abandon Progressive causes. Shortly before he left Denver, he organized a Woodrow Wilson club among local Democrats to support the candidate's run for the White House. Creel traced the beginning of what he characterized as his devotion to Wilson back to his days in Kansas City, when, in 1905—and quite by chance—he heard this professor of political science and president of Princeton University speak to a high school audience. Recalling this event on page 101 of his 1947 memoir, Creel wrote that the topic of Wilson's address was the meaning of democracy. Forty-seven pages later, he wrote that Wilson had spoken that afternoon on the cultivation of the mind and the reading of books. Creel's failure to remember precisely Wilson's subject says as much about Creel as it does about the future president. "What thrilled me was not merely the clarity of his thought," Creel wrote, "the beauty of his phrasing, but the shining faith of the man in the *practicality* of ideals. More than any other, it seemed to me that he voiced the true America—not the song that people sing when they remember the words, but the dream of liberty, justice, and fraternity." For Creel the romantic idealist, the Lochinvar, the content of Wilson's message was less important than its emotional and spiritual effect. To him, the great appeal of Wilson was not his prodigious intellect but his faith that ideals— the stuff that constituted the dream of America—could be realized practically. It was the very same faith that had long animated Creel himself, who was always far less interested in objective, balanced journalism and intellectual analysis than he was in mobilizing popular sentiment to make the ideal real in society. It is quite possible to imagine that Woodrow Wilson was for Creel but one more "character" whose appeal could not be resisted; yet Creel's response to Wilson was probably representative of the wider popular response to the man. "Sometimes people call me an idealist," Wilson declared in one of his many speeches supporting United States membership in the League of Nations. "Well, that is the way I know I am an American. America is the only idealistic nation in the world."[1]

As early as 1905, after he had first heard Wilson speak, Creel used *The Independent* to tout the man for president. He also set out to read everything he had written—Professor Wilson was a prolific historian of American government—and closely watched his fight both to improve and to democratize Princeton University. Even more closely, he monitored Wilson's entry into politics as governor of New Jersey. Ushered into office by the state's corrupt Democratic machine—the bosses believed that the academic would be the ideal front man, squeaky clean, but naive and therefore infinitely pliable—Wilson no sooner took office in 1911 than he embarked on a program of vigorous Progressive reform that proved far too popular for the bosses to stop. For the *Rocky Mountain News,* Creel wrote a series of editorials promoting the governor as the hope of the nation, and when the candidate went to Denver on the western leg of his 1912 presidential campaign tour, Creel was a guest at a luncheon honoring him. On the evening of Wilson's departure from Denver, Creel had an hour's conversation with him in his private railroad car. Other than this—writing editorials, organizing the Denver Wilson Club, and holding an hour's private conversation—Creel played no active part in Wilson's first term in office. From well outside the president's inner circle, he merely watched, with admiring satisfaction, as the president made good on his promises of reform.

However pleased he may have been with the administration of a man he deeply admired, Creel fretted much over his own transition from "married life in Colorado, where I loomed large," to "New York, where my wife resumed . . . stardom." Creel was always drawn to stage people— and he adored Blanche Bates, his wife—but the adulation actors received ultimately galled him because it was "out of all proportion to the acclaim given accomplishment in other fields. A writer may turn out the greatest book in the world, but his name will never blaze in electric lights. . . . Before I had been in New York a month, I had the feeling of a tallow dip engaged in a battle with General Electric." He could not stomach being identified as "Blanche Bates's husband," and it seemed to him that, on the street, passersby continually whispered, "There goes Man-Cannot-Support-His-Wife."[2]

Creel wanted an editorial job but, to his consternation, found no openings on the papers whose policies were congenial to his beliefs, whereas those papers that offered him a position "were odious, being opposed to every one of my social, economic, and political faiths."[3] The only alternative was freelancing. For *Harper's Weekly*, he returned to a former subject, the exposure of medical quacks and quackery, and for *Everybody's* and *Century*, he wrote some political articles. He took time out from this work to return briefly to Denver in answer to telegrams from leaders of the great Colorado coal strike, in which oppressed and exploited miners—mostly poor immigrants who spoke little English and knew nothing of their rights under American law—finally rebelled. The governor, in cahoots with the mine owners, responded by calling out the Colorado National Guard, imposing the equivalent of martial law. The fourteen-month-long strike culminated on the morning of April 20, 1914, in the so-called Ludlow massacre, in which Guardsmen, later reinforced by private mine guards, opened fire with machine guns on the strikers' tent camp. The massively outgunned strikers returned fire, but the battle did not end until dusk, when a passing freight train happened to come to a stop between the National Guard machine gun positions and the camp. This allowed many of the strikers and their families to escape into the surrounding hills. By this time, the camp was ablaze, and the Guardsmen and mine guards descended on it to loot whatever was not on fire. Of some twelve hundred striking coal miners and their families, forty-five were killed, including thirty-two women and children. In particular, four women and eleven children who had taken refuge in a pit beneath a tent became trapped when the tent was set on fire; two of the women and all of the children suffocated. Avenging these deaths became a rallying cry for the strikers, and a guerrilla war swept the state's mining district for the next ten days, ending only after President Wilson ordered regular army troops to disarm both sides.

Once back in Denver, Creel issued a call for a mass meeting on the lawn of the state house. Before a crowd of some ten thousand, he made an appeal he himself characterized as extreme. "I can still feel Senator Charlie Thomas tugging at my legs and hear him pleading, 'George! George! For God's sake, tone it down!'"[4] The main target of his attack was oil and coal magnate John D. Rockefeller Jr., who dominated the Colorado coal industry. Late in 1914, Rockefeller would be called to testify before the Commission on Industrial Relations, which had been created by Congress at the behest of the president. By then, however, Rockefeller had found a secret weapon. His name was Ivy Ledbetter Lee, a man whose suavely conservative suits made him look more like a banker than a radical pioneer, one of a tiny handful of Americans who, at the start of the twentieth century, were creating the public relations industry.

With George Parker, Lee had founded in 1904 the third PR firm in the United States, Parker and Lee, pledging to achieve on behalf of its clients "Accuracy, Authenticity, and Interest." In 1907, Lee left Parker to set up on his own. He carved out within the newly emerging PR field a specialty he dubbed "crisis communications," handling the way corporate blunders, disasters, and scandals were presented to the public. In 1906, with much ballyhoo, he had promulgated a "Declaration of Principles," proclaiming as doctrine that public relations professionals were beholden not only to their clients but to the public. He believed that it was critically important for a firm in crisis to win public confidence by getting out ahead of the problem, releasing full and frank information to the press before journalists gathered the story from other sources. The Pennsylvania Railroad engaged him in 1912 as the nation's first full-time corporate PR executive, but two years later Rockefeller hired him away, assigning him the task of "burnishing the family image" in the wake of the Ludlow massacre and the congressional hearings that followed.

To this day, students and practitioners of public relations relish what has been handed down as Ivy Lee's advice to John D. Rockefeller Jr.: "Tell the truth, because sooner or later the public will find out anyway. And if the public doesn't like what you are doing, change your policies and bring them into line with what people want."[5] In fact, the reporter of this quotation was Lee himself, who used this "advice" to promote the Rockefeller image as well as his own. While it is true that Lee counseled his clients not just to broadcast their message but also to listen to the public, it was advice he himself honored more in the breach than in the observance. He was, as George Creel came to recognize in 1914, a master of propaganda—information offered to the public both compellingly and abundantly as the truth. To counter the adverse publicity generated by the Ludlow massacre and its aftermath, Lee flooded Colorado and the rest of the nation with copies of a pamphlet he titled simply *Facts*. It was a title, Creel observed, that was precisely the antithesis of its contents, lies so egregious that, much to his delight, they backfired, ultimately resulting in the mine owners' meeting virtually all of the miners' demands.

At the time of the Ludlow affair, Creel was most keenly focused on getting fair treatment for oppressed labor, but his brush with Ivy Lee afforded him a glimpse of the potential power of effective public relations, the shaping of public opinion, which both dovetailed with and differed from his own brand of crusading journalism. His encounter with Lee taught him not just the moral value of packing propaganda with provable truth but also the persuasive power of doing so. Conversely, the fate of Lee's *Facts* was a cautionary tale on the dangers of the unethical practice of public relations and on the final ineffectiveness of propaganda based on lies.[6]

Creel's experience with the Ludlow massacre, Rockefeller, and Ivy Lee's representation of Rockefeller seems to have made him increasingly dissatisfied with mere journalism. Perhaps it made him realize that he was never really at heart a journalist, if a journalist is defined as first and foremost a reporter, one who sees and attempts to represent all relevant sides of a story and who is willing to recognize and to render the facts in all their necessary shades of gray. Rather, George Creel was always an advocate, a crusader, for whom journalism was merely a means to an end. *Collier's* editor Mark Sullivan wrote in the pages of his magazine that Creel recognized just "two classes of men. There are skunks and the greatest man that ever lived. The greatest man that ever lived is plural, and includes everyone who is on Creel's side in whatever public issue he happens at the moment to be concerned with. In Creel's cosmos there are no shadings and no qualifications. His spectrum contains no mauve, nothing but plain black and white." Reflecting on Sullivan's observation more than thirty years after it was written, Creel himself pronounced this an "exaggeration, of course, but not entirely untrue."[7]

From 1914 on, even as he continued to practice journalism for money, Creel turned increasingly to outright crusading. He and his wife agreed that after he had earned enough to cover his share of household expenses for the year, he would be free to take on pro bono projects, which included a Minneapolis campaign for commission government, work on behalf of the Colorado miners, and the campaign to secure the confirmation of Louis D. Brandeis as a member of the U.S. Supreme Court. He also worked hard on the Commission on Industrial Relations and found time to collaborate with others on *Children in Bondage,* a book exposing child labor abuses.

Creel wanted not merely to report events, but to influence—even create—public opinion. He confessed that *Children in Bondage* "was more rhetorical than factual" and his own contributions to the book "anything but objective." Moved by the tragedy of child labor, Creel wanted desperately to infuse the American public with his own feelings. It was the kind of work he needed to do, and in 1915, nothing delighted him more than having generated sufficient income from more magazine assignments to enable him to devote three months to campaigning in New York for women's suffrage. When few magazines showed any interest in printing his advocacy articles, he turned to pamphleteering, a genre in which he was free to "go as far as I liked in dealing with the leaders of the antisuffrage movement."[8]

Pamphlets were hardly new as agents of social and political change. For instance, historians almost unanimously credit Thomas Paine's pamphlet of 1776, *Common Sense,* with transforming the American Revolution once and for all into an unambiguous fight for independence. Paine's work was a classic instance of pamphleteering as public relations, the creation of popular opinion and the marshaling of that opinion to create a desired action. But it was only in 1915 that Creel discovered the tradition for himself.

Despite Creel's pamphlets, the New York campaign for equal suffrage not only failed, it left him financially strapped and looking for more of the potboiler magazine assignments he had come to loathe. Finding none, he followed up a lead that Arthur Brisbane, the editorial brains behind much of the Hearst empire, was looking for someone to ghostwrite, in a series of articles, the autobiography of Jess Willard, the six-foot-six-and-a-half-inch "Pottawatamie Giant" who had been proclaimed the "Great White Hope" after he knocked out Jack Johnson to take the World Heavyweight Boxing Championship in twenty-six brutal rounds fought at Havana, Cuba, on April 5, 1915.

The work was far from crusading, but Creel was an ardent boxing fan, who had done a good deal of boxing himself as an amateur middleweight, so the job, sure to be profitable, also promised to be at least palatable. Besides, Willard, a working cowboy who had not started boxing until he was thirty, looked to be a genuinely colorful "character."

Accordingly, Creel rushed to visit Brisbane in his office, negotiated payment at his magazine rate—a true bonanza for the writer of an extended series of articles—and then listened as the editor admonished him that Mr. Hearst, a celebrated teetotaler and abstainer from tobacco, had not purchased the rights to Willard's story "merely for the purpose of glorifying the prize ring." Far from it. His object was to "inspire the youth of the land with a *love* of clean living by portraying the life of a man who rose to fistic eminence *through* clean living." Brisbane cautioned, "There must, of course, be no faking," but, he continued, "surely, Mr. Creel, at some period in his life you will find that Willard, strong with strength that comes from never having touched liquor and tobacco, rescued the village drunkard from drowning. And you will also discover, undoubtedly, that this pure-minded young giant, taught by his good mother never to soil his lips by blasphemy, soundly trounced the town bully for using vile oaths in the presence of growing lads." Again admonishing Creel to avoid faking, he offered "a point I know you will be able to make: Mention that scientific research has proved positively that one drop of whisky put in the eye of a panther will cut his spring in half."[9]

Creel saw instantly that what Brisbane wanted was propaganda, Ivy Lee style: "no faking," which actually meant *all faking*—and every bit of it aimed at shaping public opinion in a national movement that would, before the decade was out, result in the passage of a constitutional amendment outlawing the manufacture, sale, and consumption of alcoholic beverages.

After listening to Brisbane reel off another dozen or more things that Willard "must" have done, Creel asked if he would even have to personally interview Willard. If Creel's tongue was in his cheek, Brisbane either did not notice or deliberately chose to ignore it. Interview Willard? "'Not necessarily,' Brisbane shrugged."[10]

Creel was too broke to be ashamed to take on the job, but he was also too ashamed not to call on Jess Willard personally. He tracked down the former cowpuncher in Omaha and talked with him for an hour in a dingy hotel room. What he got from the interview was not much— birthplace, the names of the towns in which he had passed his boyhood, the fact that he had had a dog, name of Rover. So Creel confabulated all the rest, leavening the outright fiction with factual accounts of Willard's fights (drawn from newspapers) and his own firsthand knowledge of training camp routine. He wrote of how Jess had lived clean, how he had whipped any number of foul-mouthed bad boys and badder men, and how he learned to despise both strong drink and tobacco. He even put into Willard's mouth the judgment that Jack Johnson's defeat in Havana was due to the "Galveston Giant's" failure to appreciate the benefits of clean living. Creel drew the line at the panther depleted by a drop of whisky in the eye—that bit did not make it into the book—but, otherwise, he blithely let himself be corrupted by easy money.

If ghostwriting is by definition a deception, framing the ghostwritten autobiography of a popular sports figure as social propaganda virtually unanchored to fact is something even less savory. Creel emerged from his Jess Willard assignment richer in cash but poorer in self-esteem. Fortunately for him, Woodrow Wilson stood for reelection in 1916, and Creel rushed to offer his services to Bob Wooley, the candidate's chief strategist. Creel was anxious to immerse himself in the cleansing bath of idealism made real.

The world situation had changed drastically since Wilson's first presidential campaign in 1912. On June 28, 1914, the chauffeur driving the heir apparent to the Austro-Hungarian throne, Archduke Franz Ferdinand, and his wife, the Grand Duchess Sophie, through the streets of Sarajevo during a state visit to the province of Bosnia and Herzegovina blundered into a wrong turn. The flustered driver stopped the automobile, and, as he shifted into reverse, dark-haired, frail-looking Gavrilo Princip, a self-proclaimed Yugoslav nationalist, already wasted with tuberculosis, rose from his seat in a shabby outdoor café, withdrew from the pocket of his outsized overcoat a Browning revolver, and fired it point-blank at the royal couple. Husband and wife died within minutes of one another, and the Austrian foreign minister, Count Leopold von Berchtold, announced that he was holding the government of Serbia, recently independent from the Austro-Hungarian Empire, wholly responsible. He demanded that Serbia make concessions amounting to a virtual renunciation of its sovereignty. When the Serbs balked, the empire attacked.

Since the late nineteenth-century heyday of Prussia's Iron Chancellor, Otto von Bismarck, the nations of Europe had been weaving a complex web of treaties and alliances, some public, others secret. Doubtless all were intended to provide security and stability; instead, they irresistibly drew the continent into the most destructive war the world had known to that time. Russia was obligated to defend Serbia; the German Kaiser instantly forged an alliance with Austria-Hungary; France honored its solemn agreement of military alliance with Russia; and Great Britain, allied with both France and Russia, was also bound to defend the neutrality of Belgium, which Germany soon violated in its wide-wheeling march against France. By August 1914, Europe and the far-flung colonies of Europe were in a "Great War," a world war. Kaiser Wilhelm II had promised his people that the soldiers would be "home before the leaves fell from the trees," and with his armies deep in France and bearing down on Paris itself, it did look as if it would be a short war. But then the German columns faltered, hesitated, turned, and dug themselves in along the river Marne, just short of the French capital. Soon the war's major theater, the Western Front, became a great, jagged scar of squalid trench extending from the English Channel in the north to the border of neutral Switzerland in the south. What had begun as a war of impulse and rapid movement became a stalemate of senseless slaughter.

By the beginning of the First Battle of the Marne in September 1914, eleven major powers were in the war. Italy would join the Allies in 1915, bringing the total to twelve, but the United States, shielded by an ocean and blissfully free from Europe's entangling treaties, stood apart and watched the madness of the Old World with a mixture of moral superiority and blessed relief. The vast majority of Americans wanted no part of what they called the "European War." In 1912's three-way race among Democrat Wilson, Republican Taft, and third-party Progressive Roosevelt, Americans fed up with the oligarchic corruption of machine politics sent Wilson (more genuinely Progressive than Roosevelt) to the White House with a solid plurality. By 1916, however, many Americans were fed up with four years of Wilson's rigorous reforms and longed for a return to a Republican administration more congenial to the interests of big business. The race for reelection against Charles Evans Hughes would be at best a close one, Wooley knew, and he and other Wilson partisans decided that their drawing card was no longer Progressive reform but an unshakable policy of continued neutrality in the Great War. Wilson's campaign slogan for 1916 became a drumbeat on a single theme: *"He kept us out of war!"*

Although Wilson's neutrality policy was in line with prevailing popular sentiment, forces were relentlessly at work to bring the nation into the war. Theodore Roosevelt and others, mostly Republicans, spoke of the necessity of upholding American honor by entering the war on the side of the Allies to oppose "Prussian autocracy" and "German atrocity." Wilson's opponents claimed that he was a bumbler who was leaving America not only unprepared to take its rightful place in the fighting but even to defend itself against what was posited as an inevitable German transatlantic invasion. President Wilson responded to such accusations by holding to the high moral road. After the German submarine U–20 torpedoed and sank the British liner *Lusitania* on May 7, 1915, with the loss of 1,198 lives, including 128 of the 197 Americans aboard, President Wilson issued a stern protest to the German government, but he did not break off diplomatic relations. He seemed to answer those who urged immediate U.S. entry into the war with a speech he delivered in Philadelphia on May 10, 1915, declaring "There is such a thing as a man being too proud to fight; there is such a thing as a nation being so right that it does not need to convince others by force that it is right."[11] Although Wilson subsequently claimed that the speech had been written before the sinking of the *Lusitania* and was not intended as a direct response to the atrocity, Theodore Roosevelt and others seized on it as evidence of a cowardly policy. Under such pressure as that exerted by Roosevelt, impartial neutrality became increasingly difficult to maintain as the 1916 election approached. The actions of the Central Powers, as Germany and its allies were called, were in fact morally repugnant, and doubtless there were many who advocated abandoning neutrality out of a sense of moral outrage.

But there were also other pressures. As a neutral, the United States had the right—indeed, the legal obligation—to trade with both sides impartially. Early in the war, there was very good money to be made supplying weapons, other goods, and general finance to the combatants.

Increasingly, however, the flow of trade and credit from the United States to the European belligerents turned away from the Central Powers and toward the Allies. High demand, an ample supply of gold, favorable shipping, and the realities of geography made dealing with the Allies far more reliable and profitable than doing business with the Central Powers. Moreover, American financial and business interests were coming to believe that the Allies would win, which made them a better credit risk than the Central Powers. By late 1916, U.S. firms had done some $2 billion in business with the Allies, and U.S. banks had made $2.5 billion in loans to them. In contrast, American banks had loaned by this time no more than $45 million to Germany.[12] Politically, the United States was neutral in 1916, but, economically, it had already taken sides. True, public sentiment still favored the man who "kept us out of war," but that sentiment was under attack, and there were signs that it was changing.

To shore up the still-favorable opinion of Wilson's neutrality policy, Wooley assigned Creel to write newspaper features in support of the president and neutrality. Creel called first on none other than Thomas Alva Edison, one of the nation's most-admired men. Although Edison had been a Republican lifelong, word had leaked that he was inclined to come out in favor of Wilson. Starstruck in the presence of the "Wizard of Menlo Park," the "Modern Prometheus," Creel was nevertheless compelled to put his "lips down to [Edison's] eardrum" so that the inventor, almost totally deaf, could hear him. The sound of his own voice bellowing in the great man's ear so discombobulated Creel that he forgot what he meant to ask. "'Never mind, son,' Mr. Edison laughed. 'I've got it all written out.'" With that, he pushed his hand into his pants pocket and pulled out some crumpled sheets of yellow paper. They were scribbled over in pencil, yet the print was clear as copperplate. In "simple, homely phrases, he had outlined his reasons for quitting the Republican party, ending up with this classic bit: 'They say Wilson has blundered. Well, I reckon he has, but I notice he always blunders *forward*.'"[13]

The Edison interview was only the first of many, but it was, in terms of Creel's understanding of public relations, the best. As Creel saw it, public relations was all about creating a popular environment congenial to whatever person or cause one espoused. The most effective way of doing this was to identify the most influential figures in the population to which you were making your appeal, get them on record as supporting your candidate or cause, and then publish that record widely and effectively. Thomas Edison was the perfect figure for this purpose. He was universally known and admired—and, what is more, he was admired specifically for having transformed the theories of cutting-edge science into the everyday reality of inventions that changed civilization itself. Popularly regarded as a latter-day alchemist, Edison was also a down-to-earth, folksy figure, a powerful industrialist who nevertheless projected the image of a common workingman, and the very incarnation of a Horatio Alger hero. For most Americans, he was not so much Everyman as he was what Everyman longed to be: revered, creative, wealthy, and successful. And if this paragon was not only supporting Woodrow Wilson but leaving the Republican Party to do so, shouldn't we all do likewise? Best of all, in contrast to Jess Willard, into whose inarticulate mouth George Creel had to put every word of a hollow message, Edison handed him the gift of a "classic bit," ready-made and original, brilliant in its eloquent homeliness. It was an utterance at once idealistic, practical, clever, and American. It was PR gold, and Creel took a profound lesson from it.

The interviews were important, but Wooley soon gave Creel an assignment he told him was even more critical. It was the task of rehabilitating the reputation of Wilson's secretary of the navy, Josephus Daniels, who had become a lightning rod for criticism of the president's military policies. A North Carolinian by birth, Daniels vigorously supported Wilson's election in 1912 and had been rewarded with a cabinet appointment. His attempts to modernize the navy, especially his encouragement of technological innovation, were overshadowed by his issuance of General Order 99 on June 1, 1914, which banished alcohol from all United States Navy ships. This provoked a certain amount of outrage among naval officers, who had long relished their "wine mess," and it gave the opposition press ammunition to use against the man the Hearst papers lampooned as the self-righteous "Holy Joe." Rendering the U.S. Navy dry, these papers claimed, had made America an international laughingstock. Other accusations followed, including charges that Daniels undermined naval discipline, ridiculed the navy uniform, and was generally incompetent.

It is true that, despite his advocacy of technological progress, Daniels, drawling in speech and deliberate in manner, cut a distinctly stodgy figure, and even his assistant secretary, the young Franklin Delano Roosevelt, grew desperately impatient with him. But the real source of the mainly Republican opposition to Daniels was his advocacy of government ownership of armor-plate factories and telephone and telegraph utilities. Private business interests (traditional elements of the Republican constituency) were loath to give up these profitable enterprises, particularly in time of world war.

Creel set about neutralizing the campaign against Daniels by mounting a countercampaign. To transform negative public opinion, he marshaled and disseminated not alternate opinion but facts—or, at least, what he judged could pass as facts. He showed that the ban on the shipboard sale or issuance of alcoholic beverages to enlisted sailors was not Daniels's innovation but had been in effect since 1899; Daniels had merely extended the ban to officers—and he had done so not out of his own moral convictions but in response to a recommendation by the surgeon general of the navy, who was alarmed by the high rate of courts-martial for drunkenness on duty. Creel also showed that, far from laughing at the liquor ban, the Russian, French, and German navies followed suit within a year. He even uncovered the text of an address Kaiser Wilhelm II made to German naval cadets: "The next war and the next sea battle demand sound nerves. Nerves will decide. These become undermined through alcohol. The nation which consumes the least alcohol wins, and that should be you, gentlemen. Take heed, and provide that indulgence in alcohol not be counted as belonging to your privileges."[14]

Creel approached other charges leveled against Daniels similarly. For instance, he claimed that the allegations that Daniels had instituted policies fomenting discontent and insubordination were based on the secretary's order instituting shipboard schools to train enlisted sailors in certain technical and academic subjects. Far from undermining discipline and morale, Creel asserted, these schools had manifestly improved both.

Since the inception of the schools, reenlistment rates had risen from 52 percent to 85 percent.[15]

To his fact-based campaign, Creel added the other mainstay of his approach to public relations: the verdict of the most influential people. He turned to retired admiral George Dewey, the commander of the "Great White Fleet" and hero of the Spanish-American War, who volunteered his full support of Daniels and his reforms.

The complete defense of Josephus Daniels quickly found its way into *Wilson and the Issues,* a small book explaining—in the kind of popular prose quite foreign to the president himself—Wilson's policies with regard to an often hostile Mexico, the sinking of the *Lusitania,* the German invasion and oppression of Belgium, and other issues for the most part related to his stance on the "European War." The ten-chapter volume was no campaign give-away but a commercial best seller. Creel donated his copyright to the Democratic National Committee, which issued a paperbound edition that included a foreword by Secretary of War Newton Baker.

Aimed at persuading the American people to stay Wilson's neutral course by reelecting him, *Wilson and the Issues* was a preview of many of the approaches Creel, beginning in 1917, would take as head of the Committee on Public Information to sell the American people on the very war the president had sought to avoid the year before. In April 1917, both Wilson and Creel would present U.S. entry into the Great War as an idealistic and ideological imperative, a fight to "make the world safe for democracy," as the president most famously put it in his War Message to Congress on April 2. A year earlier, in the 1916 book, Creel had framed the reelection campaign of Wilson—and, with it, the fate of American neutrality—as freighted with "more tremendous meaning than any other [campaign] in the history of America," save, perhaps, the campaign of 1860. Just as, in 1917, the stakes of America's entry into the war would be presented as something far more significant than influencing the military outcome of the contest, so, in 1916, Creel wrote that the "ultimates" of the presidential campaign "go far beyond the mere individual victory or defeat of Woodrow Wilson and Charles Evans Hughes, for on the decisions that must be made depends the whole future of democracy.

It is not simply a President of the United States that the people are called upon to elect; it is fundamental policies for the United States that the people are called upon to declare."[16]

This definition of the stakes was both straightforward and ideological (although the passage of a few months would render them ironic): A vote for Wilson will keep America on the peaceful, neutral course the people favor, whereas a vote for Hughes will propel the nation into a European war American big business and big financial interests want. In the next paragraph, however, Creel departed from ideology to mass psychology by way of deftly redefining partisanship as treason and betrayal: "There was never a time when the bigotries of partizanship [sic] were more akin to treason and betrayal; never a time when there was such imperative demand upon the electorate for clear, unimpassioned thinking." In his propagandizing after the United States entered the war, Creel would likewise identify partisanship with treason. He would also define his mission as the furnishing of facts to facilitate clear thought and unimpassioned decision making. In his 1916 volume, Creel complained that Wilson's opponents used raw and confusing emotionalism deliberately to obscure the clarity of Wilson's message. To counter this, Creel sought to introduce facts that would shape popular sentiment in ways that were clear and sane and strong. In April 1917, only a month after Woodrow Wilson had been inaugurated for his second term, Creel once again sought to oppose confusion with a single-minded, single-willed clarity. But whereas in 1916 the forces of hysterical obfuscation were Republicans clamoring for war, in 1917 they were antiwar holdouts unwilling to abandon neutrality.

How could Creel shift his rhetoric so completely and so effortlessly? As he saw it, there really was no shift. To Creel, it was the policy of Woodrow Wilson that mattered, whether that policy happened to be the absolute neutrality of 1916 or the absolute commitment to war of 1917. Devoted to Wilson, Creel based his public relations campaigns on the same principles employing the same techniques, whether the object promoted was peace or war.

"The whole situation," Creel concluded the first chapter of his Wilson and the Issues, "constitutes a test of democracy."

It is the capacity of a people for self-government that is on trial. It is the honesty, intelligence, and faith of the mass that are up for judgment. There is not a lie that has been told that lacks its answer; there is not a slander for which refutation cannot be found; there is not an ugly charge that does not come clean in the light of truth. It remains to be seen whether the people of the United States prefer facts to clamor, fairness to betrayal, and democracy to oligarchy; in a word, whether they are able to think for themselves.[17]

Here Creel essentially defined his conception of the role of propaganda in a democracy, unabashedly using the words *propaganda* and *democracy* in the same sentence without a trace of irony. As generally conceived, *propaganda* is the message—the picture of reality—the state wants the people to receive and to believe. Even so conceived, propaganda is not necessarily untrue, but it has little to do with people thinking for themselves. Yet it was Creel's belief that propaganda could be factually based and that, as such, it could be presented to the people as evidence, which, after weighing, would inevitably persuade them to decide correctly—that is, to make the decisions the state wanted them to make. It fell to the propagandist to find the right facts and to present them the right way, the compelling way. If this was done and done effectively, the people, ostensibly thinking for themselves, would think as the state wanted them to think.

Obviously, there is much room for abuse and corruption in this vision of propaganda. If it is easy to view Creel's paragraph as disingenuous, it is even easier to see it as downright cynical. But "Lochinvar Creel" was neither disingenuous nor cynical. He was an idealist, and he believed himself highly capable of functioning as the arbiter of truth, which he was more than willing to retail to the people, thereby countering the lies, slanders, and ugly charges of the enemy. This mission accomplished, the people would be enabled to think for themselves, which meant thinking the way President Woodrow Wilson wanted them to think.

It is, of course, not difficult to find a multitude of flaws in this view, but, in the end, only one flaw really mattered: Creel's concept of propaganda rested on the assumption that *his side* always possessed the truth whereas the *other side* always proffered falsehood. It was not unlike the Old Testament vision of good and evil as played out in the Garden of

Eden. God was good, because God was truth. The devil, especially as incarnated in the serpent, was evil because he purveyed untruth. Both the Old Testament vision and the vision of George Creel rested, first and last, on definitions flowing not from rational thought but from mythology. For a man raised on the tall tales of his Missouri "Southern colonels," mythology was not incompatible with historical truth. "The amazing thing is not that history repeats itself," Creel began Chapter 4 of his book on Wilson, "but that people learn so little from these repetitions." Neutrality, Creel went on to point out, was not invented by Woodrow Wilson, but, "as a matter of record . . . was first declared by Washington himself, and reiterated time and again by the Presidents that followed him. And just as Woodrow Wilson is abused for upholding this fixed principle of national conduct, so abuse of incredible malignity was heaped upon the Father of the Country, Jefferson, Adams, Pierce, Van Buren, Lincoln, Grant, and Harrison." Thus Creel inducted Wilson into the American pantheon of great (and some not-so-great) presidents who cleaved to neutrality, in the process defining neutrality as a fixed principle of American history as well as of American mythology, with Woodrow Wilson as one in a long line of the principle's avatars. The aim of propaganda, for Creel, was not only to convey the truth of a given policy but to reveal its essential, even mythological rightness. On this basis, Creel ended the chapter by defining any repudiation of Wilson as not only a "repudiation of the policy of neutrality," but "a return to the evil days when armed force was the one method of adjusting disputes, when every war was a world war, when blood lust ruled, and when human lives were pawns in the greedy game of territorial acquisition."[18]

In the strange logic permitted by mythology, the very thing Creel identified as the chief motive for neutrality, namely the preservation of a rational and just civilization, would soon become the motive for joining the world war. Indeed, all along, Creel had defined the struggle to defend civilization as a fight, even when peace was the chosen weapon: "It is civilization itself that Woodrow Wilson had been fighting for, and as the people of America vote, so will their stage of civilizational development be measured."[19] As with any active, living mythology, this one was not the exclusive province of the gods—Wilson and his government—but also required the support, belief, and right behavior of ordinary people.

Having developed the positive propaganda necessary to support Wilson and neutrality, Creel went on to define the opposing point of view in Chapter 5, titled "Manufacturing Hysteria." He attributed to sensationalism and yellow journalism the lurid stories of America's unpreparedness for war. They were stories planted by the "money masters," the would-be war profiteers, and, in this chapter and the next, Creel marshaled certain "facts" to counter the hysteria, including expert testimony that U.S. coastal defenses were second to none and that, under Wilson, military spending had increased greatly. Once again, Creel turned to Admiral Dewey for authoritative support, citing the old hero's opinion that the latest bill for navy funding was "the best bill ever passed by Congress."[20]

The equation of *facts* with *truth* was the keystone of the Creel mythology. It does not seem to have occurred to him—or, at least, to have mattered to him—that "fact" is by no means a synonym for "truth." Creel marshaled some facts, but he left out others. However formidable the coastal artillery may have been, the United States Army as a whole in 1916 was, in fact, puny. Together, active troops and reserves numbered just 200,000 men, tying American military might with tiny Serbia and besting, among the world's regular armies, only those of Belgium (117,000 men), Portugal (40,000), and Montenegro (50,000). At the start of 1917, the U.S. Navy could muster 4,376 officers and 69,680 enlisted sailors to man 342 warships. This made for a more substantial force than the army, to be sure, but it was still far behind the major powers in the world war. On April 6, 1917, when Congress declared war on the Central Powers, the United States military was, by any rational measure, unprepared.

Creel knew this. The war raging in Europe involved millions of men and vast arsenals. The overwhelming inferiority of America's armed forces, compared with those of the European powers, was neither a secret nor the product of hysterical rumor. The facts Creel used to counter Wilson's opponents, who pointed to the nation's unpreparedness, were not absolutely false, but they were certainly partial. Creel felt himself justified in his partiality because there was a single "fact" that trumped all others.

He revealed it the final chapter of the Wilson book, titled "The Ancient Faith":

> America is a nation of incurable dreamers. The heart of the people is not found in ledgers, their aspirations are not expressed in profits . . . .
>
> The soul of the many is found in the far-flung idealism of the Declaration of Independence, not in the cautions phrases of the Constitution. False prophets and strange gods have won no more than lip-service, for deep in the heart of the nation an abiding faith in the ultimate triumph of love, justice, and brotherhood remains untouched. Financial genius may be given its sorry day of homage, yet its right to control the destinies of America has never failed to be resisted, and the great money-makers do not live in memory beyond the reading of their wills.
>
> Vision, spirit, ideals, without the clue afforded by these dream words, the United States stammers and is unintelligible. Democracy never has been and never can be, other than a theory of spiritual progress . . .
>
> . . . All that is fundamentally big and fine has been the work of so-called "visionaries" who ran gantlets of ridicule and opposition. In the outset of every great movement, every wonderful idea, is a *dream,* and democracy was evolved to make these dreams come true.[21]

Throughout *Wilson and the Issues,* Creel countered "hysteria," which he said was built on material greed, with "facts," founded on the idealistic dream of democracy. Neutrality was part of that dream and was therefore more profoundly American than any mere materialism. These "abstractions," these "dreams," *these* were the great American truths that Wilson's noble vision of neutrality, the neutrality of a people "too proud to fight," was intended to uphold and defend against a "commercial aristocracy [that], by sinister control of government, press, and pulpit, has been able to cast the surface of things in shapes of its own desire." As for that "commercial aristocracy," it hated Wilson because "he . . . dared to stand with the exploited many against the powerful few, leading the fight of the people against their ancient enemies for the recovery of the ancient faith." Electoral victory for Wilson "means victory for democracy; it is to beat democracy back into bondage that he is being fought by the great money lords."[22]

George Creel knew that America was militarily unprepared in a world consumed by war, but that fact—those numbers, numbers of men, numbers of guns, tonnage of ships of war—was mere materialism, whereas Wilson's policies were the "decisions of one with vision to see beneath the stagnancies of materialism down to the well-springs of truth." Even as the nations of Europe wasted themselves in war, Wilson's idealism "has saved the national purse, conserved the national energies, destroyed national evils, and given us confidence in ourselves, besides inspiring the confidence of others. . . . Are these hard-won heights to be abandoned? In its hour of greatest hope, is democracy to surrender? . . . These . . . are the questions to be answered in November."[23]

So Creel concluded *Wilson and the Issues.* That he created in 1916 a work of propaganda equating Wilson's neutrality with a defense of American democracy at its most idealistic and spiritual then, in 1917, went on to create a ministry of propaganda dedicated to equating what was now Wilson's war with the defense of that very same democracy does boggle the mind and surely beggars belief. Writing more than three decades after the Great War, George Orwell posited in his masterpiece, *1984,* a world in which such shifts of thought were not only routine but formed the very basis of government. Despite his capacity for passionate idealism, the hero of Orwell's novel, Winston Smith, finally yields and comes to accept what the state tells him: that 2 plus 2 always equals 4—except when it equals 5.

For Creel, facts were the elements of effective propaganda, but the greatest fact of all was Woodrow Wilson's idealistic dream of America. In 1916, that dream demanded absolute neutrality in a world at war for material gain. In 1917, the same dream called for absolute commitment to that very war. Creel was prepared to coax the sentiment of the American millions into a shape congenial to the Wilsonian dream, whether it stood proudly against a clamor for blood one year or, the very next, exhorted the millions to shed their blood in the trenches of a faraway fight.

CHAPTER 4

SAFE FOR DEMOCRACY

O nly recently have academic historians begun seriously criticizing Woodrow Wilson for going to war. Through most of the twentieth century, certainly, American intervention in the Great War was seen as a triumph. After all, General John J. Pershing's American army rescued the Allies, who, all but bled white by three years of slaughter, were, in 1917, faltering under the blows of a series of massive and desperate German offensives. But then, it is not the military performance of the United States that the historians question; rather, it is what they consider President Wilson's naively optimistic calculus of victory versus defeat that has increasingly fallen under challenge. The president's memorable phrases still ring—that the Great War would be the "war to end all wars" and that its winning would make "the world safe for democracy"—but they now echo, it seems, hollow. We now understand that a defeated Germany, writhing under the punitive terms of the Treaty of Versailles, became ripe for the rise of Adolf Hitler, and the Great War had to be renamed World War *I* after a second, even more horrific, world war began in September 1939.

Woodrow Wilson still has many admirers and apologists, who claim with some justification that, had the president managed to wrest all that he had wanted from the peace talks that led to the Versailles treaty—that is, had the treaty been less punitive and more conciliatory and had the Senate approved U.S. membership in the treaty-mandated League of Nations—there might not have been a World War II or any other major war in the twentieth century. This we cannot know, but we do know that President Wilson, having fended off congressional and other war hawks since 1914 and having in 1916 won reelection in large part because "he kept us out of war," decided to take the nation into the most desperate and destructive armed conflict up to that time, a war for which (as he well knew) the American army was wholly unprepared.

What moved him to act?

From the very beginning of the war, in the summer of 1914, Germany and Austria-Hungary were cast in the role of aggressors. The entire world, including the United States, heard accounts of the "rape of Belgium," stories that surely had a strong element of truth but that were also amplified many fold by Britain's highly effective propaganda machine, which thickly sowed the reports with literal rapes and the wanton bayoneting of children and babies. Despite this unrelenting drumbeat of atrocity stories, most Americans between 1914 and 1916 wanted no part of the "European war." About eight months into the conflict, in 1915, the *Literary Digest* polled 367 U.S. writers and editors, of whom 105 favored the Allies and 20 the Germans, but a substantial majority, 242, called for the continuation of absolute neutrality.[1] As mentioned in chapter 3, neutrality was actually very profitable. As a neutral, the United States traded with all nations, but even though President Wilson insisted that American industry and financial institutions do business with all of the belligerents impartially, it became increasingly difficult for many Americans and most American businesses to remain impartial.

Even worse than the continual flow of atrocity stories was the irrefutable fact of German submarine warfare. The Kaiser's U-boats preyed on Allied—especially British—shipping, including commercial and passenger vessels. Whether most Americans were aware of it or not, this practice did not violate international law or even the accepted conventions of warfare. Indeed, initially at least, the German U-boat commanders surfaced to give warning before launching an attack on civilian vessels, allowing passengers and crew sufficient time to abandon ship. When this became cumbersome and exposed the surfaced U-boats to counterattack, the German navy embraced a new policy of "unrestricted submarine warfare," by which submarines were authorized to attack while submerged and without warning. That was the fate that befell the British liner *Lusitania* on May 7, 1915. True, 1,198 innocent lives were lost in the attack, including 128 Americans, but it was also true that *Lusitania* carried more than passengers. The ship had been built before the war but in strict accordance with directives laid down by the British Admiralty, which carried the luxury liner on its own Royal Navy lists as an "auxiliary cruiser." As such, on that final, fatal voyage from New York, she was loaded with American-made war materiel, including ten and a half tons of rifle cartridges, fifty-one tons of shrapnel shells, and a large amount of gun cotton (which explodes on contact with water). Also on board were sixty-seven soldiers of the 6th Winnipeg Rifles. That the *Lusitania* was functioning as a military cargo transport and even a troopship was no secret. Days before the liner departed New York, the Imperial German Embassy secured permission from U.S. Secretary of State William Jennings Bryan to publish in local newspapers a warning that because the ship was leaving port with what German agents identified as 6 million rounds of .303-caliber rifle ammunition, it would be subject to attack. Prospective passengers were cautioned accordingly.

The fact was that the Royal Navy had effectively transformed the *Lusitania* into a vessel of war, thereby placing in peril the lives of its civilian passengers. Not a single American newspaper noted this, however, but instead condemned the U-boat attack as murder. A minority of Americans, including such prominent figures as Walter Hines Page, U.S. ambassador to Great Britain, called for an immediate U.S. declaration of war. Secretary of State Bryan, however, was among the most vocal advocates of continued neutrality, and he was among the first government officials to point out that the *Lusitania* had carried contraband. In the end, Wilson's response was to condemn the attack as "unlawful and inhuman," and he sent a strongly worded diplomatic protest to the German government on May 9, 1915. When he sent a follow-up protest on June 9—even after the U.S. Customs Service had confirmed the presence of contraband onboard the *Lusitania*—Secretary Bryan resigned in protest, claiming that Wilson was acting in a deliberately provocative manner. But if the protests were too strong for Bryan, Wilson endured the barbs of pro-war champion Theodore Roosevelt and others, who mocked his comparison of the American nation to a man "too proud to fight." Moreover, other forces were at work in an effort to propel the nation into the war. As mentioned in the previous chapter, U.S. industry and finance had come to favor the Allies overwhelmingly. Whatever the degree to which Wilson's moral and strategic thinking may have inched toward war by the start of his second term, the American economy had become, in significant measure, joined to the fate of the Allies.

Early in 1916, Wilson sought to avoid any possibility of America's entry into the war by bringing the conflict itself to an end. He sent his closest adviser, Edward M. House, to London and Paris to sound out Allied leaders on the idea of the American government's acting as mediator among the belligerents. It was a good-faith offer that resulted in a tragically ambiguous agreement in the form of a memorandum drawn up with the British foreign secretary, Sir Edward Grey, on February 22, 1916. The document not only warned that the United States might enter the war if Germany rejected Wilson's efforts at mediation, it further stipulated that the right to initiate U.S. mediation rested not with the American president but with the government of Great Britain. Thus, on one hand, the House-Grey document was a sincere effort to bring about binding mediation, but, on the other hand, it was an American threat of war against Germany and a virtual announcement of impending alliance with Britain. In the end, the agreement was sufficiently disturbing to Wilson that, as the 1916 elections neared, he decided to suspend his peace initiative precisely because it might lead to entry into the war. Besides, there was, on the eve of Wilson's reelection, a positive note to report: Germany's kaiser had agreed to end unrestricted submarine warfare.

Safely reinstalled in office, Wilson made a new stab at mediation. On December 18, 1916, he invited the Allies and the Germans to clear the air by stating, once and for all, their "war aims." Nothing came of this invitation, however, and, on January 22, 1917, Wilson took a new tack, appealing for unbiased international conciliation based on the goal of achieving "peace without victory" on all sides. It is a measure of Britain's

war weariness that its government confidentially communicated willingness to accept Wilson's mediation on these grounds, as did Austria-Hungary, the nation most directly responsible for the war. Germany, however,
rejected the American president as a mediator, claiming that the United
States had effectively ceased to be neutral and unbiased. Even worse, on
January 31, the German government announced the resumption of unrestricted submarine warfare. The combination of what Wilson saw as German intransigence on the question of mediation and deliberate
provocation in the form of unrestricted U-boat aggression prompted him
to take his first unambiguous step toward war. On February 3, Woodrow
Wilson severed diplomatic relations between the United States and Germany. Later in the month, on February 26, he issued an executive order
that authorized the arming of U.S.-flagged merchant vessels. He invented
an eerily paradoxical phrase for the new policy: "armed neutrality."

Throughout late 1916 and early 1917, German attacks on British
and American merchant ships continued; no fewer than three U.S. ships
were sunk on March 18, 1917, alone. These outrages came hard on the
heels of another, which proved to be of even greater consequence. It was
the "Zimmermann Telegram," which President Wilson publicly revealed
on March 1.

On January 16, 1917, the German foreign secretary, Alfred Zimmermann, sent a coded telegram, via the German ambassador in Washington, D.C., to the German minister in Mexico. The message authorized
the minister to propose to Mexico's president, Venustiano Carranza, a
German-Mexican alliance by which Mexico would declare war on the
United States in return for a German promise of military support in a
Mexican campaign to retake the territory in Texas, New Mexico, and Ari-
zona it had lost in the Texas War of Independence of 1836 and the U.S.-
Mexican War of 1846 to 1848. As if this were not provocation enough,
the telegram also instructed the German minister to ask Carranza to in-
vite Japan to join the anti-American alliance.

From a strategic and diplomatic point of view, the proposal presented in the Zimmermann Telegram was breathtakingly harebrained,
and Carranza, wisely deciding against taking on the United States, rejected the proposal out of hand. What the German government did not

know was that British agents, monitoring cable traffic, had intercepted the message, decoded it, and handed it to Ambassador Page, who eagerly turned it over to President Wilson. Even then, it was the president's secretary of the interior, and not the president himself, who reacted first. "We can stand Germany's arrogance no longer," declared Franklin K. Lane on March 31.[2]

The next day, Wilson spoke with an old friend, Frank Cobb of the New York *World.* Later the journalist reported that he had never seen the president "so worn down." According to Cobb, Wilson remarked that entering the war would erode the very soul of America: "The spirit of ruthless brutality will enter the very fiber of our national life, infecting Congress, the courts, the policeman on the beat, the man in the street. Conformity will be the only virtue. And every man who refuses to conform must pay the penalty." Assuming that Cobb reported the exchange truthfully (and there are some historians who do not believe that he did), it was as if Wilson recognized—and was presumably willing to accept—that in order to make the world safe for democracy, it would be necessary to abridge democracy in the United States, at least for the duration of the war.[3]

Indeed, before he finally went to war, Wilson had to fight with himself. Despite Creel's assertion, in *Wilson and the Issues,* that the president had not neglected military preparedness even as he cleaved to a neutral course, Wilson had without question resolutely avoided major preparations for war. Some recent historians believe that, even as he delivered his thirty-two-minute war message to Congress beginning at 8:40 P.M. on April 2, 1917, he wistfully clung to the hope that America would not actually have to send troops to Europe. Given the exhaustion on both sides, he may have seriously believed that the mere threat of U.S. entry would be sufficient to end hostilities. Nor was the president alone in this hope. On April 6, after hearing testimony that appropriations were needed to actually deliver an army to France, Senator Thomas S. Martin of Virginia, chairman of the Senate Finance Committee and a man who had just voted for the declaration of war, gasped: "Good Lord! You're not going to send soldiers over there, are you?"[4]

If the recollections of Wilson's personal secretary, Joseph Tumulty, are to be trusted (and, as with Cobb's report, some historians do not trust them), Wilson was not quite so naive. At some level, he did face the reality that intimidation alone would not bring peace. Tumulty recalled that, at about 10:00 P.M., having returned to the White House after delivering the war message, Wilson slumped in a chair at the table in the empty cabinet room. Tumulty entered, and Wilson locked eyes on him. Reflecting on the thunderous applause that had greeted his message, the president said, "Think what it was they were applauding. My message today was a message of death for our young men. How strange it seems to applaud that." According to Tumulty, Woodrow Wilson put his head in his hands and sobbed uncontrollably.[5]

Maybe he cried afterward, and maybe he did not. In the message itself, there was not a particle of doubt. It was driven by the president's customarily confident and lofty idealism. "There is one choice we cannot make; we are incapable of making," he told Congress. "We will not choose the path of submission!" He spoke of fighting "for the ultimate peace of the world and the liberation of its people" and, of course, of making the "world . . . safe for democracy."[6]

Somewhere between the reported tears and the manifestly dry-eyed idealism the true nature of Wilson's motivation on April 2, 1917 must have been situated. He may well have been "worn down" by certain aspects of so-called public opinion as well as by the insistent reports (mostly from British sources) of "Prussian" atrocities, Germany's repeated outrages on the high seas, and, finally, the Zimmermann Telegram. He may have been worn down, but it is also apparent that, by the time of his war message, he had decided of his own volition that committing to the Great War would carry a great advantage for the United States, elevating the nation to the status of a world power. More to point, perhaps, it would give him, as president of this world power, a seat at the table around which the other powers were gathered. It would put him—like George Creel, a determined and ultimately undoubting idealist—in position to guide the other nations of the world along the path to creating what he called a "scientific peace." With the audacity of idealism, he was confident that he could reshape the senseless cataclysm of the Great War into the war that would end war itself.

For George Creel, overweening idealism often produced a degree of self-confidence that was both impulsive and even contrary to reason. If Creel justifiably recognized a kindred spirit of idealism in Woodrow Wilson, it may well be that the president reciprocated the recognition. Whatever the mix of motives that finally pressed him to war, it was idealism—and the opportunity to impose idealism on the other powers of the world—that seems finally to have pushed Wilson over the edge, prompting him to leave behind what had been a passionate desire to avoid involvement in the carnage of the Old World. And, much as idealism trumped reason in so many of the decisions made by George Creel, so it seems to have overwhelmed rationality in the case of Wilson as well as a majority of Congress. Apparently neither the president nor Congress paused to contemplate the vast chasm between the decision to declare war and the nation's manifest inability, as of April 1917, actually to fight that war. Somehow—and very quickly—Americans would have to find the will and the means to transform themselves into a nation of righteous and potent warriors.

The astounding fact is that they would do just this. By the armistice in November 1918, the United States Army would be a force of more than 4 million, having numbered, in April of the year before, fewer than 200,000.

"While America's summons was answered without question by the citizenship as a whole," Creel wrote after the war, "it is to be remembered that during the three and a half years of our neutrality the land had been torn by a thousand divisive prejudices, stunned by the voices of anger and confusion, and muddled by the pull and haul of opposed interests." *Torn, stunned, muddled.* Such are all too often the adjectives associated with a democratic people, a people free to think for themselves rather than simply obey a king or dictator. Creel continued: "These were conditions that could not be permitted to endure. What we had to have was no mere surface unity, but a passionate belief in the justice of America's cause that should weld the people of the United States into one white-hot mass instinct with fraternity, devotion, courage, and deathless determination." *One white-hot mass.* Was *this* a concept and a state of being compatible with democracy? It was a question Creel clearly asked himself. Then he offered an answer: "The *war-will,* the will-to-win, of a democracy depends upon the degree to which each one of all the people of that democracy can concentrate and consecrate body and soul and spirit in the supreme effort of service and sacrifice. What had to be driven home was that all business was the nation's business, and every task a common task for a single purpose."[7]

From the start of America's involvement in the war, George Creel exhibited a keen understanding of what needed to be done to unite America behind the fight. The passages just quoted from his own history of the Committee on Public Information, 1920's *How We Advertised America* suggest his awareness of the paradoxical nature of his mission. It was to extract from a democracy the kind of mass behavior that might be expected from people under a totalitarian regime, yet to do so without destroying democracy. It was to forge a "*war-will.*" The very word, a coinage that seemed to Creel sufficiently foreign to merit italics, could have been translated from German, the language of enemy, with its fondness for portmanteau compounds.

To create America's war-will, Creel saw that he had to instill the universal "conviction that the war was not the war of an administration, but the war of one hundred million people." The journalist Creel had always held fast to a faith in facts, the belief that these were the most powerful ammunition in the arsenal of persuasion. Now he asserted his belief that "public support was a matter of public understanding," and the creation of this understanding should therefore be the chief business of the government's propaganda machine, which, of course, would not be called a ministry, department, or bureau of propaganda, but would be known instead by a democratic term that seemed to resonate from the epoch of the American Revolution—committee, the *Committee on Public Information.*[8]

In 1920, Creel could simply write that the national "summons was answered without question by the citizenship as a whole," but, even as late as April 1917, this outcome seemed hardly inevitable or even particularly likely. For one thing, the United States was home to the largest population of Germans (many first- and second-generation immigrants) outside of Germany. Until late in 1916, various German-American *Bund* ("league") organizations raised funds for German relief and to support the German war effort. Another substantial fraction of the citizenry consisted of Americans of Irish origin, who generally regarded any enemy of England as their friend. For most other Americans—at least those who did not run a bank, a steel mill, or a munitions plant—it made little difference who won the "Great War," just so long as the United States was not caught up in it.

Like Creel, Wilson saw the necessity of creating unity and getting Americans behind the war, and, like Creel also, he believed that the nation's millions were hardly unified. Yet this champion of democracy, who had sworn an oath to uphold a Constitution that included a guarantee of freedom of speech, was inclined to favor the very thing Creel complained that "the admirals and generals" clamored for: "a hard and fast censorship law that would have put the press in leg irons and handcuffs."[9]

Woodrow Wilson was hardly the first American chief executive to urge or approve of legislation intended to defend democracy by attacking and even diminishing it. John Adams signed into law the infamous Alien and Sedition Acts of 1798, which included draconian restrictions on free speech and the right of assembly, and Abraham Lincoln was widely condemned as a "tyrant" for suspending habeas corpus more than once during the Civil War. Yet although Wilson did sign into law an Espionage Act (June 15, 1917) as well as a Trading-with-the Enemy Act (October 6, 1917) and a new so-called Sedition Act (May 16, 1918), Creel always claimed—and with great pride—that he had dissuaded Wilson from finally endorsing an outright censorship law.

Creel told the story this way. Shortly after his reelection, President Wilson sought to reward him for his articles and for *Wilson and the Issues* with an appointment as assistant secretary in one of the cabinet departments. With thanks, Creel declined the president's offer in part because bureaucratic routine was anathema to him and, even more, because he and his glamorous wife could hardly be expected to live in Washington on a government salary. As the clouds of war thickened in March 1917, however, Creel was moved to contact the president in an effort to head off the proposed censorship legislation by offering an alternative. He explained, in his private brief to Wilson, that he did not deny the need for much secrecy in fighting a war but the need for secrecy could be met "without paying the heavy price of a censorship law." As Creel saw it, with "America's youth sailing to fight in foreign lands, leaving families three thousand miles behind them, nothing was more vital than that the people's confidence in the news should not be impaired." Americans were already anxious, he argued, and anxiety naturally produces suspicion, suspicion that could only be heightened by rigorous censorship, which would "inevitably stir demoralizing fears in the heart of every father and mother and open the door to every variety of rumor." Beyond this strategic imperative for eschewing outright censorship, Creel urged Wilson to bear in mind the constitutional guarantee of freedom of the press, nevertheless admitting that "[n]o other right guaranteed by democracy has been more abused"—abused, that is, by those claiming the right—but concluding that "even these abuses are preferable to the deadening evil of autocratic control."[10] He had chosen his adjective, "autocratic," carefully; Wilson and his government consistently painted Germany and the other Central Powers as exemplars of "autocracy" at its most wicked, and the administration further defined *autocracy* as the precise antithesis of *democracy*.

To his strategic and idealistic arguments against censorship, Creel added three more pragmatic reasons to reject it. First, it would almost certainly prove difficult, probably impossible, both to police and enforce effectively. Second, censorship laws might effectively muzzle the smaller papers, but, as the European experience with censorship demonstrated, they would do little to rein in the biggest, most influential newspapers, even in cases of "bold infraction." Finally, while it is true that those who frame censorship laws always claim to be doing nothing more than protecting military secrets, the legislation has a "way of slipping over into the field of opinion," thereby infringing on free speech. "Arbitrary power grows by what it feeds on," Creel wrote to Wilson. Laws governing censorship would soon become so elastic that the classification "[i]nformation of value to the enemy" would be "stretched to cover the whole field of independent discussion." Creel believed that suppressing "independent discussion" in wartime was especially destructive because "the people did not need less criticism in time of war, but more. Incompetence and corruption, bad enough in peace, took on an added menace when the nation was in arms."[11]

Having detailed the harm a censorship law would do, Creel proposed his alternative: a "voluntary agreement that would make every paper in the land its own censor, putting it up to the patriotism and common sense of the individual editor to protect purely military information of tangible value to the enemy." He went on to argue that, in any event, it was "idiocy to assume that the enemy would depend on the indiscretions of newspapers for their information." Given Creel's absorbing interest in the American Civil War—he had been raised on the tales of the "Southern colonels" who had fought it—this last point may have been disingenuous. He must have known that Civil War commanders on both sides derived a great deal of their intelligence concerning enemy troop strength, movements, and even battle plans precisely from the "indiscretions of newspapers." Nevertheless, Creel suggested to Wilson that the far graver threat came from out-and-out spies in our midst, and he recommended strict control not of the press, but of private cable and wireless communications in and out of the country.[12]

Concluding the pragmatic, practical aspects of the case against censorship, Creel ended on an idealistic note clearly designed to appeal to the president, arguing that "*expression*, not *suppression*, was the real need." The problem was not to stop potentially dangerous communication but to flood every possible media outlet with positive communications useful to the Allied war effort. This was necessary because the "sentiment of the West was still isolationist; the Northwest buzzed with talk of a 'rich man's war,' waged to salvage Wall Street loans; men and women of Irish stock were 'neutral,' not caring who whipped England, and in every state demagogues raved against 'warmongers.'"[13] The irony is, of course, inescapable. All of these objections to war—save the Irish animosity toward the English—were raised very persuasively by George Creel himself in his 1916 propaganda for Wilson's reelection, especially *Wilson and the Issues*.

Now these very sentiments, which had been essential to Wilson's retention in the White House, were liabilities.

Expression, Creel proposed, would not be confined to America and Americans but would be directed toward "an even greater task beyond our borders." The "war-weary peoples of England, France, and Italy" required the rejuvenating benefit of a "message of encouragement," whereas "the peoples of the neutral countries [had] to be won to our support, and the peoples of the Central Powers to be reached with the truth." The mission was to produce and disseminate propaganda on a global scale and through every medium—not "propaganda as the Germans defined it" but "propaganda in the true sense of the word, meaning the 'propagation of faith.'"[14]

Needless to say, this was no task for some legislated board of censors. In his brief to the president, Creel proposed establishing an agency to fight for what Wilson himself had called "the verdict of mankind." It would "reach deep into every American community, clearing away confusions," and it would simultaneously "seek the friendship of neutral nations and break through the barrage of lies that kept the Germans in darkness and delusion."[15]

It did not take Wilson long to respond to the Creel brief. The president had delivered his war message on April 2, Congress declared war on April 6, and a week later, on April 14, 1917, President Woodrow Wilson issued a terse executive order, number 2594 (which was backdated to April 13):

> I hereby create a Committee on Public Information, to be composed of the Secretary of State [Robert Lansing], the Secretary of War [Newton Baker], the Secretary of the Navy [Josephus Daniels], and a civilian who shall be charged with the executive direction of the Committee.
>
> As Civilian Chairman of this Committee, I appoint Mr. George Creel. The Secretary of State, the Secretary of War, and the Secretary of the Navy are authorized each to detail an officer or officers to the work of the Committee.[16]

The very day the executive order was issued, April 14, Creel took an oath as chairman of the Committee on Public Information. Within weeks it would be the largest, most ambitious propaganda program any nation had ever developed to that time, and it would rival even the formidable propaganda machinery of the brutal totalitarian regimes that came into being in the years following World War I.

As Creel told it, the Committee on Public Information—which Creel usually called the CPI, but the public soon referred to as the Creel Committee—was created as an ethically more palatable and strategically more useful alternative to censorship. As Creel told it, then, his committee existed *instead of* censorship.

But this last point was not exactly true, and the ambiguous position of George Creel and the Creel Committee with regard to censorship is both a symptom and a measure of the fate of democratic rights even in a war undertaken in defense of democracy.

A version of the Espionage Act was introduced in the House and Senate on February 5, 1917, four days after Germany announced the resumption of unrestricted submarine warfare and two days after Woodrow Wilson severed diplomatic relations with Germany. The Webb-Overman bill would have punished by imprisonment of up to twenty years and fines as high as $10,000 anyone who in wartime and without lawful authority should "collect, record, publish, or communicate" certain types of information that the bill broadly and vaguely defined as of a military nature or otherwise "directly or indirectly, useful to the enemy." Even more draconian was the provision of this same dire penalty for the communication or publication of "false reports or statements" or "reports or statements likely or intended to cause disaffection in, or interfere with the success of, the military or naval forces of the United States." A version of the bill passed in the Senate, but it died in the House upon the adjournment of the lame duck session of the 64th Congress on March 4. It had been hotly debated, and a number of champions of free speech, including Norman Thomas (a New York pastor associated with the American Union Against Militarism), Robert L. Hale (Columbia University economics instructor), John D. Moore (of the Friends of Irish Freedom), and Arthur E. Holder (lobbyist for the American Federation of Labor), appeared before Congress to present criticism of the bill. The general public, however, was either indifferent to the proposed legislation or tended to support it. [17]

More bills would follow, as would more debate. With each new legislative proposal, newspaper editors became more outspoken in defense of freedom of the press and objection to censorship, yet the public, fearful of enemy agents, tended increasingly to welcome restrictive legislation. Creel had worried about divisiveness and a lack of unified *war-will*. There was good reason for this. Thanks in no small part to Creel's own efforts, Wilson had gained reelection on a platform of neutrality. Yet by the time of the resumption of unrestricted submarine warfare and the severance of diplomatic relations, indifference, debate, and outright protest quickly turned to a rush among German-American societies, Socialist assemblies, labor groups, and even many pacifist organizations to pledge their allegiance and absolute loyalty to the American government. Indeed, in March, Nicholas Murray Butler, president of Columbia University and director of the Carnegie Endowment for International Peace, proclaimed his advocacy of military force, suspended the activities of the endowment, then, early in the war, turned over endowment headquarters to accommodate—rent free—some of the offices of the Creel Committee.

Even as the public and organizations representing various factions of the public rallied to the flag, newspaper publishers and editors continued to report on the debate over an espionage bill, admitting the necessity of strong laws to expose, arrest, and punish spies—the nation was in the grip of spy hysteria, with some papers wildly claiming that 100,000 German agents were at work in the United States—but decrying portions of the bill that would censor the press. Not that the mainstream press was ever actually critical of the war, the war effort, or war preparations. For example, newspaper support for the Armed Ship Bill, which President Wilson had requested on February 6, 1917, to arm merchant vessels, was virtually universal as well as intemperate. After passing the House by a large majority, the bill bogged down in the Senate thanks to a filibuster led by Wisconsin's iconoclastic Progressive Robert M. LaFollette Sr. and failed to pass by the time the 64th Congress adjourned. President Wilson responded by arming the ships through an executive order on March 9 amid a newspaper outcry, which accused LaFollette and others who had endorsed the filibuster of nothing less than treason. The response was typical of the mainstream press, which generally was committed to promoting national unity, even if this meant suppressing debate and dissent by branding them treason. When the new Congress reconvened and the Senate adopted, on March 8, cloture—which could end a filibuster by a two-thirds Senate vote—the nation's newspapers overwhelmingly approved what they hailed as a means by which any future "thwarting of the national will" might be suppressed.[18] Yet these same papers, while advocating the suppression of debate in Congress, continued to protest against censorship of the press.

As one version after another of the espionage bill and related legislation was debated, the nation's papers devoted extensive coverage to proposals of censorship, opposition to censorship, and defeat of censorship. "America will never submit to the suppression of information to which the people are plainly entitled," the *Philadelphia Public Ledger* cried out. "The American people are not accustomed to wearing muzzles," said the *Hartford Courant*.[19] Yet, despite the claim of each paper that it spoke on behalf of the American people, expressing their collective outrage, it was the editors, not the people, who protested. In the end, the press simply declared victory. On May 15, 1917, after the Senate passed a version of the espionage bill without an amendment explicitly authorizing press censorship, the *New York Times* triumphantly headlined its story:

SPY BILL PASSES;
NO CENSORSHIP
Amendment for Press Supervision Is Beaten by Vote of 48 to 34.

But, on May 23, the paper followed up by printing a letter President Wilson had written to Edwin Yates Webb, chairman of the House Judiciary Committee, under the headline "WILSON DEMANDS PRESS CENSORSHIP" and followed this on May 24 with an editorial asking "Does the Administration really feel that this Prussian edict would be a proper return for the services the newspapers have rendered the authorities in Washington?"[20]

On June 1, the *Times* was again able to exult:

HOUSE DEFEATS CENSORSHIP LAW BY 184 to 144.
Spy Bill Goes Back to Conference,
with Orders to Eliminate Press Gag.[21]

According to the newspapers, the espionage bill as passed and signed on June 15, 1917, was an antispy law, nothing more and nothing less. This leads one to wonder if any of the reporters or their editors had actually read the legislation that was finally enacted. For example, Title I, Section 3 of the law forbade anyone from making or conveying "false reports or false statements with intent to interfere with the operation or success of the military or naval forces of the United States or to promote the success of its enemies." It barred any "attempt to cause insubordination, disloyalty, mutiny, refusal of duty, in the military or naval forces of the United States" or to "wilfully obstruct the recruiting or enlistment service of the United States." Punishment for violating these proscriptions included a fine of up to $10,000 and/or imprisonment for up to twenty years.[22] True, there is no mention of censorship of the press here, but there is a powerful incentive to self-censorship and what Creel himself would have characterized as "voluntary" curtailment of freedom of the press and freedom of speech. "False reports," "false statements," and attempts to "interfere with the operation or success" of the U.S. military or to "promote the success of its enemies"—all of this language was breathtakingly broad, vague, and subject to an extremely wide range of interpretation. Before the end of the war, Title I, Section 3 would be used by the U.S. Department of Justice to prosecute some two thousand cases under the Espionage Act—very few of them for spying as such. Moreover, Title XII of the act forbade the mailing of any material that violated other provisions of the act. This ensured potentially tight government control over magazines and other subscription matter that was transmitted via the U.S. mails.

During and after the war, George Creel deeply resented and vigorously fought accusations that the CPI and he himself were agents of censorship. He pointed out, quite correctly, that neither he nor the CPI had any authority of enforcement or prosecution under any law. The CPI, he always said, did nothing more than produce and disseminate information and advise the press on guidelines for voluntary self-censorship, all without government interference or sanction. Yet the reality was that editors universally came to feel that the Creel Committee—and George Creel in particular—did wield very potent authority under the Espionage Act and therefore could coerce and compel censorship. Not only did these editors believe (and quite correctly) that Creel had the ear of many in the administration, from President Wilson on down, they also recognized his very close ties with the Department of Justice, which wielded the power of prosecution.

Repeatedly Creel asserted that he was nothing more than chairman of CPI and had no other official authority. Actually, he was also a member of the Censorship Board, which Wilson established pursuant to authority granted by the Trading-with-the-Enemy Act of October 6, 1917. This legislation authorized censorship of all messages that passed between the United States and any foreign country. The transmission of transatlantic news was included and therefore subject directly to the outright censorship Creel had, in a domestic context, disavowed.

On May 7, 1918, the Espionage Act was amended in a manner so far-reaching that the *amendment* was informally referred to as the Sedition *Act* of 1918. Title I, Section 3, of the Espionage Act was substantially expanded by the amendment, which extended the $10,000 fine and twenty-year prison term to anyone who might

> make or convey false reports, or false statements, or say or do anything . . . with intent to obstruct the sale by the United States of bonds . . . or the making of loans by or to the United States, or whoever shall wilfully utter, print, write, or publish any disloyal, profane, scurrilous, or abusive language about the form of government of the United States, or the Constitution of the United States, or the military or naval forces of the United States, or the flag . . . or the uniform of the Army or Navy of the United States, or any language intended to bring the form of government . . . or the Constitution . . . or the military or naval forces . . . or the flag . . . of the United States into con-

tempt, scorn, contumely, or disrepute . . . or shall wilfully display the flag of any foreign enemy.

The amendment also effectively barred strikes or work slowdowns, the urging, incitement, or advocacy of "any curtailment of production in this country of any thing or things . . . necessary or essential to the prosecution of the war."[23]

This was draconian censorship indeed, and yet the Sedition Act provoked little public objection. Creel liked to believe that compliance with voluntary censorship was in large part due to the high esteem in which the nation's newspapermen held the integrity of his word. After all, he was one of their own. In part, this was doubtless the case, but it is also an inescapable fact that editors got the message—they got the message behind the Espionage and Sedition acts, and they understood that George Creel was the man with power and authority—unofficial though it might be—to impose and to enforce censorship under those potent acts.

George Creel always pointed with pride to the CPI as a timely alternative to censorship, an alternative that defended democracy without abridging it. It seems likely that he himself believed this. Nevertheless, it was by no means the whole truth. The Creel Committee was not so much an alternative to censorship as it was an alternative form of censorship. Nor was its authority founded solely on the potency of factual truth in achieving moral suasion; there was certainly an element of this, but the authority of the CPI also derived from the looming presence of the heavy penalties embodied in the Espionage and Sedition acts.

And it also derived from something even more compelling.

When he proposed to Woodrow Wilson establishing an agency to create, promote, disseminate, and generally manage *expression* instead of merely imposing *suppression*, Creel defined his mission as creating a single, white-hot *war-will*, yet by the time the Creel Committee came into being, the nation was actually in the throes of war fever, even war hysteria. The vast majority of the American people rallied to the war effort. Creel found that his mission was not so much to manage public opinion as it was to manage those who could do much to influence public opinion: the press. He had believed that the big job facing him would be to recruit the press in support of a grand appeal to the people. Instead, he discovered that he could count on the people to back his efforts to manage the press. The people were behind the war. The CPI would work to maintain and direct their support—and it would work as well to ensure that the press cooperated and collaborated in this campaign by avoiding anything that might raise questions or create doubt about the war. The people, it seemed, were as hungry for propaganda as they were for news—perhaps even hungrier—and Creel did not want the press to kill their appetite.

The *people* neither distrusted nor protested the real or perceived authority of George Creel. Many putative *representatives* of the people—the legislators—did distrust and protest, but Creel was always less concerned with winning over legislators than he was with persuading the press that he could be trusted and that they should therefore voluntarily comply with CPI guidance and directives. But what Creel offered as a democratic alternative to absolute "Prussian" censorship was never actually free of coercion, the coercion embodied in law as well as in the surprising unity of public opinion. To understand both the American home front in World War I and the role and practice of propaganda in democracy, it is necessary to acknowledge that the operations of the Creel Committee, including the program of "voluntary" censorship it administered, were quietly backed by coercive legislation predicated on "crimes" broadly and vaguely defined but punishable by very harsh penalties. However, to understand George Creel—and the manner in which he created and managed his committee—it is also necessary to acknowledge that, for all his implied authority, this habitually impulsive, temperamentally mercurial man was a model of self-restraint. He could have raised himself to the heights of a most dangerous demagoguery, had he wanted to do so. He was, after all, in an ideal position to exploit a popular patriotism that often crossed the line into war hysteria. This is precisely what might have been expected of him, a writer risen from the ranks of yellow journalism, a fiery reformer who had once called for the lynching of corrupt city officials and who had once fanned the flames of violent rebellion in the great Colorado coal strike, a man who saw the world in terms of good (those on his side) and evil (everyone else). Instead, George Creel brought to the work of the committee a spirit of democratic passion tempered by liberal rationality. America's first and only ministry of propaganda would prove to be an enterprise of great inventiveness and boundless exuberance, yet also of thoughtful deliberation and remarkable integrity.

CHAPTER 5

CONJURING THE COMMITTEE

Audacious, impulsive, imaginative, and heedless of most limits, George Creel may have been the only man in America capable of creating the Committee on Public Information. Authorized by President Wilson's executive order issued on April 14, 1917, before the end of the year the Creel Committee was a plainclothes army of more than 100,000. Outwardly it appeared to be a massive, albeit instant, bureaucracy. It was in fact an organic entity rather than a bureaucratically structured government agency. Its explosive growth was marked by what Creel himself called an "accidental quality." The committee was improvised on the job, a string of "lucky accidents" consistently figuring "in the work."[1] The principal mission of the Creel Committee was established from the outset: to oversee a program of voluntary censorship and to flood the media with news from essentially official sources in a comprehensive effort to manage the war information that reached the public. With this double mission as a constant, it seemed that scarcely an hour passed without a new idea being offered—and acted on—for accomplishing it. Committee departments and bureaus were created in the morning and closed down or merged with others by the afternoon. Before quitting time, fresh entities were already spawning. The time span between idea and action was infinitesimal.

As Creel told the story, the idea for the committee was all his. As others told it, however, the idea—or at least the germ of the idea—came from Woodrow Wilson's cabinet, namely the secretaries of state, war, and the navy. According to Navy Secretary Josephus Daniels, he, Secretary of War Newton Baker, and President Wilson (with the other cabinet members giving their assent) "were very anxious that we should not fall into the stupid censorship which had marked the action of some countries in dealing with the war news." In fact, as we saw in chapter 4, Wilson was by no means opposed to censorship. It is unclear whether Daniels, writing some twenty years after the fact, misremembered the president's position, wanted to "revise" that position, or was recalling the president's position as it existed *after* the Creel brief. Whatever his motive, Daniels's version of the story was that he called into his Navy Department office immediately after the declaration of war "all the newspapermen in Washington" to tell them that there would be no censorship and that, on the contrary, "we would give them freely the information that would let them know what was going on." From time to time, however, "we" would request that the papers "publish nothing which might fall into the hands of the enemy or embarrass war operations." In this recollection, Daniels made no mention of Creel, so, again, it is unclear whether he was taking credit for the idea of voluntary censorship, whether he met with the newsmen *after* reading the Creel brief, or whether he simply misremembered the sequence of events. Whatever the truth may be, Daniels, at this point, apparently saw no need for a special committee or other agency—until, that is, he judged that he was not getting 100 percent compliance with the self-censorship request. "Ninety-nine per cent of them [the newsmen] patriotically accepted this suggestion but we soon found out that now and then the zeal for scoops outran patriotism." This imperfect compliance was the genesis of the Committee on Public Information, according to Daniels, and, at this point—finally—enter George Creel: "No other name was suggested as the executive head of that committee except that of Mr. Creel."[2]

Perhaps the general agreement on Creel's appointment resulted from the fact (if we accept Creel's version) that he had already proposed creating an agency to "make the fight for . . . 'the verdict of mankind.'" Yet agreement was not quite universal. "[Secretary of State Robert] Lansing, I think, would have preferred a sort of censorship," Daniels wrote, "and never warmed up to Mr. Creel or to the work of the Committee." Apparently, this was an understatement. Creel wrote that Lansing "was terribly upset for fear that people might think that he was 'under' me," and in his 1947 memoir went on to suggest that Lansing's objections grew out of a combination of envy, egotism, turf protection, and a pompous absence of humor.[3]

Whether by intention and design or not, Creel's demeaning of Lansing obscures the legitimate gravity of the issue the secretary of state had raised. Lansing was concerned that a civilian, a journalist, a man elected to no office, a man with no constitutional standing whatsoever had been put in a position to abridge, at will, the prerogatives and operations of the cabinet, including, most especially, those of the Department of State. In his *War Memoirs,* published in 1935, Lansing complained that Creel "soon assumed all authority and ran the Office of Public Information in accordance with his own ideas. I do not think the change to a 'one man' office was distasteful to Mr. Wilson, as he had great confidence in Creel's ability and personal loyalty . . . [but] Creel was hostile to me personally . . . and sought in various ways to discredit me as Secretary of State." In his own memoir, Creel quoted then dismissed this comment with the single expletive "Bosh!"[4]

Lansing was indisputably right about one thing. President Wilson was not disturbed by Creel's "one man" leadership of the Committee on Public Information. Nor were Daniels and Baker. All three knew Creel personally. Creel had been instrumental in gaining Wilson a second term. As part of the Wilson reelection campaign, Creel had defended Daniels against an outrageous smear campaign. As for Creel's acquaintance with Baker, the two had become friends and colleagues years earlier, at the turn of the century, when they both zealously waved the banner of Progressive reform. None of the three saw any danger in turning over a major wartime government operation to a man who could, with justification, be labeled their mutual political crony. As Daniels explained it two decades after the war, "Baker, saying that I was a journalist by profession [Daniels owned the Raleigh (North Carolina) *News & Observer*], largely turned over to me the work of the Committee, and never a week passed that I was not in consultation with Mr. Creel."[5] In effect, then, two of the three cabinet members who served on the CPI blithely ceded their authority to George Creel—although, twenty years after the fact, Daniels added the essentially cosmetic comment that he was always "in consultation" with Creel. If the Creel Committee was a "one man" office, this had come about less through any ambition Creel may have had to build an empire than through the passivity of Baker and the compliance of Daniels. We are left, then, to wonder whether the blurring of chronology—did the idea for the CPI originate with Creel or with Daniels?—might have served another purpose. Daniels may have been anxious to blunt the impression Lansing clearly had, that government officials were ceding authority and abrogating responsibilities willy-nilly to a mere journalist.

Daniels and Baker freely yielded authority to Creel. Lansing both carped and raised serious objections but apparently did little of substance to countermand the other two secretaries. Perhaps this was because the cabinet members' original conception of the CPI was modest. As Lansing, Baker, and Daniels wrote to President Wilson on April 13, 1917, the committee was to do no more than frame *regulations* and create *machinery* to safeguard potentially sensitive information while preserving a general openness suited to a democratic government. James R. Mock and Cedric Larson, the authors of *Words That Won the War,* a study of the CPI published in 1939, as the United States struggled fitfully to maintain neutrality in what looked to be yet another "European war," observed that "the original purpose of the CPI was to supervise the handling of government news," period. Mock and Larson credited Daniels, Baker, and Lansing with presenting the "germ of an idea" to President Wilson, who immediately cut an executive order establishing the committee, "but it was the brilliant and restless mind of George Creel that took this idea and created a vast and complex organization of which the President and his advisers could not have dreamed." The authors of *Words on War* elaborated on this by explaining that Creel not only did what they called the CPI's "primary job of directing the release (or sometimes the suppression) of news of the American people at war," he also "moved into the far less restricted field of opinion management," what we today would call public relations. It was toward this end that Creel and the CPI "invented new techniques and perfected old ones, and first to last built up a stupendous propaganda organization." Sweeping, even breezy, this description is nevertheless accurate. But where Mock and Larson showed greatest insight was in their interpretation of the real purpose of Creel's "stupendous propaganda organization": "to make President Wilson's theories known to every village crossroads in this country and in remote corners of foreign lands."[6]

The mechanics and methods of the CPI represent important innovations in opinion management, public relations, propaganda, or whatever else one chooses to call it; however, the most profound direction in which Creel took the CPI enterprise was not in the control of information but the creation of thought. Creel believed that Woodrow Wilson was dead serious about making the Great War an ideological contest, a struggle for the hearts and minds of the whole world, and the CPI chairman therefore intended the committee to function, above all else, as an instrument to broadcast the Wilson ideology. His intention was not merely to excite and galvanize patriotism but to ensure that the war would be what Wilson wanted it to be: a theory of democratic government ratified in blood.

As observed in chapter 4, Creel described the mission of the CPI as bringing unity of public opinion, forging a white-hot *war-will*. By the time the committee came into existence, popular enthusiasm for the war was already at a high—even hysterical—pitch, and the more immediate problem for the CPI was managing the press rather than the people. Beyond this, the very highest committee priority soon became the inculcation of ideology. Creel saw himself as more than the nation's cheerleader. A cheerleader urges victory for the sake of victory. Creel proclaimed himself a propagandist—a propagator of the faith. His mission was to urge victory for the sake of Wilson's ideologically established gospel of democracy. This often required CPI activities to take a nuanced rather than an all-out approach. Patriotic enthusiasm continually threatened to degenerate into demagoguery and mob action. Even victory verged on becoming nothing more than an empty mantra, its attachment to democratic ideology sometimes fragile, imperfectly understood by the people.

Brainwashing is a term that did not come into the English language until 1950, but it describes what most people believe is the purpose of propaganda.[7] In the popular understanding, propaganda is the means a government, a state, a head of state, even a large corporation uses to "brainwash" a given population—that is, to instill in them certain attitudes, beliefs, or loyalties without regard to individual intelligence, will, or even consciousness. This was far from how Creel defined propaganda and, therefore, far from how he defined his mission. The mass of messages the CPI delivered were not intended to seduce, deceive, or hypnotize but to educate Americans and others in the gospel of Wilsonian democracy. Brainwashing molds belief by overcoming, even nullifying consciousness. Creel's propaganda, in contrast, was aimed at heightening consciousness for the purpose of creating a set of ideologically based beliefs, individual by individual, yet with perfect uniformity.

While it was true that enthusiasm for the war ran surprisingly high by April 1917, cultivating the sophisticated degree of uniform ideological understanding across the American population was a very tall order. Mock and Larson invited their readers to imagine the situation of a midwestern family living "on a quarter-section of farmland a dozen miles from the railroad, telegraph, and post office. The nearest daily newspaper was published at the far end of the next county, seventy-five miles away. No through road passed near their farm, they had seen pavement only a few times in their lives, and they had no phone. Normally they paid scant attention to public affairs. Their only aim in life, so it seemed, was to bring in the golden harvest."[8] It was these people—among many others—that the Creel Committee had not only to reach but to reach so effectively, so thoroughly, and so consistently that they would emerge not brainwashed or bullied, nor even simply charged with a zeal for victory, but *educated* in the fine principles of Wilsonian political ideology. They needed not merely to support the war but to understand it—the way Woodrow Wilson understood it.

Creel achieved this transformation of mind, even in a remote midwestern farm family, by ensuring that every item of war news they saw—in the county weekly, in magazines, or in the city daily picked up occasionally in the general store—was not merely officially approved information but precisely the same kind that millions of their fellow citizens were getting at the same moment."⁹ The CPI made sure that every story had been vetted, whether at the source or "voluntarily" by the newspaper that printed it; however, virtually all stories ultimately flowed from CPI sources. The patriotic advertisements that appeared in the nation's newspapers were the work of many hands, but all of those hands worked for the CPI. Even straight commercial advertising took a cue from the CPI, which networked with ad agencies and business leaders at every level, feeding them guidelines for the inclusion of a patriotic slant in hawking everything from soap to life insurance. Indeed, there was not a single significant media outlet that failed to carry a CPI message. In addition to newspapers and magazines, county fairs, movies, classrooms, post office walls, churches, synagogues, union halls—virtually every physical interface with the public—was a venue for a CPI message. The result was a torrent of news and other information, but it was not brainwashing. It was reasoned, rational exposition and argument made overwhelmingly powerful by dint of sheer volume, repetition, and ubiquity.

To achieve this level of saturation required an extraordinary apparatus, which came into existence with nearly unbelievable speed. It seemed as if the Creel Committee was not so much created as it was conjured out of thin air.

The sole conjurer, without question, was George Creel. "Putting the Committee on Public Information together," he admitted, "was like asking the Babylonians to build a threshing machine, for there was no chart to go by." Yet with his customary impulsive optimism, he found a great advantage even in this. "Starting from scratch seemed a hardship at the time, but on looking back, I see it as my salvation. With the organization put together man by man, I knew it from top to bottom and could keep an eye and hand on every division."¹⁰ Writing in 1947, he contrasted his situation to that of Elmer Davis, the popular newspaper and radio journalist who was appointed to head the Office of War Information (OWI) at the outbreak of World War II in 1941. Davis, Creel pointed out, had been saddled with the staff of three dysfunctional existing agencies, the

Office of Government Reports, the Office of Coordinator of Information, and the Office of Facts and Figures. As a result, the propaganda effort in World War II was not nearly as pervasive or thoroughly coordinated as the work of the CPI in World War I. Even more frustrating was the position of Assistant Secretary of State William Benton, who was assigned to run the Office of International Information and Cultural Affairs, created immediately after the end of World War II. It was an unwieldy conglomeration of the wartime Office of Strategic Services (OSS) and the OWI.

But "starting from scratch" really did mean beginning with nothing. For the first several weeks of operation, the CPI did not even have an office. Initially, Creel and the CPI were assigned temporary quarters in the U.S. Navy Library, "a shadowy, shelf-filled room peopled by quiet, retiring gentlewomen, who shuddered in corners while noisy mobs invaded their sanctuary." Here Creel was assailed by "hundreds of callers—eager patriots, duty-dodgers, job-hunters, cranks, inventors, Congressmen with constituents to place—buzzing like a locust swarm and devouring time with much the same rapacity." At length, Newton Baker came to the rescue by lending Creel the services of Douglas MacArthur, at the time a "handsome young major" in the regular army, who quickly located space for the CPI at 10 Jackson Place, once the dwelling of either Daniel Webster or John C. Calhoun (tradition was divided on the identity of the occupant), across the street from the White House. Later, after Creel was forced to shoehorn personnel into basement cubbyholes and the attic, the town house next door was leased as well, and when office workers overflowed into the kitchen and hallways of this domicile, a third Jackson Place dwelling was commandeered. Later still, some of the operation would spread to the Treasury Building and elsewhere. Even Mock and Larson, the two scholars who devoted the greatest effort to documenting the history of the CPI (and who had liberal access to all of the living principals, including George Creel himself) despaired of ever being able to "draw a definitive outline of its work" or its development: "no one can." That is because the CPI did not so much develop as it exploded into existence. "A 'come at once' telegram would be dispatched to some journalist, scholar, or public figure, he would catch an afternoon train; and presto! the next dawn would break on a brand new unit of the CPI."[11]

Among the first to receive such a telegram was Arthur Bullard, like Creel a Missouri native, who, after two years as a student at Hamilton College, went to work in New York City as a probation officer and wrote highly practical essays on criminology. He left this work in 1904 to become a foreign correspondent for several U.S. and European magazines, and by 1914 was editor of *The Outlook*. The author of a number of travel books and political studies, including *The Diplomacy of the Great War* (1916), Bullard suspended his busy career to answer Creel's call. Close behind him came Ernest Poole, a Chicago-born Princeton man, who graduated in 1902, the very year in which Professor Woodrow Wilson was named to the presidency of the institution. Creel knew Poole as a crusading journalist, who vigorously promoted a roster of social reforms, especially in the area of child labor. By 1917, when he responded to his Creel telegram, Poole was best known for his 1915 novel, *The Harbor*, which portrayed life and death on the rough Brooklyn waterfront. The pro-union, frankly Socialist slant of the book was red meat to the conservative Robert Lansing, who complained in his *War Memoirs* of Creel's "well known . . . Socialistic tendencies . . . evidenced by some of the people he employed."[12]

Harvey O'Higgins, Edgar Sisson, W. L. Chenery, and Charles Hart were also in the very first wave of prominent figures Creel drafted. A Canadian by birth, O'Higgins was a highly successful freelance journalist and literary jack-of-all-trades, whose muckraking nonfiction included *The Beast* (1910), a sensational exposé of the social environment of city-bred children, and *Under the Prophet in Utah* (1911), a sensational exposé of the Mormon Church. In 1914, he wrote a play—sensational, of course—*Polygamy*, on the subject of Mormon plural marriage. Creel claimed that O'Higgins gave up an annual income of $15,000 to work for the CPI.[13]

Edgar Sisson had entered journalism as a reporter and drama critic, and he served as city editor of the *Chicago Tribune* and managing editor of *Collier's*. He left the editorship of *Cosmopolitan* to work for the Creel Committee. William Chenery was, like Creel himself, an alumnus of the

Rocky Mountain News, then went on after the war to become editor of *Collier's.* Charles S. Hart left a $10,000-a-year post as advertising manager of *Hearst's Magazine* to work for the CPI at $3,900, Creel having intercepted him on his way to a high-level position in the U.S. Army Ordnance Department.

These men—the first of many prominent figures to turn their backs on the private sector for the sake of the war—worked, Creel said, day and night, to get the CPI up and running by the end of its very first week of existence. It established itself first and foremost as the source of guidance for the voluntary censorship program. The CPI struggled into birth during the height of press outrage over the prospect of censorship legislation. Creel must have seen himself and the CPI in a perilous position at this point. Yes, the press was up in arms over censorship, but the fact was that, even with the war under way, as yet no censorship was being imposed. This notwithstanding, Creel knew that that the Espionage Act, still under debate, would inevitably bring some form of censorship with it. On one hand, he had to discuss and define the censorship issue in a way that would mollify the members of the press, but, on the other, he had to create a sufficiently credible program of "voluntary censorship" that would satisfy bureaucrats, military men, and lawmakers sufficiently to ward off the inclusion of outright censorship of the press in the Espionage Act. The first step in this high-wire act was a statement Creel crafted and immediately distributed to every member of the Washington press corps. "It will be necessary at times to keep information from our own people in order to keep it from the enemy," Creel wrote frankly, "but most of the belligerent countries have gone much farther." He cited European censorship of reports concerning outbreaks of epidemics in training camps and articles "tending to raise unduly the hopes of the people as to the success" of anticipated military movements as examples of the "sort of suppression [that] had obviously nothing to do with the keeping of objectionable news from the enemy." European-style censorship betrayed "distrust of democratic common sense," Creel wrote. What is more, it failed to solve the problem. "A printed story is tangible even if false. It can be denied. Its falsity can be proven. It is not nearly so dangerous as a false rumor"—the very thing that grows in an "atmosphere created by common knowledge that news is being suppressed." In short, Creel pledged, only information that is of direct military use to the enemy would be censored. Everything else would be left to the patriotic common sense of editors.[14]

After distributing the statement, Creel, Bullard, and Sisson met with the press, explaining that a program of voluntary censorship would not only be genuinely voluntary but fully public. The assembly of newspapermen was hostile at first, but Creel believed that it became "more friendly as understandings were reached, and when we left it seemed a certainty that the plan would be approved." But the next day, the newspapers published a letter from President Wilson in which he denied having withdrawn support for a full-blown censorship law, and, with that, the trust and goodwill of the editors instantly collapsed. Worse, Secretary of State Lansing issued a statement declaring that the "Department of State considers it dangerous and of service to the enemy to discuss differences of opinion between the Allies and difficulties with neutral countries." Likewise, "Speculation about possible peace is another topic which may possess elements of danger, as peace reports may be of enemy origin put out to weaken the combination against Germany." As far as the press was concerned, these objections pushed the envelope of censorship, but the real deal breaker came at the conclusion of Lansing's statement: "Generally speaking, articles likely to prove offensive to any of the Allies or to neutrals would be undesirable."[15] The vague adjective "offensive" gave the government censors license to stop publication of just about anything.

Editors roundly declared that they were being set up as the victims of an administration plot to gag them. In vain, Creel pointed to the concluding portion of the statement he and his colleagues had presented to the press: "Nearly all the European belligerents have also tried to prevent the publication of news likely to offend their allies or create friction between them. The Committee is of the opinion that the more full the interally [inter-ally] discussion of their mutual problems the better. . . . If any case arises where one of our papers uses insulting or objectionable language against our comrades in arms it had best be dealt with individually. But so far as possible this Committee will maintain the rule of free discussion in such matters."[16]

This was not sufficient to appease the press, which was relieved only after the latest "censorship bill" was defeated. Although the CPI had been in existence for only a week, Creel decided to put the entire issue to rest by promulgating an authoritative policy fully defining voluntary censorship. It was printed on a ten-by-twelve card and distributed to the nation's editors:

WHAT THE GOVERNMENT ASKS OF THE PRESS

The desires of the government with respect to the concealment from the enemy of military policies, plans, and movements are set forth in the following specific requests. They go to the press of the United States directly from the Secretary of War and the Secretary of the Navy and represent the thought and advice of their technical advisers. They do not apply to news despatches censored by military authority with the expeditionary forces or in those cases where the government itself, in the form of official statements, may find it necessary or expedient to make public information covered by these requests.

For the protection of our military and naval forces and of merchant shipping it is requested that secrecy be observed in all matters of—

1. Advance information of the routes and schedules of troop movements. (See Par. 5.)
2. Information tending to disclose the number of troops in the expeditionary forces abroad.
3. Information calculated to disclose the location of the permanent base or bases abroad.
4. Information that would disclose the location of American units or the eventual position of the American forces at the front.
5. Information tending to disclose an eventual or actual port of embarkation; or information of the movement of military forces toward seaports or of the assembling of military forces at seaports from which inference might be drawn of any intention to embark them for service abroad; and information of the assembling of transports or convoys; and information of the embarkation itself.
6. Information of the arrival at any European port of American war-vessels, transports, or any portion of any expeditionary force, combatant or non-combatant.

7. Information of the time of departure of merchant ships from American or European ports, or information of the ports from which they sailed, or information of their cargoes.

8. Information indicating the port of arrival of incoming ships from European ports or after their arrival indicating, or hinting at, the port at which the ship arrived.

9. Information as to convoys and as to the sighting of friendly or enemy ships, whether naval or merchant.

10. Information of the locality, number, or identity of vessels belonging to our own navy or to the navies of any country at war with Germany.

11. Information of the coast or anti-aircraft defenses of the United States. Any information of their very existence, as well as the number, nature, or position of their guns, is dangerous.

12. Information of the laying of mines or mine-fields or of any harbor defenses.

13. Information of the aircraft and appurtenances used at government aviation-schools for experimental tests under military authority, and information of contracts and production of air material, and information tending to disclose the numbers and organization of the air division, excepting when authorized by the Committee on Public Information.

14. Information of all government devices and experiments in war material, excepting when authorized by the Committee on Public Information.

15. Information of secret notices issued to mariners or other confidential instructions issued by the navy or the Department of Commerce relating to lights, lightships, buoys, or other guides to navigation.

16. Information as to the number, size, character, or location of ships of the navy ordered laid down at any port or shipyard, or in actual process of construction; or information that they are launched or in commission.

17. Information of the train or boat schedules of traveling official missions in transit through the United States.

18. Information of the transportation of munitions or of war material.

Photographs.—Photographs conveying the information specified above should not be published.

These requests to the press are without larger authority than the necessities of the war-making branches. Their enforcement is a matter for the press itself. To the overwhelming proportion of newspapers who have given unselfish, patriotic adherence to the voluntary agreement the government extends its gratitude and high appreciation.

COMMITTEE ON PUBLIC INFORMATION,
By GEORGE CREEL, Chairman.[17]

The statement is worth quoting in its entirety as evidence of the incredible speed and efficiency with which the CPI worked. At the time that the card was created, the CPI did not even have a permanent office and was in the feverish process of recruiting personnel at every level. Yet the content, the completeness, the form, the very tone of this communication conveyed the authority of a long-established branch of the government. It was the opening act, the debut feat, of Creel the conjurer.

Any attempt to chronicle the evolution of the CPI is doomed, partly because some three-quarters of the committee's records were lost when operations were precipitously shut down after the armistice by a mistrustful, resentful, and angry Congress, and partly because there simply was no "evolution." The development of the Creel Committee was an explosive improvisation. Nevertheless, the CPI had a certain contour.

As Creel saw it, the mission dictated the priorities. The first imperative was to create, issue, and win approval for the rules of voluntary censorship. After this was accomplished by the end of the CPI's first week of existence, "the next step, obviously, was the fight for national unity." For Creel, this meant forming public opinion, which, in turn, implied a necessary preparation: "before a sound, steadfast public opinion could be formed, it had to be *informed*. Not manipulated, not tricked, and not wheedled, but given every fact in the case." The object was to avoid creating the impression that the war was "the war of the administration or the private enterprise of the General Staff" but was, rather, "the grim business of a whole people." To create this popular attitude and collective sentiment, Creel believed he had to give every man, woman, and child "a feeling of partnership." This feeling was to be based on the dissemination of "every fact in the case," and the way to accomplish this feat "was to put trained reporters in the War Department, the Navy, and every other agency connected with the war machine."[18]

To use the terminology associated with Iraq War that began in 2003, Creel *embedded* media personnel with the administration of the armed forces. Because the work of the CPI was mainly news gathering and news publishing, among the earliest activities of the committee was the recruitment and deployment of the journalists who made up the first major unit of the CPI, the Division of News. What came after this unit was established Creel admitted "was inspirational rather than planned." Highlights of this "inspirational" sequence included the creation of the Division of Pictorial Publicity, after the celebrated graphic artist Charles Dana Gibson (creator of the iconic "Gibson Girl") walked into CPI headquarters on or shortly before the morning of April 17, 1917, with a poster he wanted to contribute. Creel welcomed the contribution and immediately pressed Gibson into service to recruit an army of famous artists for the production of many more paintings and posters. That very same afternoon, Creel was also visited by another walk-in, "a rosy-cheeked youth by the name of Donald Ryerson," who presented his plan for putting public speakers in the movie theaters of Chicago. Before he left Creel's office, Ryerson had been given a brief to assemble a national organization to be called the Four-Minute Men. It would become the most visible and vocal of the CPI's operations. Further inspired by Ryerson's idea of using speakers to manage public opinion, Creel "reached for the telephone and drafted Arthur Bestor," president of the Chautauqua, the celebrated nationwide program that presented public speeches by prominent Americans, to create a Speaking Division.[19]

Within days of the visits by Gibson and Ryerson and the call to Bestor, four other men called on Creel. Herbert Houston, the influential publisher of *Our World,* William H. Rankin, another editor-publisher, Thomas Cusack, owner of a major billboard advertising company, and William H. Johns, an advertising executive, urged Creel to begin purchasing vast expanses of advertising space in newspapers and magazines, and on billboards. The result of this counsel was the instantaneous birth of the Division of Advertising, headed by Johns.

These units formed the operational core of the CPI—at least for its first few months. By the armistice, it had become possible to outline something resembling a rational organizational structure, although no one who has ever written about the CPI agrees on the details. By the end of the war, committee operations could be seen as broadly divided between two main sections, the Domestic Section and the Foreign Section. Offices were on Jackson Place—the row houses Douglas MacArthur had secured—and the Treasury Building as well as elsewhere in Washington, New York, and other cities.

The Executive Division consisted of Chairman Creel and associate chairmen (Sisson, O'Higgins, and Carl Byoir, remembered as one of the founding fathers of modern public relations). Its function was to plan, initiate, and coordinate all CPI operations.

The Office of Business Management was set up in October 1917 to relieve the Executive Division of various routine administrative functions. Under this office were a Division of Stenography and Mimeographing and a Division of Production and Distribution, which, between them, handled much of the actual, physical production and distribution of printed material.

Within the Domestic Section, the Division of News was originally headed by newspaper man John W. McConaughy, who was succeeded by Leigh Reilly, former managing editor of the *Chicago Herald.* Before the end of the war, the division had issued some six thousand major releases published in about twenty thousand newspaper columns per week.

Associated with, but independent from, the Division of News was the office that published the *Official Bulletin,* the first official daily newspaper of the U.S. government, intended to be a record of the nation's participation in the war, written "without color or bias." The first issue was published on May 10, 1917.[20]

Before the April 1917 ended, a Foreign Language Newspaper Division had been established for two purposes: to monitor every foreign-language newspaper in the United States (in this, it would later work to enforce the licensing provisions of the Trading-with-the-Enemy Act—despite Creel's frequently repeated insistence that neither he nor the CPI possessed any enforcement authority) and to translate CPI pamphlets and other publications into foreign languages. In March 1918, the division was absorbed into the Division of Work with the Foreign Born.

Guy Stanton Ford, a distinguished historian and dean of the Graduate School of the University of Minnesota, was pressed into service to create the Division of Civic and Educational Cooperation, which commissioned, edited, and published 105 books and pamphlets, mostly by eminent scholars. Distributed through schools and colleges, these volumes achieved a staggering circulation of 75 million. The division also issued a sixteen-page newsletter, *The National School Service,* which had an effective circulation of 20 million households.

The Picture Division, established in October 1917, managed the production and distribution of war-related still photographs. It is unclear whether the Bureau of War Photographs, established somewhat later, was organized under the Picture Division or separate from it, but it served essentially the same function. Part of the bureau was a Department of Slides, which produced and distributed lantern slides for public lectures and school programs.

Established along with the Picture Division in October 1917 was a Film Division, which at first was responsible only for distributing motion pictures produced by the U.S. Army Signal Corps. Later it acquired its own Educational Department and Scenario (i.e., script) Department and, working closely with commercial film studios and personnel, began making original movies. In March 1918, the Picture Division and the Film Division merged.

A Bureau of War Expositions was established to organize, mount, manage, and circulate exhibits of the weapons of war as well as battle trophies captured by U.S. forces. Twenty-one cities hosted major exhibitions, and the bureau also staged parades and smaller presentations.

Related to the Bureau of War Expositions but independent from it (organized directly under the Executive Division) was the Bureau of State Fair Exhibits, which also displayed weapons and war trophies, but did so in order to draw attention to its principal exhibits promoting conservation programs to aid in the war effort.

The Division of Industrial Relations, created late in the war, was intended to secure the ongoing cooperation of labor. After only a month of operations, the work of the division was taken over by the U.S. Department of Labor; however, the CPI continued to run an American Alliance for Labor and Democracy (headed by famed labor leader Samuel Gompers) and a Labor Publications Division, operating out of offices at 51 Chambers Street in Manhattan.

During most of its first year of operation, CPI staff frequently received telephone calls from citizens seeking "information." Such inquiries were natural, given the organization's title, Committee on Public *Information,* but the CPI was neither equipped nor staffed to answer routine questions from the public. Accordingly, on March 19, 1918, President Wilson authorized the creation of a Service Bureau under the aegis of the CPI for the purpose of providing the public with information on "the function, location, and personnel of all government agencies."[21] The bureau maintained a central office at 15th and G streets in Washington and set up information booths in the city's Union Station and elsewhere.

As already mentioned, the Division of Pictorial Publicity was among the first CPI units to be established, operating out of headquarters at 200 Fifth Avenue, New York City. Separately, the CPI's Executive Division created and directly supervised a Bureau of Cartoons, which issued the *Weekly Bulletin for Cartoonists* to "guide" political cartoonists in creating messages useful to the war effort.

The Division of Advertising was created under the directorship of William H. Johns in December 1917 and was headquartered in the Metropolitan Tower in New York City. Authorized to purchase advertising space, the division consistently managed to secure most space for free.

The Four-Minute Men recruited and coordinated more than 75,000 volunteer speakers who gave patriotic talks in movie theaters during the four minutes projectionists required to change reels when showing feature-length films. Established in September 1917 as an instant outgrowth of the Four-Minute Men, the Speaking Division was merged with its parent operation in the fall of 1918. It functioned as the government's national lecture bureau.

The Division of Syndicate Features enlisted leading novelists, popular essayists, and short-story writers to contribute syndicated feature material to the nation's newspapers and magazines. Creel estimated that the CPI reached 12 million readers each month through this division.

The Division of Women's War Work created and distributed news stories and other information relating to the role of women in the war effort. Division personnel also wrote some 50,000 personal letters to wives and mothers in response to issues and concerns raised by conscription, conservation, and other war-related matters.

The Division of Work with the Foreign Born was formally established in May 1918 to promote the patriotism of various national and ethnic minorities living in the United States.

The Foreign Section of the CPI was smaller than the Domestic Section and began operations somewhat later, in October 1917. There were essentially three units in this section. The Wireless and Cable Service cooperated with U.S. Naval Communications and commercial cable operators to prepare and transmit news dispatches to practically every country in the world. A significant portion of this material even penetrated into Germany and Austria and appeared in newspapers there. The Foreign Press Bureau, directed by Ernest Poole, delivered to CPI press agents stationed abroad a steady stream of feature articles and photographs (often in "mat" form, ready for reproduction) to be offered to foreign newspapers and magazines. Finally, the Foreign Film Division managed the export of movies from the Division of Films (under the Domestic Section), using the provisions of newly passed U.S. export licensing laws to force commercial film distributors to export CPI movies along with their own productions.

The major divisions and operations of the CPI, in their ideological as well as functional dimensions, will be discussed in the chapters that follow. The outline just presented, broad and sketchy as it is, can do no more than hint at the remarkable scope and comprehensiveness of the

Creel Committee. The speed with which it all came into existence was very much in sync with tempo of the times. The demands of war on a nation almost entirely unprepared for large-scale armed conflict drastically accelerated every aspect of government, the military, industry, and daily life. In George Creel, the nation had found the very man whose impulsive, sometimes reckless, always improvisatorial nature was most perfectly geared to the extraordinary demands made by the extraordinary times.

CHAPTER 6

A MONOPOLY ON THE NEWS

In the heady days of Progressive reform, George Creel was squarely on the side of the "trustbusters," who fought Standard Oil and the other infamous monopolies during the long twilight of the Gilded Age. Now that America was in the Great War and he was in charge of managing the nation's ration of news, it was Creel's turn to become a monopolist. On the face of it, he had successfully fought to substitute for government-imposed censorship a "voluntary censorship" imposed solely by the press upon itself. Such, at least, was the fiction Creel sold and most editors bought—if somewhat grudgingly.

As has already been discussed, although the nation's press declared victory on the eve of the passage and signing of the Espionage Act of June 15, 1917, with headlines proclaiming the defeat of censorship, the act incorporated all of the authority necessary for controlling the news yet was silent on the mechanics of enforcement. This actually gave the Committee on Public Information far more implied power than Chairman Creel ever officially claimed. In default of assignment of authority to any other agency, the Espionage Act left George Creel as the government's most visible agent of judgment and enforcement in matters of censorship. Combined with Creel's close ties to the War and Navy departments and the Department of Justice as well as the Post Office Department, this meant that his CPI held a very heavy club to wield against any newspaper that did not submit voluntarily to censorship.

Even before passage of the Espionage Act, the Post Office Department had been operating under a directive issued on April 25, 1917, by First Assistant Postmaster General J. C. Koons, ordering all local postmasters to report on "suspicious characters, disloyal and treasonable acts and utterances" and, indeed, on "anything which might be important during the existence of the present state of war."[1] In addition, almost immediately after the declaration of war, President Wilson ordered the U.S. Navy to seize all commercial "wireless establishments" (radio stations) and ordered radio operators, amateurs and professionals alike, to cease broadcasting. On April 28, three days after Koons's order to postmasters, Wilson issued an executive order tightly clamping down on cable, telephone, and telegraph messages leaving or entering the United States. Thus, Creel's "voluntary" press censorship came amid extensive censorship of materials sent via the U.S. mails and virtually total censorship of international messaging by electrical means. It was well known that Commander David W. Todd, the director of Naval Communications who was in charge of cable censorship, and Brigadier General Frank McIntyre, among whose intelligence duties was the supervision of telephone and telegraph lines at the Mexican border, were in continual close touch with Creel and used the CPI as a clearinghouse through which they coordinated the activities of Military Intelligence and Naval Intelligence with other branches of the government. By the end of April 1917, censorship was by no means genuinely voluntary. American newspapers did not enjoy unrestricted access to news from Europe or any other theater of the war.

Nevertheless, strictly speaking, there was no official censorship of domestic news when the CPI came into existence and before the passage and signing of the Espionage Act. In effect, then, there was no federally administered domestic news censorship in the United States for the first seventy-one days of the nation's involvement in World War I. Yet while passage of the Espionage Act was still pending, it was George Creel, self-proclaimed enemy of mandatory censorship and champion of voluntary censorship, who heralded the arrival of something more coercive than self-policing of the press. On May 28, 1917, as chairman of the CPI, he issued a document entitled "Preliminary Statement," which appeared first in pamphlet form and then in the CPI's government newspaper, the *Official Bulletin* of June 2. The cover of the pamphlet bore a passage from President Wilson's letter to Hearst manager Arthur Brisbane: "I can imagine no greater disservice to the country than to establish a system of censorship that would deny to the people of a free republic like our own their indisputable right to criticize their own public officials. While exercising the great powers of the office I hold, I would regret in a crisis like the one through which we are now passing to lose the benefit of patriotic and intelligent criticism."[2] Creel followed this up with his own italicized foreword:

> *Belligerent countries are usually at pains to veil in secrecy all operations of censorship. Rules and regulations are issued as "private and confidential," each pamphlet is numbered, and the recipient held to strict accountability for its safe and secret keeping. The Committee on Public Information had decided against this policy, and the press is at liberty to give full publicity to this communication. It is well to let people know just what it is that the committee proposes and desires, so that there may be the least possible impairment of public confidence in the printed information presented to it.[3]*

It was a most telling juxtaposition: Wilson's disavowal of the censorship of critical opinion was positioned as an immediate prelude to Creel's promise that the only items that would absolutely *not* be subject to censorship were the *rules* of censorship. By publishing these two statements in tandem, Creel clearly intended to ease the press and the nation into a system of quite rigid information control.

For their part, newspapers such as the *New York Times* seem to have accepted as a wartime necessity operating in a twilight world in which the First Amendment, although not entirely abrogated, was deeply compromised. Consider the sequence of headlines and subheads under which the *Times* reported on the "Preliminary Statement":

Censor Creel Gives Out Rules For Newspapers
Would Bar Speculation About Possible Peace,
or Differences of Opinion

WITH ALLIES OR NEUTRALS
Articles "Likely to Prove Offensive" Likewise Put Under the Ban
OTHER RULES OBEYED NOW
They Are Such as the Newspapers Voluntarily Adopted—
Censorship Bill Likely to be Defeated.[4]

After somewhat indignantly bestowing on Creel the title of "censor" ("Chairman Creel has been commonly referred to as the Government censor," the article went on to explain, "but he has always insisted that his purpose is to increase instead of curtail the amount of information furnished to the press for the benefit of the people in the war period"), the headlines and subheads employed a proscriptive vocabulary— "Would Bar," "Under the Ban"—and seemingly warned readers that major editorial topics, including speculation about peace and differences of opinion among allies and neutrals, as well as *anything* likely to prove offensive, would be squashed. Yet the final subhead reiterated the press's general claim of victory over censorship, implying that, repressive though the censor's rules might be, they were really no different from what the press had already voluntarily adopted. Wounded though the First Amendment might be, the important thing, the *Times* seems to say, was that the censorship bill would go down in final defeat.

The ambiguity of the press's response may be explained by the belief among editors that even though they had already agreed to voluntary censorship and had (as the *Times* put it) consistently "demonstrated . . . patriotism and loyal discretion by the [voluntary] suppression of news of possible benefit to the enemy," the Wilson administration continued to push "for a drastic press censorship law."[5] By contrast with what the administration wanted, the CPI's "Preliminary Statement" must have appeared almost liberal. Thus, even though Creel was the first government official to lay down actual censorship regulations, he benefited from comparison to what the press called the "Wilson proposal." Embracing Creel allowed the press to save face with the reasonably plausible fiction of voluntary censorship.

The truth was that even George Creel lacked absolute confidence in what the *Times* called the "patriotism and loyal discretion" of the nation's editors. In May, he phoned the editor of the *Washington Herald* to complain about an editorial titled "Defective Shells," which had followed news of the explosion of a gun aboard the armed navy transport USS *Mongolia*. The blast killed two nurses, Edith Ayers and Helen Wood, on their way to Europe. Apparently prodded by the U.S. Navy, which feared that stories about defective ammunition would undermine public confidence, Creel told the editor that there was no factual substance to the charge that the explosion had been caused by bad ammunition. In response, on May 24, the *Herald* printed a new editorial, on page 1, complaining that the CPI was part of Woodrow Wilson's "campaign to shackle the press . . . to rob it of the right guaranteed by the Constitution, to establish an autocratic menace to those organs of public opinion which may have the courage to criticize the conduct" of the war.[6]

Even as this controversy erupted, the Department of the Navy complained to Creel that Berlin had had four days' advance notice of the arrival of the first U.S. destroyers at Queenstown, Ireland. On May 26, Secretary of the Navy Josephus Daniels issued a statement directly to newspaper editors, warning that the "premature publication of ship movements is particularly a source of danger." But—and this is important—he went on to acknowledge his awareness that no American newspaper had actually given out the information. His only purpose in issuing the statement (he wrote) was to point out to editors the "extreme care . . . required in shielding military information from the enemy."[7]

The *Mongolia* affair alerted Creel to the weaknesses of voluntary censorship, even as the security breach involving the destroyers suggested that the imposition of wholesale mandatory censorship could be triggered by almost any incident, even if no newspaperman were actually at fault. He saw, therefore, a need to step beyond the mere spirit of voluntary censorship based on vague notions of patriotism, loyalty, discretion, and good sense. The "Preliminary Statement" was this step. In it, Creel assured the press that the "only news which we wish to keep from the authorities at Berlin *is the kind which would be of tangible help to them in their military operations.*"[8] Toward this end, the "Preliminary Statement" included a section called "Regulations for the Periodical Press of the United States during the War." These regulations—they were *not* billed as "Guidelines" or "Suggestions," but as "Regulations"—carefully divided news into three categories, "Dangerous, Questionable, and Routine," each to be treated differently.

Within the "Dangerous" category were three subcategories, "General, Naval, and Military." The list of forbidden items under the "General" rubric included all stories of naval and military operations in progress, except for what was officially given out; the movements of official missions; threats against the life of the president; news relating to the Secret Service or confidential agents; and the movements of "alien labor"—that is, foreign-born U.S. workers. Under the "Naval" category, journalists were forbidden to report on the position, number, and identification of U.S. and Allied warships; informational details relating to lights and buoys; the names of arrival and departure ports; data relating to marine mines and mine traps; signals, orders, and radio messages to and from ships; anything relating to submarine warfare; general information on ports, dry docks, and repairs; anything relating to convoys, including their makeup and schedules. Forbidden under the "Military" category were stories about fixed land defenses and fortifications; troop movements; the assignment of small detachments; the concentration of troops at ports of embarkation; and experimental weaponry or aircraft. Of course, any information furnished by the CPI was always acceptable.

The "Regulations" placed under the "Questionable" heading all matter that might be acceptable for publication, but only with caution—and, usually, only with the explicit approval of the CPI. Here Creel fudged, declining to offer a detailed listing, but instead suggested some example subjects, including training camp routine, technical inventions, and the publication of rumors, especially those of a sensational nature (such as the outbreak of an epidemic in a camp). Anything outside of the "Dangerous" and "Questionable" categories was deemed "Routine," which meant that it could be published without prior approval; however, Creel urged editors to submit to the CPI anything about which they entertained even the slightest doubt. Such articles would be reviewed and stamped "Passed by the Committee on Public Information," which meant that they contained no objectionable material but had not been checked by the CPI for accuracy, or "Authorized by the Committee on

Public Information," which meant that the material had been both cleared in terms of security and, after investigation, had also been found to be factually accurate.

After what amounted to a substantial list of don'ts, Creel closed with "The Committee on Public Information was given its name in no spirit of subterfuge, but as an honest announcement of purpose." Yet the *New York Times* found that the "most interesting" part of the "Preliminary Statement" was neither the enumerated list of forbidden matter nor the CPI's assertion of its positive, informative mission but, rather, the inclusion of notes "submitted by the Departments of State, War, and the Navy," which, under the heading "Explanation," followed the "Regulations." The notes outlined a vast gray area that substantially extended the reach of government censorship. In this section were included a declaration by the Department of State that it was "dangerous and of service to the enemy to discuss differences of opinion between the allies and difficulties with neutral countries." As for speculation about possible peace, it also "may possess elements of danger, as peace reports may be of enemy origin, put out to weaken the combination [alliance] against Germany." Here, too, was the classification as "undesirable" of any article "likely to prove offensive to any of the allies or to neutrals."[9]

Strictly speaking, none of this—not the "Regulations," with its list of "Dangerous, Questionable, and Routine" subjects, and not the broader topics included under the "Explanation" heading—had the absolute force of law on May 28, 1917. But editors and reporters took it all as if it had. The coming into force, on June 15, of the Espionage Act made everything in the "Preliminary Statement" unambiguously matters of law, even as the newspapers greeted that very act as a triumph of the First Amendment because it did not include an explicitly titled censorship amendment.

The Espionage Act did not *require* a censorship amendment. Implied censorship powers were part of the body of the act, and these were enlarged by the subsequent amendment popularly called the Sedition Act and by the Trading-with-the-Enemy Act. All of these acts of Congress included law directly based on Creel's "Regulations," and yet Creel repeatedly invoked what a later generation of government bureaucrats would call "plausible deniability," claiming that the CPI was "without the slight-est authority to decide what constitutes seditious utterances or disloyal attitudes," but then adding "Only in cases of absolute misstatement of fact have we ever intervened, scrupulously avoiding all appearance of control over opinion."[10] One is left to wonder whether the phrase "all ap-pearance" was the product of conscious self-irony, an intention to de-ceive, or entirely unconscious ambiguity. In any event, having denied possessing enforcement authority, Creel nevertheless left the door wide open to intervention. And as if this were not sufficient to put the iron in his velvet glove, every editor knew that, as chairman of the CPI, Creel also sat on the Censorship Board, which most certainly did have the ex-plicit statutory backing of the full force of the Wilson administration and the United States government. Moreover, the CPI chairman had the ear of the Department of Justice and could suggest prosecutions; he was also closely connected to the War Trade Board, which had the authority to do any number of things to put an uncooperative newspaper out of business, including cutting off its shipments of newsprint, which was strictly ra-tioned during the war.

Even more important than possessing unspoken but real and univer-sally understood coercive power, Creel had on his side what he under-stood as the logic of self-censorship. This empowered him to substitute an even more potent control over the news than any government-decreed program of censorship could ever apply. "With the press depended upon to protect military information of tangible benefit to the enemy," Creel wrote, "it became an obligation to meet the legitimate demand for all war news that contained no military secrets."[11] It is a remarkable sentence, worthy more of a sharp lawyer than a crusading journalist. The formula it presented was this: To reward the press for its patriotic self-restraint ("vol-untary," albeit reinforced by $10,000 fines and twenty-year prison terms), the Creel Committee would supply virtually all the news the press would get.

Supplying this news was an "obligation" and a "duty," but "not a duty . . . that could be left safely to the peace-time practice of the press with its uninterrupted daily swing of reporters through the various de-partments, the buttonholing of clerks, and the haphazard business of per-

mitting minor officials to make unchecked and unauthorized statements."[12] Yet another extraordinary twist of logic. The danger, it seemed,
was not a free press but a motley assortment of government clerks and
minor officials who were apt to be too free in what they might let slip to
reporters. As Creel put it, the war effort did not require protection from
the press so much as from the government bureaucracy.

And there was even more. News had to be retailed to the press
equally and universally. There was no longer "room for the 'scoop,'" not
because some reporter might get hold of exclusive information that
would be of value to the enemy, but because "war news could not be
looked upon in any other light than common property calling for common issuance."[13] Under the CPI war regime, news was not to be the result of investigation, the proprietary product, as it were, of private
enterprise, but public property to be apportioned equally to all. The
Creel Committee effectively nationalized the news. Not only did it come
from a government source, it was treated as government property.

In justice to George Creel, this description of his alternative to censorship, which was, in fact, an alternative form of censorship, may seem
ironic to a reader today, but it was almost certainly instituted and administered in good faith by Creel himself. Yes, a chaotic welter of editors, reporters, and loose-lipped federal functionaries posed a threat to wartime
secrecy, but even greater dangers came "from the other side," from the
"admirals and generals . . . reared in a school of iron silence," who
"looked upon the war-machinery as something that had to be hidden
under lock and key. To the average military mind everything connected
with war was a 'secret,' and the press itself had no rights that needed to be
respected." As if this were not bad enough, the "few . . . officials [who]
appreciated the value of publicity" lacked all "news sense," so that "trivi-
alities were brought forward and real importances buried."[14]

The U.S. Army and Navy thought they needed near-absolute secrecy.
Creel believed that what they really needed was a good press agent, an
"official machinery for the preparation and release of all news bearing
upon America's war effort . . . a running record of each day's progress."

The objective was not to serve history but to create among the "fathers and mothers of the United States . . . a certain sense of partnership," what a later generation of PR professionals would call "buy-in," buy-in to a war to which American parents were yielding up their young men.[15]

To accomplish this mission, Creel instantly grasped that the government could not impose itself on the press but would have to co-opt the press, not merely by hiring journalists but by identifying newspapermen "of standing and ability" and *swearing them in* to government service, placing them "at the very heart of endeavor in the War and Navy departments, in the War Trade Board, the War Industries Board, the Department of Justice, and the Department of Labor." The media would be thoroughly integrated into the government, made one with it. Whereas conventional censorship was designed to keep the press out, Creel's plan was to take the press in. Whereas conventional censorship was designed to stop the flow of information, Creel's army of journalists, pledged to government service, were "to take the deadwood out of the channels of information, permitting a free and continuous flow."[16] The trouble with censorship as conventionally conceived was that it created a vacuum where the people's perception of reality should be. Popular opinion, sentiment, and belief all abhor a vacuum. Denied information, the people will look to whatever sources present themselves—enterprising reporters, rumor mongers, panic-stricken parents, spies—to fill the vacuum. The CPI would make sure that the mental and emotional space of the American people was always full, full of the reality *it* supplied.

The thorough co-option of the press was a task "more delicate and difficult" than anyone could have conceived, "for both the press and the officials viewed the arrangement with distrust, if not hostility." Government and military officials believed that "necessary concealments were being violated," whereas editors and reporters suspected they were being snowed, subjected to "'press-agenting' on a huge scale."[17]

No amount of definition, redefinition, and patriotic rhetoric would succeed in moving either side in this contest of values and motives. Words alone would not avail. The only means of selling the mission of the CPI was to take bold action. Once he persuaded the military to loose its grip on items arbitrarily deemed secret, Creel had to drive home his insistence that more than "only 'favorable news' . . . be given out for publication." He demanded of the military and the government "that the bad should be told with the good, failures admitted along with the announcements of success." Moreover, while the press was expected to accept on good faith the CPI as a reliable source, the CPI itself would not regard its own government sources the same way. Committee personnel were to be given "the unquestioned right to exercise their news sense and to check up every statement in the interest of absolute accuracy."[18]

Creel went even further. Good newspapermen developed a nose for hype and could instantly sniff out the subtly perfumed work of the press agent. What the press agent peddled as news was really puffery, and good journalists either rejected it outright or held it at arm's length. Creel, the crusader whose writing style had been honed in the heyday of sensational yellow journalism, demanded that CPI writers and editors eschew "the slightest trace of color or bias, either in the selection of news of the manner in which it was presented." More than any other promise Creel could have made to the press, the consistency of this colorless approach to the stories persuaded "correspondents . . . that we were running a government news bureau, not a press agency."[19] Creel's "spin" (to use a modern PR term) was the conspicuous absence of spin.

Supplying news was a twenty-four-hour-a-day, seven-day-a-week occupation. Stories were typed on mimeograph stencils, reproduced, then put out on a table in the pressroom, where the news associations stationed men at all times and which correspondents visited regularly. The stories were intended to be sent out on the wire as "live news." This meant not only that CPI personnel had to write them quickly, but that any concerned branch of government had to sign off on a given article without delay.

The Division of News was more than a distribution channel. It also functioned as a central information bureau, the only source a correspondent needed to visit for authoritative information. Creel understood that the natural relationship between journalists and an official news bureau/censor was hostility and suspicion. One way he sought to overcome this was by making the reporter's job easy for him. Before the Division of

News had come into existence, reporters had to scramble all over town to run down a story, visiting office after office, making one phone call after another, often waking weary and wary officials out of bed in the middle of the night. Now the Division of News "desk men," who were billed as being in touch with everyone and everything of any importance night and day, could confirm or deny a story or rumor with a single phone call. This not only gave the CPI unprecedented control over information, the arrangement was "sold" to the press as a great time-saving service for *their* benefit.

Creel insisted that, despite the centralization of the pressroom and the desk men, the Division of News never tried to thwart independent news gathering or even interfere with reporters' individual contacts. Yet *intervene* it certainly did. It was at the "insistence and arrangement" of the Division of News that each correspondent had a daily interview with division "executive heads" and told them what story or stories he wanted. In response, the appropriate division either supplied the correspondent with the facts or orchestrated an appropriate interview.

Centralization of information was relatively straightforward among the close-knit Washington press corps and the Washington-based wire services. Thus newspapers big enough to have Washington correspondents or to subscribe to Washington-based wire services were both in the official information loop and under CPI control. The rural press was another matter. Creel put it this way: The small country weeklies were "experiencing a sense of neglect."[20] What he refrained from saying was that, because these modest rural papers could afford neither to maintain Washington correspondents nor to subscribe to the major wire services, they were effectively beyond the direct reach of the CPI. To bring the country papers under government control, the Division of News hired a "country editor," who put together a weekly digest of the official war news and mailed it to the rural weeklies in galley form, which made typesetting and composition a cinch. No weekly was legally required to subscribe to this service, but more than twelve thousand, always hungry for big news, did so, and in this way some six thousand columns were distributed each week.

Counterbalanced against the supply side of its operations was the censorship function of the Division of News. Again, the CPI disclaimed any policing authority and instead presented itself as an advisory service to correspondents and editors, interpreting, on request, government secrecy requirements. Any difficult or doubtful cases were referred to Brigadier General Frank McIntyre or a representative from the Department of the Navy. Creel insisted that the CPI never issue any "direct order" in response to a query. It was always to be left to the individual correspondent to "comply with the wishes of the government or reject them, the decision being left entirely to his common sense and patriotism." That seemed crystal clear, but Creel continued: "The Committee itself was at all times careful to avoid any appearance of censorship."[21] Once again, that phrase "appearance of" introduced an element of ambiguity into the statement of CPI policy and function.

Although he was occupied with directing what rapidly became a vast and varied enterprise, Creel took a personal, hands-on approach more often than an executive one. In many cases, it was he who responded directly to the queries that came into the Division of News. Typical was this from Hugh J. Hughes, editor of the Minneapolis-based magazine *Farm, Stock and Home.* In January 1918, Hughes wrote: "Do you think we are concealing anything from Germany when we withhold from publication the approximate number of men now in France? Isn't that number quite as well known to Wilhelmstrasse as to Washington? Is not the location of American units on the front perfectly well known to Germany, likewise the ports of entry in France?" It was a provocative question, which illustrated the degree to which cynical assumption, not a greed for a scoop, ruled the thinking of journalists and editors. In typical fashion, Creel replied personally and directly, man to man, as it were, and without resorting to a "canned" statement based on official policy: "I tell you quite frankly, as the Secretary testified, that Germany does not know how many men we have in France, or does not know their location. On the theory that the Germans are bound to find out everything, and that therefore there is no point in attempting any secrecy, we might as well send advance information of our plans in carbon to the German War Office and have done with it. Merely because we may fail in some essential of secrecy is not a reason why common prudence should be thrown to the winds."[22]

Replying to queries from editors and correspondents such as Hughes, Creel might be blunt, but he was also always warmly collegial. He could be much sterner, however, when it came to an actual transgression. On August 4, 1917, the *San Francisco Examiner* published a feature story titled "Why the U-Boats Can't Get Our Troopships," which included diagrams illustrating how marine mines were laid and exploded, where British minefields were located, and how Allied convoys were organized. All of this information had been clearly defined in Creel's "Preliminary Statement" and in the Espionage Act as prohibited from publication. On August 16, Creel sent a telegram to the editor of the *Examiner,* asking him to "PLEASE WIRE AT ONCE WHERE YOU SECURED THIS MATERIAL AND PHOTOGRAPHS AND BY WHAT AUTHORITY YOU PUBLISHED INFORMATION ABSOLUTELY PROHIBITED BY LAW."[23] In this way, Creel asserted his presence as a monitor. His message was unmistakable—*you are being watched*—yet, even in this case, he left enforcement to other agencies. While the Division of News functioned throughout the war to advise editors and reporters, it was the Departments of State, War, and the Navy that actually issued orders and directives relating to the nitty-gritty of censored subjects.

To the government, Creel promoted the Division of News as a means of control and an aid to censorship, but, even more, as the great outlet for "a flood of positive news" to overwhelm "the negative and destructive." To the newspapers themselves, Creel presented the Division of News as a service that saved them time and money while also "making daily and vigorous fight against unnecessary secrecies."[24]

The fight was quite real. When General John J. Pershing left for France with the first contingent of the American Expeditionary Force (AEF), he insisted that no correspondents accompany him. The CPI protested that this would arouse both indignation and suspicion from press and public alike, and Secretary of War Baker responded by overruling Pershing. The Division of News vetted the correspondents selected by the various news associations and ultimately approved twenty-three men to be lodged at AEF headquarters in France. After all twenty-three were in place, Pershing cabled angrily that there were now twice as many correspondents with the as-yet tiny AEF as there were with the gargantuan armies of France and Britain. Creel admitted that this was probably the case, but it was also true that neither France nor Britain were sending their troops thousands of miles across an ocean, far from their families, to fight a "European" war, and it was true as well that the United States had many, many more newspapers than France and Britain combined. Thanks to CPI efforts, the correspondents remained, and their number grew as more and more AEF troops arrived in theater.

Not that the American press was duly grateful for the services and support rendered by the Division of News. Creel often wrote of having developed "cordial" relations with the press, but, just as often, he complained that the press "thundered at the Committee as an 'agency of repression.'"[25] In truth, the mission of the CPI in general and the Division of News in particular was even more thankless. When, in March 1918, the War Department, in the interests of secrecy, insisted that casualty lists be stripped of all detail before they were issued to the press, Creel and the CPI protested. Since the beginning of the war, the Division of News had reported casualties in this format:

> Wounded: Private John Jones. S. J. Jones (father)
> 2 Yale Street, Brooklyn, N.Y.

The new War Department directive pared the format to:

> Wounded: Private John Jones

"We realized at once that the thousands of identical names in the United States made it certain that the new form would work anxiety and suffering on countless homes. Merely to announce that John Jones or Patrick Kelly was killed or wounded meant that the parents, relatives, and friends of innumerable John Joneses and Patrick Kellys would be given over to fear and grief, since there was nothing to indicate exact identity."[26] Creel appealed to the War Department to change its policy, and when he ran up against a stone wall, he directed the Division of News to flatly refuse to issue casualty lists in the new form. To Creel's stunned chagrin, instead of hailing this as a stand against military insensitivity and stupidity, the same press that had condemned the CPI as an agency of repression now excoriated it for daring to question the prudence and wisdom of War Department policy. Nevertheless, Creel stood firm and took the issue to President Wilson himself, who, after hearing Creel out, ordered the old form of the casualty lists to be restored.

For all their suspicion and protest, the nation's newspapers did come to rely on the Division of News, and this is precisely what Creel had hoped for. In the spring of 1918, in testimony before a perpetually skeptical and hostile Congress, Creel was asked by a member of the House Committee on Appropriations to defend the CPI against charges that it effectively *commanded* papers to print the news it offered. Creel responded that every item produced by the Division of News was made available to all Washington correspondents. They, in turn, were free to file the stories "with the telegraph operator or the trash man at their own discretion." Overwhelmingly, the papers chose to print the division's releases. Far from commanding publication, the only direct threat the CPI wielded was cutting a paper off from all releases if it chose to break news before the authorized date. The Division of News was determined that all papers would have equal access to the news it issued. There would be no scoops.

Newspapers were not forced to print CPI material, but, in the case of almost all war stories, it was the only source available. Judging from the sheer volume of releases produced and published—some six thousand, which filled more than twenty thousand newspaper columns every week of the war—the Division of News was an overwhelming propaganda triumph. The cost of this was ridiculously small. From the beginning of operations, just weeks after the declaration of war, until the armistice, the Division of News rang up $76,323.82 in debt.[27] It was, after all, little more than a "city desk," compact and efficient, yet nevertheless an information nexus that functioned simultaneously as *the* news source and *the* choke point by which the flow of news could be controlled. Certainly, no government agency in American history—perhaps in the history of any nation—has ever leveraged resources to greater effect.

CHAPTER 7

INVASION OF THE FOUR-MINUTE MEN

Given the history of the century recently ended, it is nearly impossible to divorce the word *propaganda* from sinister images of secret bureaus hidden within the bowels of anonymous gray buildings and administered by cadres of unsmiling men in the black leather trench coats favored by Hitler's Gestapo. The Creel Committee's far-reaching Division of News, however, presented no such image. It was a suite of small, ordinary offices staffed by a few newspapermen, with a "pressroom" that was nothing more imposing than four walls surrounding a table stacked with freshly mimeographed official releases, there for the taking. More impressive by far was another CPI operation, the Division of the Four-Minute Men, the committee's largest propaganda department. No mere cadre, this division was, at 75,000, a veritable army, yet its "soldiers" wore nothing more menacing than the uniform of the man in the street, and its headquarters was neither a monolith nor a bunker, but tens of thousands of neighborhood buildings, the nation's union halls, churches, synagogues, and, most of all, its nickelodeons and movie houses.

Call the Four-Minute Men a secret army, perhaps, but its most potent secret was that it was hidden in plain sight. On a day late in April 1917, the vanguard of that army, in the person of one Donald Ryerson—

a "handsome rosy-cheeked youth," Creel called him—strode deliberately into the neat, small white brick Navy Library on Dahlgren Avenue in the Washington Navy Yard, the quarters into which the bustling Committee on Public Information had been shoehorned during the first days of its existence. Ryerson "burst through the crowd and caught my lapel in a death-grip," Creel recalled.[1] He devoted but few words to an introduction before describing a plan for the organization of volunteer speakers who would give patriotic talks in motion picture theaters. Ryerson explained that such a group, assembled by the civic-minded young Chicago businessmen he represented, had been speaking in his city's theaters since April 1, even *before* the declaration of war. Their goal back then was to sell the idea of urgent voluntary military training, and they called their band of speakers the "Four-Minute Men," both in reference to the Minuteman militia of Revolutionary Lexington and Concord and in acknowledgment of the special requirement of the job: to deliver an informative and persuasive speech in no more than four minutes, the time it took a professional projectionist to change reels when showing a feature-length film.

Creel the crusading journalist had certainly seen and heard more than his share of crackpots, phonies, and scams, but he offered absolutely no skeptical resistance to Ryerson. Ten minutes after the young man released his lapel, Creel appointed him national director of the Four-Minute Men. Creel was always a soft touch for idealists; moreover, his own impulsive nature lurched in step with the frenetic tempo of wartime Washington to move him to say yes more often than no.

Yet Creel's decision cannot be wholly ascribed either to idealism or impulse. Seeing his primary mission as flooding the nation with news from a single government source, Creel understood that to conduct as well as accommodate this torrent he needed to command every possible sluice, the broader the better. In 1917, three major information outlets—newspapers, magazines, and silent movies—could lay claim to the title of "mass media." The basic technology of radio was almost two decades old, but Guglielmo Marconi saw his invention as a means of station-to-station communication and apparently never imagined that it would be used for public broadcast. For this reason, perhaps, the world's first commercial radio station broadcasting to an audience, KDKA of Pittsburgh, would not take to the air until after the war, on November 2, 1920, when it delivered the returns of the Harding-Cox presidential election. But if radio had yet to be born as a mass medium in 1917, the Four-Minute Men would nevertheless "broadcast" nationwide, live and direct to the ready-made audiences drawn to the nation's movie houses. It was, manifestly, a very good idea.

We might speculate whether Creel would have seen a role for the Four-Minute Men had broadcast radio been an established fact in 1917. Probably he would have, because they gave the Creel Committee something no other mass medium could have delivered: pure propaganda.

Creel wore many hats in his colorful prewar career, but he was never a philosopher or theoretician. In connection with his war work, he spoke frequently of "propaganda," a word to which he always gave a quasi-religious meaning. For Creel, *propaganda* was the gathering and dissemination of facts for the purpose of *propagating* truth among the faithful. He never ventured intellectually beyond this distinctive and emotionally charged definition. Creel operated from his gut, and it would be several months before the Committee on Public Information had a member capable of appreciating analytically the significance of the Four-Minute Men as a vehicle of propaganda in its fullest sense.

Edward L. Bernays was a dapper little man of five foot four with a thick but neatly trimmed black mustache and a taste for snap-brim hats and broad silk neckties. He had the look of success and was indeed very successful, having become by World War I the youthful dean of American public relations, a field he was still very much in the process of helping to invent. Flat feet and poor eyesight kept him out of the army when he tried to enlist on April 6, 1917. Nor was it a help that he had been born in Vienna, in 1891, the son of Sigmund Freud's sister Anna, although he had lived in New York City since the age of one. Rejected by the army, he tried the Red Cross, the Commission on Military Training (offering to recruit popular musicians to perform at camps), and his local draft board (presenting himself as a statistical manager). Rebuffed by all, he organized several patriotic programs on his own, then at last cadged an interview with Ernest Poole, who headed up the Creel Committee's Foreign Press Bureau under the Division of News. Poole was impressed by the massive bundle of testimonial letters Bernays handed him, but he cautioned that his foreign birth, in the land of the enemy no less, might well prove an insurmountable obstacle. There would have to be an investigation.

It took several months for the Military Intelligence officers attached to CPI to conclude that Bernays was a loyal American. After graduating from high school at age sixteen, he had paid homage to his grain-merchant father by earning from Cornell University a degree in agriculture, a subject in which the Manhattan-bred boy had absolutely no interest. That done, he dipped a toe into the grain market, quickly withdrew it, then began editing *The Medical Review of Reviews* and *The Dietetic and Hygienic Gazette* in 1912. For Bernays, this was hardly a more congenial vocation than buying and selling grain, but he always managed to find something to interest him in the work. For example, he used the pages of the *Review* to persuade physicians to prevail upon their female patients to abandon wearing corsets with stays. It was not so much that Bernays had a passion for liberating women from their whalebone corsets—although he made no secret of his admiration for the female form *au natural*—but that he had an emerging passion for what he would call, unapologetically, *propaganda.*

As Bernays saw it, advertisers pleaded with prospective customers. Propagandists, in contrast, identified the leaders in a population, then appealed strictly to them, seeking to influence the key people who are the creators of influence. To tell women directly that they should shed their corsets might well produce some level of compliance, but Bernays knew it was far more efficient and effective to persuade their doctors to tell them.

Of course, the opportunities for such social leverage—propaganda—were few and far between for an editor of a "medical review of reviews." Nevertheless, just two months after he had begun editing it, that journal unexpectedly brought Bernays something new. A physician submitted a review not of an article reporting on some medical experiment, but a rave for a new play. Eugène Brieux's *Damaged Goods* told the story of one George Dupont, a man who, on the eve of marriage, is diagnosed with syphilis. Postpone your wedding, and you can be cured, Dupont's doctor tells him. But profound social embarrassment propels him into the ceremony, he marries without delay, fathers an infected child, and gives his wife a disease that renders her sterile.

Not only did Bernays publish the review, in itself a daring step at the time, he and his partner in the journal, a high school chum named Fred Robinson, decided to get *Damaged Goods* produced on Broadway. They discovered that Richard Bennett, one of the stars of turn-of-the-century American theater (and better known to later generations as the father of film actress Joan Bennett), had expressed interest in backing a production of the play. Bernays wrote to him: "The editors of the *Medical Review of Reviews* support your praiseworthy intention to fight sex-pruriency in the United States by producing Brieux's play *Damaged Goods.* You can count on our help." Bennett replied enthusiastically, promising to furnish a cast of marquee stars who would work without pay in this crusade against crippling Victorianism. However, it would be up to Bernays to raise money for renting a theater, hiring a crew, and myriad other expenses. He would also have to persuade New York's watchdogs of decency not to shut the play down on opening night.[2]

Bernays reflected on the nature of the project at hand. By presenting *Damaged Goods,* he hoped ultimately to effect social change. However, he reasoned that in order even to get the play to the stage, he would have to effect some degree of social change from the get-go. Controversy always poses a threat, but it also presents an opportunity, the very opportunity to convert controversy into a cause. This, Bernays understood, would not happen on his say-so alone, any more than women would cast off their corsets because he told them to. As with the corset crusade, he decided to identify and appeal to the leaders of influence in the community, and he did so not in the person of a twenty-one-year-old editor but as the director of the *Medical Review of Reviews* Sociological Fund Committee. To this organization, which had a name before it had a membership, Bernays drew Mrs. William K. Vanderbilt Sr., John D. Rockefeller Jr., Franklin and Eleanor Roosevelt, prominent Unitarian minister the Reverend John

Haynes Holmes, and Dr. William Schieffelin, who had developed a new drug treatment for syphilis. The participation of these leading figures transformed local society just enough to yield a flood of contributions to the fund. Moreover, it made the play, from its premiere, a red-hot ticket.

Most drama reviewers were, however, unimpressed. They did not find *Damaged Goods* obscene and offensive, but (in the words of one) "dull and almost unendurable."[3] That hardly mattered. Drama critics are not society's leaders. They might be able to kill most plays, but not this one, which mounted the boards already anointed by society's moral, civic, and commercial luminaries, who created a social context in which the play simply could not be condemned or rejected. In 1913, less than a year after its New York stage premiere, the muckraking author Upton Sinclair published a novelization of the play. In his preface, he quoted the *Washington Post*'s review of its first performance in the nation's capital:

> In many respects the presentation of this dramatization of a great social evil assumed the aspects of a religious service. Dr. Donald C. Macleod, pastor of the First Presbyterian Church, mounted the rostrum usually occupied by the leader of the orchestra, and announced that the nature of the performance, the sacredness of the play, and the character of the audience gave to the play the significance of a tremendous sermon in behalf of mankind, and that as such it was eminently fitting that a divine blessing be invoked. Dr. Earle Wilfley, pastor of the Vermont Avenue Christian Church, asked all persons in the audience to bow their heads in a prayer for the proper reception of the message to be presented from the stage. Dr. MacLeod then read the Bernard Shaw preface to the play, and asked that there be no applause during the performance, a suggestion which was rigidly followed, thus adding greatly to the effectiveness and the seriousness of the dramatic portrayal.[4]

By the time the play had reached Washington, it was no longer a controversy but a cause. Rabbi Abram Simon, of the Washington Hebrew Congregation, confessed, "If I could preach from my pulpit a sermon one tenth as powerful, as convincing, as far-reaching, and as helpful as this performance of *Damaged Goods* must be, I would consider that I had achieved the triumph of my life." Police Commissioner Cuno H. Rudolph remarked, "I was deeply impressed by what I saw, and I think that the drama should be repeated in every city, a matinee one day for father and son and the next day for mother and daughter." The Surgeon General of the United States, Dr. Rupert Blue, pronounced it "a most striking and telling lesson. For years we have been fighting these conditions in the navy. It is high time that civilians awakened to the dangers surrounding them and crusaded against them in a proper manner."[5]

Bernays not only found a way to open to discussion a sensitive issue of public health, he also found a way to get sex onto the American stage or, as one editorial put it, to make the hour strike "sex o'clock in America." And he had done so with the blessing of society's religious, legal, political, and medical leaders. Such was the power of propaganda. After he joined the Creel Committee four years later, Bernays would define it as "a consistent, enduring effort to create or shape events to influence the relations of the public to an enterprise, idea or group."[6]

Edward L. Bernays was not a central figure in the CPI bureaucracy, but no other member of the committee so clearly defined its principal purpose and task. It was not to tell people what to think or what to feel but to "create or shape events" themselves so that *these* would favorably influence how the public thought and felt about the war. "It was," Bernays wrote in his 1928 book *Propaganda,* "the astounding success of propaganda during the war that opened the eyes of the intelligent few in all departments of life to the possibilities of regimenting the public mind." The Creel Committee "developed a technique which, to most persons accustomed to bidding for public acceptance, was new."

> They not only appealed to the individual by means of every approach—visual, graphic, and auditory—to support the national endeavor, but they also secured the cooperation of the key men in every group—persons whose mere word carried authority to hundreds or thousands or hundreds of thousands of followers. They thus automatically gained the support of fraternal, religious, commercial, patriotic, social and local groups whose members took their opinions from their accustomed leaders and spokesmen.[7]

In no other of the CPI's many activities was the "technique" Bernays defined more in evidence than in the Four-Minute Men. They were never passive messengers, mere broadcasters, but individual human instruments of propaganda, all 75,000 of them. Creel and Ryerson authorized the creation of Councils of Defense for each state, to be chaired by a prominent individual chosen by the governor. This leader would, in turn, nominate or sanction county, town, and neighborhood chapters and chairmen. To merit recognition from the state chairman, each local chairman was required to furnish written endorsements from "three prominent businessmen, bankers, professional, or public men." Thus certified as community leaders, the local chairmen were tasked with choosing speakers. The official *Four-Minute Men Bulletin,* issued from Ryerson's office (moved from Chicago to Washington on June 10, 1917), cautioned against recruiting professional speakers, who were "too accustomed to longer speeches with room for anecdotes and introduction." Instead, "young lawyers and businessmen" were to be sought, men capable of presenting "*messages* within the four-minute limit." Thus social authority flowed downward in a kind of cascade of command, from Washington headquarters, to the governors of the states, to the chairmen of the State Councils of Defense, to the local Four-Minute Men chapters. Prominent in the community but not *too* prominent, these speakers were nevertheless social leaders on a local level, a notch or two above the audiences they addressed. In Livingston County, Michigan, for example, a rising attorney named Willis L. Lyons organized the local Four-Minute Men chapter, then, according to a commemorative publication, stepped down "after becoming a candidate for Prosecuting Attorney . . . so that the Four Minute Men's work might not be said to be connected with political affairs." Another attorney, A. Riley Crittenden, was appointed to replace him, having "been engaged in the Four Minute Men activities in St. Charles, Michigan, previous to his work in Livingston County. As a member of that team he had spoken in four states besides Michigan."[8]

The position of Four-Minute Man was an avidly sought after job during the war years, despite its being entirely unpaid. Men on their way up in the community saw it as a means of gaining recognition and prominence. Doubtless because most of the Four-Minute Men were of an age to be in uniform, the position also offered a comfortable explanation for remaining a stay-at-home. After all, no Four-Minute Man could be accused of being a "slacker." On the negative side, Creel observed, the position sometimes brought out the "secret William Jennings Bryan" in many men, including those "of the most unlikely sort."[9]

The *Four-Minute Men Bulletin,* distributed to speakers and chairmen alike, was very specific on the subject of would-be "great orators": None need apply. There was to be no pomposity, no empty verbiage, no hollow patriotism, no vague idealism, and nothing that would try the patience of people who had come to the movies to be entertained. In an age of neighborhood movie houses, chairmen were cautioned to rotate assignments so that no speaker would go stale with the nickelodeon's regulars. "The speech must not be longer than four minutes, which means there is no time for a single waste word"; the speaker could never "break in on a photoplay," and was obliged to deliver his speech only during the first four-minute intermission occurring after 8 P.M.[10]

Performing as a Four-Minute Man was hard work. While speakers were issued model speeches and lists of approved topics, they were expected to compose the actual speech themselves. None was assigned canned talks; nor were speakers allowed to read their speech on stage. As the first *Bulletin,* issued on May 22, 1917, explained, it was to be delivered with neither script nor notes. Speakers were advised to divide their talks: "say 15 seconds for final appeal; 45 seconds to describe the [Liberty Loan] bond [issue]; 15 seconds for opening words, etc., etc.," and they were admonished never to "be satisfied with success. Aim to be more successful, and still more successful."[11]

In 1928, Edward L. Bernays would define propaganda, in part, as "regimenting the public mind," and yet there was remarkably little regimentation in the Four-Minute Man propaganda enterprise. Untrained local speakers read guidelines and tips in each issue of the *Four-Minute Men Bulletin,* but they were never actually given speeches to deliver. Creel Committee professionals could easily have written and issued talks to 75,000 Four-Minute Men, which would have given George Creel a very high degree of control over the message his CPI was "broadcasting." But that would have been advertising, not propaganda. Advertising delivered a message. Propaganda created or shaped reality.

And that was the genius of the Four-Minute Men idea. By 1917, the nickelodeon had become the people's palace, a portal between nation and world on one side and neighborhood and home on the other, a territory partaking equally of official culture, collective myth, shared fantasy, secret desire, and personal belief. Into this very special cultural, social, and emotional space came not a paid government hack or a professional politician delivering the party line but a man of the community, who, apparently and to all appearances, simply spoke his mind. Now, precisely because he was of the community, he could be heard as giving voice to the ideas already present in it. But he was also a *Four-Minute Man,* slightly above his audience, his speech preceded by a lantern slide projected on the screen announcing "John Doe will speak four minutes on a subject of national importance. He speaks under the authority of The Committee on Public Information, Washington, D.C."[12] What he had to say, therefore, arose from the community but was also government certified as authoritative and worth listening to.

Like the movie theaters in which they spoke, the Four-Minute Men were hybrids, crosses between central authority and a community of neighbors. The words of a politician or even the president might be eloquent and moving, but they were words nonetheless, a form of advertising, however exalted. The words of a respected member of the local community, especially if perceived as spontaneous and heartfelt, came across less as mere words than as reality itself. Seamlessly, unobtrusively connected to the central authority of the government, yet produced locally, this was precisely what Edward Bernays meant by propaganda.

To ensure that each speaker always connected with his audience, the *Four-Minute Men Bulletin* advised, "Get your friends to criticize you pitilessly. We all want to do our best and naturally like to be praised, but there is nothing so dangerous as 'josh' and 'jolly.' Let your friends know that you want ruthless criticism. If their criticism isn't sound, you can reject it. If it is sound, wouldn't you be foolish to reject it?" Yet speakers were admonished not to let themselves be led by their audience: "Don't yield to the inspiration of the moment, or to applause to depart from your speech outline. This does not mean that you may not add a word or two, but remember that one can speak only 130, or 140, or 150 words a minute, and if your speech has been carefully prepared to fill four minutes, you can not add anything to your speech without taking away something of serious importance." They were further advised to remain of the people yet also, as leaders of the community, just a little ahead of the people. After all, some of the people's language was stale. The *Bulletin* counseled: "Cut out 'Doing your bit.' 'Business as usual.' 'Your country needs you.' They are flat and no longer have any force or meaning." The alternative, however, was not radical originality but "a new slogan, or a new argument, or a new story, or a new illustration" found in newspapers or magazines. "So keep your eyes open. Read all the papers every day, to find a new slogan, or a new phraseology, or a new idea to replace something you have in your speech."[13]

While the Four-Minute Men clearly believed they were contributing to the war effort, they did not feel that they were being asked simply to deliver a government message. As a former Four-Minute Man in Livingston County, Michigan, observed, "Their rule was that their cause was strong and that they could afford to be frank and open, ready to concede doubt, wherever doubt rightfully existed, and making no claims beyond what they knew to be true, and thus standing on the rock of fairness, honesty being their armor, frankness and fairness their weapons."[14]

Propaganda is most powerful when it is perceived to be fact. It loses effect in proportion to its seeming coerced, and so Ryerson and Creel did indeed put much trust in the individual Four-Minute Man. Nevertheless, they also vigilantly sought to rein in eccentricity, idiosyncrasy, and individual imagination. The *Bulletin* instructed local chairmen personally to monitor the performance of their speakers. As Creel approvingly observed, "The ax fell heavily whenever a speaker failed to hold his audience, or injected a note of partisanship, or else proved himself lacking in restraint or good manners."[15]

But the fall of the ax did not impede the explosive growth of the Four-Minute Men. At the time of the First Liberty Loan campaign,

which began in April 1917, the Four-Minute Men was a national organization with 1,500 members. By September 1918, the ranks had bur-
geoned to 40,000. By Armistice Day, November 11, 1918, there were
75,000 volunteers organized into 7,629 formally established branches,
including 217 colleges and universities and 51 granges (in a nation that
was still largely agricultural).[16] Every state in the union and the District
of Columbia had branches, as did the territories of Alaska, Panama Canal
Zone, Guam, Hawaii, the Philippines, Puerto Rico, and Samoa. In
Alaska, it was reported that one dedicated speaker labored 60,000 miles
back and forth over the territory, delivering talks in established and improvised nickelodeons as well as any other places people assembled, including general stores, saloons, mining camps, and the village halls of
remote fishing communities.

Between April 1917 and November 11, 1918, the Four-Minute Men
delivered 7,555,190 speeches, mostly to movie theater audiences, but
speakers were also sent into churches, synagogues, Sunday Schools, fraternal lodges, labor unions, social clubs, civic organizations, lumber
camps, and even assemblies of Indian tribes. Thomas J. Rouillaurd, described by the *Bulletin* as a full-blooded Sioux, was a Four-Minute Man
in South Dakota. "I think the Indians are doing their best for the country," he said, "but more could be done if they understood more fully
what this war means to us."[17] A cadre of U.S. Army officers was also recruited as Four-Minute Men to speak "at ease" to the troops in camps,
forts, and cantonments throughout the United States and France, ad-
dressing such subjects as "Why We Are Fighting," "Insurance for Soldiers," and home-front matters.

Like the Hydra of Greek mythology, the Creel Committee sprouted
head after head, and each head then produced heads of its own. The
Four-Minute Men soon gave rise to a Women's Division, which sent
speakers not only to address women's clubs but to speak at matinee performances in movie houses. These performances, after all, were attended
mainly by women, whose husbands, at midday, were at work—if not
serving in the camps or the trenches. While many of the speakers in the
Women's Division were men, this was the only Four-Minute Men subor-
ganization that recruited women speakers. There also soon appeared a

Junior Division, which issued a special *School Bulletin*. Contests for the best junior speeches were held in more than 200,000 schools across the country, the winners receiving a special certificate from the government. The nation's colleges were covered by a subgroup called the College Four-Minute Men, organized in September 1918, typically chaired in each institution by a professor of public speaking. Students pored over the *Four-Minute Men Bulletin* and other assigned material, each expected to deliver at least one speech per semester.

Local Four-Minute Men organizations took pains to tailor speeches to the community. In New York City alone, some sixteen hundred speakers addressed half a million people each week in their native tongues. Italian was popular, but it came in second to Yiddish. On the Lower East Side, Rabbi A. G. Robinson, executive director of the Young Men's Hebrew Association, organized the Yiddish-Speaking Four-Minute Men to address Yiddish movie theaters and playhouses as well as various businesses "where Jewish people are largely employed." The *Four-Minute Men Bulletin* reported: "At the present time the Jewish section is operating in 30 theaters, sending speakers to each twice a week. Among these are all the large Jewish playhouses of the city, each one of which has an average attendance of 2,000 at a performance. In this way we are reaching about 25,000 people per week. We expect soon to have every Jewish audience in a motion-picture house or a Jewish playhouse addressed by a Jewish speaker. Both Yiddish and English are used in accordance with the character of the audience."[18] At a Fourth of July program in Hartford, Connecticut, Four-Minute Men delivered speeches on "The Meaning of America" in Italian, Polish, Hungarian, Ukrainian, Armenian, and Czech.

For all of this outreach, movie houses remained the principal venues of the Four-Minute Men, and the Creel Committee took steps to ensure the continued cooperation of exhibitors. Theater managers were neither more nor less patriotic than anyone else, but many worried that giving the stage to a Four-Minute Man would open the gates to a flood of speakers and fundraisers from other government agencies or private patriotic groups. To address this issue, Creel once again applied the Bernays principle. Instead of relying on the authority of official committee requests made directly from a government agency to each theater manager, the Creel Committee secured the endorsement of a leader directly relevant to every manager. William A. Brady, president of the National Association of the Motion Picture Industry, was prevailed on to name the Four-Minute Men as the "official and authorized representatives of the United States Government in the movie theaters of America."[19] The exhibitors fell into line.

The trouble with staffing an agency with up-and-coming young men in 1917–1918 was that many of them would, sooner or later, disappear into uniform. Doubtless there were some who used their position in the Four-Minute Men to postpone or avoid service, but despite the rapid growth of the organization, the turnover (for which no figures are available) must have been high. One of the first to leave was the creator of the Four-Minute Men, Donald Ryerson, who, before the end of June 1917, accepted a commission in the United States Navy. He was replaced by fellow Chicagoan William McCormick Blair, a young stock and bond broker, who, in the worst days of the Great Depression in 1935, would go on to found a highly successful LaSalle Street brokerage. If anything, Blair was even more energetic and focused than the admirable Ryerson. He formalized the state organizations and introduced a more rigorous and regular "inspection service" to monitor speakers and cull out those who did not measure up. Not content to trust the individual speaker quite as fully as Ryerson had, Blair created a National Advisory Council, which included Professor S. H. Clark of the University of Chicago's Department of Public Speaking and, in addition to other prominent figures, Samuel Hopkins Adams. Adams would earn fame and wealth as a popular novelist in 1926 with his *Revelry,* based on the exuberantly lurid scandals of the administration of Warren G. Harding. Even more successful was his 1942 *Harvey Girls,* about the adventures of the young waitresses that the restaurateur Fred Harvey sent to the Wild West with his expanding chain of railroad station dining halls; the novel was the basis of a 1946 Judy Garland movie of the same name. At the time of World War I, however, Adams was best known as a muckraking journalist in the vein of

Creel himself. In 1905, he wrote a series of eleven articles for *Collier's* magazine, in which he analyzed the ingredients of some of the country's most popular patent medicines. He argued that the patent medicine industry was built almost exclusively on false claims about its products and, worse, that many of the medicines were actually harmful. Collected into a book, *The Great American Fraud,* the articles were, along with Upton Sinclair's novel *The Jungle,* instrumental in the passage of the Pure Food and Drugs Act of 1906. With Adams, Blair thus added a new layer to the Bernays propaganda sandwich. While the University of Chicago professor lent his authority to the forensic skill of the speakers, the presence of Adams on the Advisory Board seemed to certify the authenticity of the message itself. His was not the imprimatur of the U.S. government or a Washington functionary, but the seal of approval of a man who had taken on a huge industry, had shaken up the federal bureaucracy, and had gamely defended the interests of the American public.

On August 21, 1918, William McCormick Blair also left the Creel Committee, to enlist at Camp Zachary Taylor as an infantry volunteer. William H. Ingersoll, a businessman who was already on the National Advisory Council, took over until the Four-Minute Men were demobilized on December 31, 1918.

If Blair's National Advisory Council had helped make the message of the Four-Minute Men unassailable as far as the American public was concerned, the organization did not escape an assault by Congress. From the beginning, many in government opposed the elevation of a "radical journalist," a "campaign huckster," "depraved hack," and "licensed liar" to the post of national "censor." Always headlong and impulsive, George Creel, it is true, did nothing to endear himself to Congress. But it is also true that Creel, through no fault of his own, found himself in the uncomfortable position of lightning rod for the Wilson administration. In the throes of the war effort, few representatives and senators were willing to risk their political capital on direct criticism of the president. Instead, they engaged in what the press—often as not also hostile to Creel— dubbed "jumping on George." Creel was repeatedly called before this or that congressional committee, typically to answer questions about purported breaches of national security or misappropriation of funds. He was accused of being an agent for the IWW—the "subversive" International Workers of the World—a Socialist, and a Communist, as well as pro-German. "Never very patient under attack," Creel later wrote, "particularly when unjust, I made the blunder of fighting back." In May 1918, while Creel was answering questions after a speech before a New York forum, somebody asked whether he "thought all Congressmen were loyal." Creel impulsively blurted out: "I do not like slumming, so I won't explore the hearts of Congress for you."[20]

The demands for Creel's resignation poured in from Congress. Claude Kitchin, North Carolina Democrat and fiery chairman of the House Ways and Means Committee, condemned the CPI chairman as "unworthy of the respect of any decent citizen," and when Creel issued a public letter of apology, the volume of congressional outrage only increased. Creel offered his resignation to President Wilson, who refused to accept it, but did insist that he "put a padlock" on his lips. The president declared, however, that he would not allow one indiscretion to outweigh a year of useful service, and when a group of senators formally called on Wilson to order Creel's removal, he stood firm: "Gentlemen, when I think of the manner in which Mr. Creel has been maligned and persecuted I think it a very human thing for him to have said."[21]

Creel kept his job, but that summer of 1918 he approached the president with a bold gambit he hoped at last would placate Congress. Up to this time, the work of the Creel Committee had been paid for out of a $50 million appropriation Congress put directly into the president's hands as an emergency fund for the national security and defense. The president, not Congress, dispensed monies from this fund. Reasoning that this situation was galling to Congress, which must have felt, quite rightly, that it had no control over the CPI, Creel decided to let Congress take hold of his purse strings. This, Creel urged President Wilson, "would give me my day in court, and bring lies out into the open. . . . Anything is better than being nibbled to death by ducks."[22]

Thus Creel attempted to deal with Congress as he was dealing with the American public through the Four-Minute Men. Just as speakers drawn *from* the community could deliver a message that seemed to be *of* the community, by giving Congress control of CPI funds, Creel hoped Congress would come to feel that the Creel agenda was actually its own. It was an imaginative gamble, to be sure, but it failed miserably. Congress not only proved parsimonious, appropriating for the committee and its activities exactly one-half of what Creel requested in June 1918, but representatives and senators dogged him over every penny, repeatedly accusing him—and always doing so in the pages of the nation's newspapers—of mismanagement and even outright fraud.

Under fire from Congress, Creel produced a meticulous cost/benefit accounting of all the operations of the Committee on Public Information. By the end of the war, the Four-Minute Men had cost the government of the United States a paltry $140,150.40. Creel estimated that newspaper publicity generated by the Four-Minute Men was worth $750,000, calculated at the going rate of such advertising. He produced the report of a single clipping bureau, which, in the space of eighteen months, noted some 900,000 lines of free publicity. Creel went on to calculate the value of other "contributed expenditures." Figuring the contributed cost of 1 million speeches (in fact, *seven* times this number had been delivered) at $4 each, he came up with a contribution of $4 million. Rent of theaters and other venues—all contributed gratis, of course—he estimated at $2 million. Publicity contributed by the press amounted to at least $750,000. Total contributed expenditures, then, were $6,750,000 against just $140,150.40 out of pocket.[23]

In the Four-Minute Men, Ryerson, Blair, and Creel created an extraordinary instrument of propaganda, entirely new to American life and never to reappear again, at least not on such a vast, reality-shaping scale. But how was such an instrument to be used? What reality did it create?

Even as the CPI made emotional appeals to patriotism, Creel became increasingly alarmed by the pitch and intensity of anti-German, anti-foreign feeling on the streets of America. The *Four-Minute Men Bulletin* cautioned speakers to avoid "strong rhetoric that appeals only to those already more than convinced." Illegal acts of discrimination, harassment, and outright violence against German-Americans and other "foreigners" grew increasingly common as the war continued, and the *Bulletin* admonished: "No hymn of hate accompanies our message."[24]

The early issues of the *Four-Minute Men Bulletin* clearly sought to preempt inflammatory speeches, suggesting such useful but unemotional topics as "Universal Service by Selective Draft," "First Liberty Loan," "Red Cross," and "Food Conservation." Yet even Four-Minute Men headquarters began to stray into sensationalism by the beginning of 1918. For example, the *Bulletin* of January 2, 1918, drew the attention of speakers to what it called "Prussian 'Schrecklichkeit' (the deliberate policy of terrorism)" and printed this "Illustrative Four-Minute Speech":

> While we are sitting here tonight enjoying a picture show, do you real-ize that thousands and thousands of Belgians, people just like ourselves, are *languishing in slavery* under Prussian masters? . . .
>
> Read the stories of deliberate *governmentally ordered* brutalities as told in the book, *German War Practices,* recently published by the Gov-ernment's Committee on Public Information. . . .
>
> Prussian "Schrecklichkeit" (the deliberate policy of terrorism) leads to almost unbelievable besotten [*sic*] brutality. The German soldiers—their letters are reprinted—were often forced against their wills, they themselves weeping, to carry out unspeakable orders against defenseless old men, women, and children, so that *"respect"* might grow for German "efficiency." For instance, at Dinant the wives and children of 40 men were forced to witness the execution of their husbands and fathers. . . .[25]

There were also always plenty of speeches on policy subjects, such as "Why We Are Fighting" and "The Danger to Democracy"; on avoiding rumor and gossip, "Unmasking German Propaganda" and "Where Did You Get Your Facts?"; and on such practical matters as "Fire Prevention" and "Farm and Garden." But some speakers insisted on pushing the en-velope by appealing to wartime paranoia. This speech is from October 1917:

> Ladies and Gentlemen:
> I have just received the information that there is a German spy among us—a German spy watching us.

He is around, here somewhere, reporting upon you and me—
sending reports about us to Berlin and telling the Germans just what
we are doing with the Liberty Loan. From every section of the country
these spies have been getting reports over to Potsdam—not general reports but details—where the loan is going well and where its success
seems weak, and what people are saying in each community.

For the German Government is worried about our great loan.
Those Junkers fear its effect upon the German morale. They're raising a
loan this month, too.

If the American people lend their billions now, one and all with a
hip-hip-hurrah, it means that America is united and strong. While, if
we lend our money half-heartedly, America seems weak and autocracy
remains strong.

Money means everything now; it means quicker victory and therefore less bloodshed. We are in the war, and now Americans can have
but one opinion, only one wish in the Liberty Loan.

Well, I hope these spies are getting their messages straight, let-
ting Potsdam know that America is hurling back to the autocrats
these answers:

For treachery here, attempted treachery in Mexico, treachery
everywhere—one billion.
For murder of American women and children—one billion more.
For broken faith and promise to murder more Americans—bil-
lions and billions more.
And then we will add:
In the world fight for Liberty, our share—billions and billions and
billions and endless billions.[26]

A "vast enterprise of salesmanship," George Creel called the work of his
Committee on Public Information, and while it is quite valid to look at
the Four-Minute Man army as a massive instrument of propaganda, in
many ways it more closely resembled a troupe of traveling salesmen.

During the years of 1917 through 1918, America was a nation criss-
crossed by "commercial travelers," and the traveling salesman—the
"drummer"—was a familiar cultural icon. Before the Four-Minute Men,
there were the Fuller Brush Men, selling door to door a line of brushes

developed by Nova Scotia-born entrepreneur Alfred C. Fuller. So pervasive did these salesmen become that it was the *Saturday Evening Post,* not the Fuller Company, that coined the "Fuller Brush Men" epithet. In 1906, Fuller had begun making brushes in his sister's basement. By the end of World War I, his company's annual sales were $15 million, and his Fuller Brush Men were fixtures of American life. In coming years, they would be featured in such comic strips as *Dagwood and Blondie* and *Mutt and Jeff* and in many movies. It is estimated that, between 1906 and 1950, Fuller Brush Men had called on nine out of every ten American homes, selling these households more than $800 million worth of brushes. The Four-Minute Men sold the Great War much as the Fuller Brush Men sold brushes: with speeches that were finely tuned sales pitches.

By the war era, American companies had smoothly honed the art of the pitch, and it was the rare salesman who was not thoroughly familiar with something called AIDA. It was not the Verdi opera but an acronym: *A*ttention, *I*nterest, *D*esire, *A*ction. This was the skeleton on which early-twentieth-century salesmen, Fuller Brush Men or Four-Minute Men, were typically admonished to flesh out their appeals to prospects, and in the vast majority of Four-Minute Men speeches that skeleton can be readily discerned. Look, for instance, at the "German spy" speech just quoted. The opening sentence, "I have just received the information that there is a German spy among us—a German spy watching us," cannot fail to get attention. The next two paragraphs develop interest, and the material beginning with "If the American people lend their billions now" is calculated to arouse desire. Like all effective sales pitches, the speech ends with a call to action: "In the world fight for Liberty, our share—billions and billions and billions and endless billions." *Our* share. Like so many other Four-Minute Man speeches, this one ends with an appeal for cash. Take action. Buy a bond.

Many facets of the Creel Committee's work were dedicated to selling the government's Liberty Loans, but none more intensely or directly than the Four-Minute Men program. The overwhelming success of the four national Liberty Loans and the culminating Victory Liberty Loan may be taken as a quantitative measure of the effectiveness of the Division of the

Four-Minute Men. Two billion dollars in bonds were offered in the First Liberty Loan. More than $3 billion was subscribed by 4 million Americans. Three billion dollars in bonds was offered in the Second Liberty Loan, to which $4.6 billion was subscribed by 9.4 million people. Another $3 billion was offered in the Third Liberty Loan, and almost $4.2 billion was subscribed by 18,308,325 men and women. Nearly 23 million Americans bought bonds in the Fourth Liberty Loan. Six billion dollars' worth was offered, and nearly $7 billion was sold. The final Victory Liberty Loan, which came after the armistice, was more modest—$4.5 billion in bonds—but even that was oversubscribed to the tune of $5,249,908,300 by almost 12 million purchasers.[27]

The Four-Minute Men were at the core of the genius that drove Creel's program of propaganda. They were literally born of a culture of salesmanship, and they labored among a people accustomed to salesmen. Although they hawked patriotism and the precepts of Wilsonian democracy, their principal merchandise was not nearly so abstract. They sold war bonds. They did what salesmen do. They asked for money.

And like all good salesmen, they did not put their appeal in terms of cost but in terms of value. Like all good salesmen, they did not so much sell a product as they sold the benefits of a product. War would create a better world, a world without war. The Four-Minute Men offered the American public the opportunity to buy into that world—with their loyalty, their service, their sacrifice, and their cash.

A few years later, Adolf Hitler and his henchmen—especially propaganda minister Joseph Goebbels—studied Creel and his Committee on Public Information. They admired and emulated many of the mechanical aspects of the Creel program, such as the use of vivid graphics and brilliant posters, the exploitation of film, and the creative control of all avenues of news and information. They understood what Creel had understood: that the task at hand was not so much mass advertising—broadcasting a message—as it was public relations, the very creation of public opinion, the shaping of an environment receptive to the vision of the leader.

Yet the Nazi managers understood their nation's culture even as George Creel understood his. In contrast to America, Germany was not a nation of salesmen and consumers. The name "Four-Minute Men" was intended to evoke images of the nation's first citizen army, it is true, but the modern version of that band was unmistakably an "army" of salesmen, whereas the citizen army the Nazis created was unmistakably paramilitary, ranging from the Hitler Youth to the brown-shirted Storm Troopers of the Sturmabteilung (SA). The object of Nazi propaganda was to ensure that no German thought of himself or herself as a civilian. Whereas Creel sought to decentralize the message of the central government, making it a local matter, the Nazis used propaganda to wholly absorb the local within the central, to make them one and the same. Hitler wanted Germany to become an army—forever. Creel wanted Americans to act like an army—for a time.

CHAPTER 8

THE LOOK OF WAR

George Creel was a man of words, who had made his way in life by writing and by talking people into believing what he wanted them to believe. In his view, it was mainly through language that the public's perception of reality was created, and the first telegrams he sent to muster a staff when he was authorized to create the Committee on Public Information were to journalists and writers like himself. But he also sent one more telegram. It was addressed to Charles Dana Gibson, the most famous name in American popular illustration, and it asked him to gather together a "committee" of artists to aid the government in war-related "pictorial publicity."

In one of those you-can't-make-this-stuff-up moments, Gibson was handed Creel's telegraphic summons just as he was chairing a dinner meeting of the Society of Illustrators, which had gathered at New York's Hotel Majestic to discuss how they, the artists of the United States, might help their country win the war. It was April 17, 1917, eleven days after Congress had voted to declare war and four days after George Creel had been appointed to create and head the CPI. "If it had all been prearranged it could not have happened better," Gibson later wrote to Creel.[1]

On the following Sunday, April 22, Gibson went to Creel's house for a meeting and there, before the evening had ended, the Division of

Pictorial Publicity was born. That a government organization marshaling artists into war service should have come into being just nine days after the CPI itself was authorized is extraordinary, of course, but it is also of a piece with rest of the Creel Committee's efforts. Indeed, by the time Creel came calling, a contingent of the nation's best-known and most highly paid artists and illustrators were already zealous advocates of preparedness. A number had organized themselves into a patriotic artist group they called the Vigilantes, whose purpose had been to oppose neutrality and pacifism well before President Wilson called for war.

The best known of the Vigilantes was Howard Chandler Christy. Born in Morgan County, Ohio, in 1873, Christy studied at New York's National Academy and the Art Students League, where his mentor was the celebrated painter William Merritt Chase. Christy made a popular hit when he was just twenty-two with the "Christy girl," whose debut incarnation was published in the November 1895 issue of *The Century* magazine. She was a more delicately and conventionally feminine version of Charles Dana Gibson's own "Gibson girl," an image virtually contemporaneous with the Christy girl, but which proved to be an even more enduring idealization of American femininity. Well into the early twentieth century, the Gibson girl—statuesque, lean, athletic, yet amply endowed in bosom and hips—appeared not only in magazines but on a staggering array of everyday merchandise, ranging from saucers to ashtrays to fans and umbrella stands. The Gibson girl made her creator a household name, elevating him to the status of dean of American illustrators and therefore the obvious person for Creel to have contacted. Yet it was Christy, younger than Gibson by half a dozen years, who had the bona fides as a wartime artist, having produced exciting front-line illustrations of the Spanish-American War in 1898 for *Scribner's, Harper's,* and *Leslie's Weekly.* Even before he joined the Vigilantes, Christy made a great show of his patriotism, hoisting the Stars and Stripes in his front yard daily and purchasing a cannon he ceremonially fired every Fourth of July.

Not that Christy's fellow illustrator and Vigilante Gibson was any slouch when it came to flag waving and military preparedness. He had favored U.S. entry into the Great War from the moment in 1914 when

Germany violated the neutrality of what British propagandists invariably referred to as "little Belgium." From about 1916, Gibson had begun publishing pro-war cartoons. Unlike Christy, he had not seen war firsthand, but news of the Great War, especially accounts of German atrocities, "moved him as politics never had been able to do," according to his biographer, Fairfax Downey, who remarked of Gibson's wartime cartoons that a new "power . . . surged genii-like from his ink bottle. Never had he drawn with such vigor and verve. His soldiers fixed bayonets and leapt into action." Even the "Gibson girl" was drafted for patriotic combat, transformed into an athletically voluptuous Columbia.[2]

Artists like Christy and Gibson burned with patriotic fervor, and, as the nation's most prominent illustrator, Gibson was just the magnet to attract all the other big names. He immediately established the headquarters of the Division of Pictorial Publicity at 200 Fifth Avenue in New York, with branches soon to spring up in Chicago, Boston, and San Francisco. Before a month was out, he had signed on most of the prominent illustrators working in the nation. He appointed Frank De Sales Casey, art manager for *Collier's,* to be his vice chairman and secretary. "Casey knows every artist in town," Gibson explained to a *New York Times* interviewer early in 1918. "He's familiar with their work, knows the tendency of every one of them, and the conditions under which each has worked and can produce his best. Casey will know just the man to assign to do a certain picture when a particular request is made by one of the Government departments at Washington." Also in the division's inner circle were the Indiana-born graphic artist, lithographer, and designer Charles Buckles Falls; Henry Reuterdahl, whom President Theodore Roosevelt had chosen to document the 1907 to 1909 circumnavigation of Admiral Dewey's "Great White Fleet," intended to exhibit American naval might to the entire planet; Louis D. Fancher, prominent book and magazine illustrator; Charles D. Williams, a stylish book and magazine illustrator who contributed to *Sunday Magazine, Collier's, American Magazine,* and others; Robert J. Wildhack, another prominent illustrator; and illustrator-cartoonist Fred G. Cooper. More big names in illustration and commercial art were recruited to serve as "associate chairmen," including Herbert Adams, Edwin H. Blashfield (the leading American muralist and mosaic artist of his time), Ralph Clarkson, Oliver D. Grover, Francis Jones, Arthur Matthews, Joseph Pennell (best known for his magnificent lithographs and etchings), Edmund Tarbell (distinguished painter and teacher), Douglas Volk, and Cass Gilbert, architect of Manhattan's Woolworth Building, at the time the tallest skyscraper in the world.

It was Gilbert who put into words the mission of the Division of Pictorial Publicity: "To . . . make the story of the war and what it meant a story that 'one who runs may read,' and to place upon every wall in America the call to patriotism and to service." [3]

The artists of the Division of Pictorial Publicity would fight what Creel called the "Battle of the Fences," their principal mission to create striking posters of aesthetic and emotional merit to be displayed in every available outdoor public space, including the high board fences that were ubiquitous in American cities and towns of the period. As Gilbert had written of creating "a story that 'one who runs may read,'" so Creel observed that the "printed word might not be read, people might not choose to attend meetings or to watch motion pictures, but the billboard was something that caught even the most indifferent eye."[4]

It was hardly an opinion peculiar to Creel. By the late nineteenth century, French lithographers, in particular the commercial lithographer-artist Jules Chéret, had perfected very-large-format lithography capable of producing mural-size posters that introduced into visual advertising many of the techniques and much of the quality of fine-art lithography. In 1889—by which time the commercial posters of Chéret and his many followers had been slapped onto every Parisian wall and post—Chéret was awarded the Legion of Honor for "creating a new branch of art." More accurately, however, he had created a new medium for advertising. In an age before people were accustomed to seeing moving images on screen—and long before the advent of television and other forms of video—Chéret had found a way to make public visual impressions that were sufficiently powerful to move people to buy the merchandise of whoever had commissioned his posters. By 1917, commercial lithographed billboards were ubiquitous in the United States as well, and the best were universally recognized as peerlessly effective means of making sales. The most successful commercial artists produced graphics that were appealing, aggressive, and persuasive. The head of the wartime United States Fuel Administration remarked that he could "get authority to write a column or a page about fuel," but he could not "make everybody or even anybody read it. But if I can get a striking drawing with or without a legend of a few lines, everyone who runs by must see it." Division of Pictorial Publicity associate chairman Joseph Pennell explained that the capacity to transmit meaning without words was "the whole secret of the appeal of the poster."[5]

Of course, for that appeal to work successfully, the poster, Pennell observed, had to incorporate a "design [that] is effective and explanatory." The artists of the Division of Pictorial Publicity, he wrote, "are working with and for the government of their country . . . they are at work for the people, at work which the people can understand, for if they cannot it is worthless." Again, George Creel, a Populist journalist who knew nothing about art, understood perfectly. "The old-style poster, turned out by commercial artists as part of advertising routine," he wrote, "was miles away from our need." Washington bureaucrats "imagined art as a sort of slot-machine"; that was a "mistake that had to be rectified. What we wanted—what we had to have—was posters that represented the best work of the best artists—posters into which the masters of the pen and brush had poured heart and soul as well as genius."[6] To convey the nobility of Woodrow Wilson's war vision and to win the hearts and minds of the American people was no job for an advertising hack. It required genuine artists. Gibson and Casey recruited the best and the most successful—ultimately 279 artists and 33 cartoonists in all. Included were some of the most distinguished names in modern American painting, such as William Glackens and George Bellows of the "Ashcan School" (both among the most acclaimed artists of their generation); the respected realist painter Kenyon Cox; Arthur G. Dove, one the nation's first significant abstractionists; and the great book illustrator-painter N. C. Wyeth.

Creel always aimed to recruit the best, the brightest, and the most widely respected—not just because they would create the most effective works of propaganda, whether journalistic, educational, literary, or artistic, but precisely because they were the most influential people in their line of work, the generally acknowledged arbiters of public opinion and sentiment.

―――――――――――――

As was the case with most of what the CPI did, moving the masses often proved easier than dealing productively with Congress and the Washington bureaucracy. Creel asked H. Devitt Welsh, a Philadelphia-based illustrator, to join him in the Washington offices of the CPI to serve as full-time liaison between the Division of Pictorial Publicity and all the heads of the key government branches. Creel wanted all administrators and bureaucrats to know that the artists were at their disposal, and he was eager for the various government agencies to communicate their needs and requirements. Welsh canvassed Washington and came away with a list of requirements for most of the major departments. He sent these to Gibson in New York, who used them to make assignments to his artist army, carefully matching artist to assignment as if he were the art director of a major magazine. Yet neither Gibson nor Creel wanted to stifle individual creativity, and division artists were invited to submit ideas of their own, "so that government routines were soon broken up by the inrush of new and more vivid thought." The result of this flow of creativity was something of a backlash. Government functionaries often resisted suggestions from the CPI's stellar staff, and Gibson frequently found himself languishing in the corridors of Washington for days "actually begging for the privilege of *submitting sketches* from men and women whose names stood for all that was finest in American art."[7]

If Gibson was discouraged, he never let on. He and his colleagues devoted themselves faithfully and furiously to their work. "We have a meeting every Friday night," Gibson told the *New York Times,* "at our headquarters, 200 Fifth Avenue, where we meet men who are sent to us with their requests by the different departments in Washington." Casey would hear his Washington "clients" out, then would select "two of the best men he thinks can be found for the work," and, after the meeting adjourned to Keene's Chop House, he would place the two "on each side of the official emissary. In the course of the dinner views are exchanged on all sides, and we come to understand one another pretty thoroughly."[8]

Gibson made the process seem both rational and collegial, but, in reality, a gulf separated the bureaucrats and the artists. Gibson went on to share with the *Times* interviewer his belief that the "making of posters, heretofore . . . has been colored too much with the merely material view of things." Gibson did not want his top-flight artists wasting "time in the picturization of coal, wheat, ammunition, clothing, and the thousand other things that must be conserved to bring victory. . . . These were not the things with which to fire the imagination and stir the heart of the great American people." Instead, he wanted them to create "pictures that would cause the same emotions as are felt when one sees a Belgian child dying for want of food, or an American soldier slain for lack of ammunition." He wanted to depict

> the spiritual side of the conflict. . . . the great aims of the country in fighting this war. They already have been pictured in words by the President, and I want to say now that he is the greatest artist in the country today, because he is an idealist. He is the great Moses of America. He points out the promised land, the milk and honey. The work of the artist will be made easy by putting into pictorial form the last message of the President.[9]

Like both Creel and Wilson, Gibson understood that the subject of propaganda was not the mere surface of reality but its emotional and spiritual dimensions. The bureaucrats wanted a picture of food or of ammunition. Gibson wanted to give the people a picture of what a lack of food or a dearth of ammunition creates: the death of a child, the death of a soldier. The bureaucrats wanted documents; Gibson wanted poems. The bureaucrats wanted to tell; Gibson wanted to show—and to inspire, to move, to urge. For those who possessed the minds and hearts and imaginations to understand, propaganda was the sovereign instrument of idealism, and it was idealism, not a thirst for martial glory or fear of "the Hun," for which America was—according to Wilson and his disciples, Creel among them—fighting this war.

By Creel's meticulous accounting, fifty-eight U.S. government departments and committees directly requested work from Division of Pictorial Publicity Artists. Seven hundred poster designs were accordingly created, along with 122 designs for cards for streetcar and window display, 310 items intended to be published in newspapers and other forms of print advertising, 287 cartoons, and 19 designs for "Seals, buttons, etc.": a total of 1,438 graphic works. When one reviews surviving examples of this material today, it is apparent that neither side—neither the government bureaucracy nor Gibson and Creel—absolutely prevailed in determining the nature of the artwork. Most of the posters produced by the CPI's Division of Pictorial Publicity are of significant, in some cases exceptional, aesthetic merit. Many deserve to be described without condescension as works of art. Yet even of these, a large number are devoted to the utilitarian and instructional subjects the heads of various government departments demanded. Common subjects included conservation (save coal by using heat and electricity sparingly; don't waste food; grow your own vegetables; join the Woman's Land Army to raise crops), support the troops (knit socks, send books), support the American Red Cross (give money), enlist in the army or navy, and, at the very least, contribute to the Liberty Loan programs.

Liberty Loan appeals and recruiting posters were subjects that gave artists the greatest license for patriotic emotion. Liberty Loan posters often depicted America's fighting men in action or used cherished national symbols—images of the Statue of Liberty, Columbia, and Uncle Sam—to stir hearts and open wallets. A few exploited the pressure to conform that was abundantly present in wartime America. Historians have frequently pointed out the irony of the American home front, which typically used highly coercive, distinctly undemocratic means to rally support for a war that was intended to make the world safe for democracy. Dissent was generally greeted with disdain and social ostracism; offenders were branded as "slackers" and sometimes suffered violent vigilante justice, ranging from vandalism to physical assault. In 1918, the Division of Pictorial Publicity issued a "car card" (a streetcar advertisement) depicting a row of passengers seated on a streetcar bench beneath car cards advertising the Fourth Liberty Loan, food conservation, and the Red Cross War Fund. All of the passengers, men, women, and children, proudly sport "Honor Buttons" on their lapels, marking them as contributors to the Liberty Loan—all, that is, save one man, who sits in dour misery, head down, arms folded across his chest to hide his unadorned lapel. "You'll be uncomfortable without your Honor Button," the poster's headline warns. In one of his own posters, Charles Dana Gibson put it both more poetically and more pointedly. Columbia strides toward the viewer, right fist clenched, left arm upraised, her head topped by a tiara emblazoned with the words "Public Opinion." She delivers an uncompromising message about buying bonds: "if you have the money to buy and do not buy, I will make this No Man's Land for you!"[10]

A number of the Liberty Loan posters went in a very different direction, stabbing at the popular heart with demonic portrayals of the enemy. A widely published example by division artist Fred Strothmann shows a German soldier creeping over the edge of what is either a trench or an abstracted landscape of general ruin, his fingernails stained with blood and blood dripping from his bayonet, the lurid red contrasting monstrously with the uniform dark gray of his face, shoulders, and spiked helmet, beneath the visor of which his eyes glow with a murky green light. "Beat back the HUN with LIBERTY BONDS," the legend beneath him runs. Another poster, this one by J. Allen St. John, reduces the enemy to an even lower level of inhumanity. Beneath a stark, larger-than-life-size bloody handprint is the simple legend:

> The Hun—his Mark
> Blot it Out
> With
> LIBERTY BONDS

Recruiting posters, naturally, were a numerous category, ranging from beautifully rendered realistic depictions of men at arms to images of Columbia, arrayed in flowing robes, making an appeal for volunteers. Portraits of women abounded, such as Howard Chandler Christy's picture of a sassy lass arrayed in a windblown petty officer's middy blouse, sailor cap perched jauntily atop a head of bobbed hair, kerchief waving pertly below the plunging neckline of the blouse. "Gee!!" the caption runs. "I wish I were a man. I'd join the Navy, Naval Reserve or Coast Guard." Other posters took a sterner approach. Frank Brangwyn contributed a dramatic scene of sailors in a longboat fiercely rowing to the sinking hulk of a merchant vessel freshly torpedoed by a German U-boat. "Help Your Country Stop This," the legend admonishes. "Enlist in the Navy."

Many recruiting posters made a special appeal to conscience. Laura Brey, one of a handful of female artists recruited by Gibson and Casey, created an elegant scene showing a young man in civilian suit, with stiff celluloid collar and trim bowtie, standing in the shade of a darkened room, looking somewhat wistfully through a large window at a sun-drenched parade of khaki-uniformed doughboys who march beneath the vivid red, white, and blue of an American flag. "On Which Side of the Window are YOU?" the caption demands.

Charles Dana Gibson was an artist, and George Creel a journalist, but, of course, both men were more than the sum of their ostensible professions. Both conceived of what they did not as ends in themselves but as the means to an end, vehicles capable of moving men and women to action. They understood what government bureaucrats could not understand but what came to any talented American salesman as second nature: People responded to what moved and motivated *them,* not what anyone else thought they should respond to. For that reason, the artists of the Division of Pictorial Publicity took many approaches to creating recruiting posters. In addition to those that evoked patriotism, righteous vengeance, doing one's bit, and self-sacrifice, others appealed to more pragmatic motives. Charles Livingston Bull's recruiting poster for the Army Air Service promised to endow volunteers with the magnificent self-image of a winged warrior, Bull depicting aerial combat between an American bald eagle and a Teutonic dark gray hawk with the forked tongue of a serpent:

JOIN THE
ARMY AIR SERVICE
BE AN AMERICAN EAGLE!

Some posters did nothing more than advertise the opportunity to learn an advanced and profitable skill. One by Otto Cushing promised "Mechanical Training," while a number of unsigned posters touted the opportunity to "LEARN—EARN."

James Montgomery Flagg's posters for the U.S. Marines also put the emphasis on self-interest. One shows a Marine astride a snarling leopard—on which he is mounted facing *backward*—his rifle, bayonet fixed, held at porter arms, his campaign hat set at a jaunty angle, and his mouth in a broad smile across his handsome face:

> travel? adventure?
> answer—join the Marines!

It was Flagg who created the most famous of all recruiting posters, a classic rendering of Uncle Sam (actually a self-portrait, to which was added a white goatee), his index finger leveled straight at the viewer, just above the caption: "I Want YOU for U. S. Army." Flagg had drawn his inspiration for this icon from a British recruiting poster, which showed Lord Kitchener in much the same pose. Flagg's version was printed and distributed during the war in a quantity of over 4 million. Less familiar but even more dramatic was another Flagg masterpiece, which, against a plain white background, depicts a red-headed young man, jaw set, chin outthrust, feet firmly planted apart in pugnacious outrage. He sheds his suit jacket as if preparing for a fistfight. At his feet is his crumpled fedora, obviously flung down in rage and lying beside an open newspaper with the headline "HUNS KILL WOMEN AND CHILDREN!" Above it all is the poster's stark caption:

> TELL THAT TO THE MARINES!
> At 24 East 23rd Street

For all the stark economy of its presentation, the poster is an especially rich example of graphic propaganda. The image evokes righteous outrage, even as it demonstrates precisely what to do about that outrage. As a work of realism, it shows a man preparing for a fight by taking off his jacket. As a work of symbolism, it conveys the necessity of shedding the garments of civilian life to don the uniform of a warrior. The word *enlist* appears nowhere. Instead, there is the paraphrase of a familiar expression of defiant outrage—"Tell it to the Marines!"—and the address of the Manhattan recruiting station.

Effective propaganda evokes and shapes thought and emotion, then shows just what to do with the thought and how to act on the emotion.

Not all of the artists who worked for the Division of Pictorial Publicity remained in their studios. At the request of General John J. Pershing, division leaders chose eight of their number to receive commissions as U.S. Army captains and go to the trenches of France to draw the war firsthand. Three hundred drawings were exhibited throughout the United States, and many were reproduced in magazines.

But the Great War was fought in an age that demanded the documentary immediacy and objectivity of camera and film more than the impressions of artist and pencil. On September 25, 1917, President Wilson had issued an executive order creating within the CPI a separate Division of Pictures and a Division of Films; from the beginning, however, the two divisions overlapped, and in March 1918, the Division of Pictures became the Bureau of War Photographs within the Division of Films. These units were responsible, respectively, for all still photographs and motion pictures relating to the war, including combat photography and the small amount of combat motion picture footage that was produced. U.S. Army Signal Corps and U.S. Navy photographers as well as photographers from commercial photo agencies covered the front. It was the job of the division and the bureau not only to create and distribute material but also to vet everything produced, whether by military or civilian photographers.

The Bureau of War Photographs received Signal Corps and U.S. Navy pictures, cleared them for distribution—consulting with relevant government departments in cases of doubt—and made prints on demand from the original negatives for a charge of ten cents each. Most were distributed through commercial agencies, including the Photographic Association, Underwood and Underwood, Harris and Ewing, Brown Brothers, and the Western Newspaper Union. Schools and public libraries were also major customers, but other organizations and individuals were free to purchase prints as well. The bureau also issued permits to nonmilitary photographers who wanted to photograph military and naval installations and equipment. Such requests were never handled as matters of routine. Those seeking permits were subjected to rigorous investigation. Yet the bureau made it a matter of policy to avoid creating unnecessary red tape. While censorship and security were important, the main mission of the CPI was granting access and obtaining distribution rather than withholding access and limiting the circulation of materials. The public wanted to *see* the war, and the Creel Committee wanted to show it to them.

Whereas the Bureau of War Photographs handled photographic prints intended mainly for publication, another Division of Films subsidiary, the smaller Department of Slides, drew on material furnished by the Bureau of War Photographs to supply schools, churches, and public and private organizations with magic lantern (projector) slides for fifteen cents each—about half the cost of commercially available slides. At first, the department merely distributed slides processed by the U.S. Army Signal Corps, but demand soon became so heavy that the department set up its own laboratory at 1820 18th Street, N.W., Washington, DC.

As originally established, the Department of Slides simply filled orders for individual images. Later in the war it assumed a more sophisticated role, creating entire slide shows. Experts were hired to write formal "scenarios" to accompany ordered sequences, including *The Ruined Churches of France,* a set of fifty slides assembled by Stanford University professor John Tatlock, who also composed an accompanying narrative text. Other sets included *Building a Bridge of Ships to Pershing, To Berlin via the Air Route, Making the American Army, The Call to Arms, Airplanes and How They Are Made,* and *The Navy at Work.* Most of the slides produced by the department were distributed domestically, but a good many shows were also sent abroad through the CPI's Foreign Section.

In all, the Committee's Picture Division became virtually the only source of war photographs seen by the American people. These were fed to newspapers and magazines at the rate of some seven hundred different images a day. As for the Department of Slides, it produced and distributed a total of 200,000 individual lantern images.

Given the near-miraculous speed with which so much of the CPI was conjured into being in the early spring of 1917, we may wonder why the unit assigned to deal with the most significant mass medium of the day, the movies, was not formed until September 25, 1917. Was the Division of Films an afterthought, a somewhat belated realization that, in the rush to create the Creel Committee, something very big had been left out?

Not at all. The fact was that the American film industry had enlisted in the Great War well *before* President Wilson even asked Congress for a declaration. As early as 1915, the Vitagraph Company released *The Battle Cry of Peace,* which a *New York Times* review described as an "animated, arresting, and sometimes lurid argument for the immediate and radical improvement of our national defenses." The film depicted the invasion of the United States, facilitated by the naiveté of American pacifists and heralded by the bombardment of New York City.[11]

By April 1917, when war was finally declared, at least a dozen films described as "war pictures" were already in the nation's theaters. They ranged from literal-minded documentaries such as *How Uncle Sam Prepares* (made "by authority of and under the direction of military experts") to broader, more suggestive allegories. Geraldine Farrar, star of Cecil B. DeMille's *Joan of Arc* (released in March 1917), told the *Exhibitor's Trade Review,* "I knew when I played Joan of Arc for Mr. DeMille's picture that it would be, as it is, the greatest of all pro-Ally propaganda."[12]

To all appearances, there was little need for a government agency to persuade the American film industry to join up. On April 21, 1917, an *Exhibitor's Trade Review* editorial urged moviemakers to "have ready and waiting on their shelves pictures of happiness, pictures of cheerfulness, and pictures that show the brightness and sunshine of life" specifically for the purpose of maintaining popular morale during the "time of strife and turmoil, of suffering and sorrow that is approaching." Yet, in the very next issue, on April 28, the *Review* warned motion picture producers "who are contemplating productions with war as their theme . . . to see to it, before those pictures are released, that they are not likely in any particular to exert an influence prejudicial to the government's prosecution of the war." The consequences of failing in such diligence? "There is every indication that the federal authorities will suppress such pictures without hesitation." Far from urging studios to fight against such impending censorship, the *Review* insisted that this was no time to discuss what it called "a producer's abstract right to make and market any kind of picture he pleases." Yes, the *Review* conceded, "Probably he possesses that right. But public right takes precedence over any private right, especially in time of war."[13]

Unlike the nation's newspapers, which protested the prospect of government censorship as an infringement on freedom of the press—and protested it even in the face of wholesale public indifference to the censorship issue—the movie industry almost welcomed it. Not only did studios begin to produce propaganda before the government did, they volunteered their services before being asked to do so, and at least one of their principal industry organs, the *Exhibitor's Trade Review,* urged voluntary self-censorship before George Creel asked them for it. The fact was that, in contrast to the newspapers, the movie industry was already in the propaganda business, retailing to the public on a weekly basis, in matinees and evening shows, various incarnations of the American dream and democratic ideals. These were the industry's bread and butter, and the advent of war merely intensified the demand for a more concentrated and direct form of such fare. As Creel quickly came to realize, movies were a most natural and readymade medium for propaganda.

Movie folk also plunged into direct fund raising for the war. William A. Brady, president of the National Association of the Motion Picture Industry, responded to Secretary of the Treasury William Gibbs McAdoo's request for industry aid in arousing public support for the First Liberty Loan by convening a high-level meeting on May 23, 1917, which voted to create a program to pay for 30,000 Liberty Loan slides to be shown in movie theaters all across the country. At the same time, the screen's top stars made whirlwind national tours, staging outdoor Liberty Loan rallies in major cities and towns. Working from a booth in front of the New York Public Library on Manhattan's Fifth Avenue, Theda Bara sold $300,000 in bonds in a single day. Douglas Fairbanks hired a private train to crisscross the country and took in $1 million. His leading lady (and, after the war, his wife), Mary Pickford, "America's Sweetheart," beat him by 100 percent, taking in $2 million as a result of touring California.

Finally, on July 11, 1917, Brady and members of what was now called the War Cooperating Committee called on George Creel (and other officials) in Washington. Creel was ready for them. He asked the committee to assign delegates to act as liaisons with each government department so that moviemakers would know on an ongoing basis just what the government wanted from them. Pressed into this service were the giants of the early film industry, directors, producers, and studio heads including William Fox, D. W. Griffith, Thomas Ince, Jesse L. Lasky, Carl Laemmle, Marcus Lowe, Joseph M. Schenck, Louis J. Selznick, and Adolph Zukor.

Contrary to what critics such as Secretary of State Robert Lansing and many congressional Republicans frequently said of him, Creel did not assume dictatorial, hands-on control of every aspect of America's propaganda effort. Recognizing that the film industry was very much on board with the campaign to support the war, he was largely content to allow it to continue its good work without his interference. Having conferred with industry leaders and connected them with the heads of the most important government departments, Creel turned next to the U.S. Army Signal Corps to secure "the best photographers [i.e., cinematographers] in the United States" to film the war not just for the historical record but to show immediately to the American people. Creel was also eager to secure film coverage of camps, factories, and fields in the United States, to make a film "record, as far as we could, representing democracy's preparation for war." Distributed nationwide, these films were also captioned in many languages and sent "to all parts of the world so that other peoples might see what our country is, what our institutions are, and how America is rallying to the colors."[14]

In this way, the CPI got into the movie business. The Division of Films was directed by Charles S. Hart, who, in eight months, created an organization staffed by forty-five people, including film industry professionals, operating out of a main office in New York and a satellite office in Washington.

Originally the division was intended to work with the Signal Corps and navy to create documentaries, which would not compete with commercial films and would be shown mainly in public meetings rather than in movie theaters, except for the occasional benefit show. Under Hart's leadership, however, and with George Creel's blessing, the Division of Films rapidly outgrew its initial brief. Before the end of the war, it had taken on six principal functions: (1) cooperating with Signal Corps and navy film makers to create documentaries; (2) writing original "scenarios" (scripts) for *commercial* films about government work; (3) issuing permits for commercial films about the war; (4) producing original feature-length documentary films; (5) distributing and promoting all war films, whether the U.S. government had produced them or they were the work of commercial studios or Allied governments; and (6) cooperating with the CPI's Foreign Film Division to export pictures from government as well as commercial sources through CPI agents abroad.

The Division of Films had an Educational Department, which supplied movies to army and navy meetings, patriotic rallies, and schools either free of charge or for the nominal rental fee of $1 per reel per day. Soon, however, this operation was almost totally eclipsed by commercial distribution nationwide. Except in three states—California, Michigan, and North Dakota, all of which used a government distributor—CPI films were distributed by Pathé, First National, and World Film, all major commercial firms, which took a percentage and made money for themselves as well as for the CPI. Rental fees charged exhibitors were generally less than what was paid for standard studio fare, and the distributors agreed on a sliding scale that allowed small-town movie houses to show CPI films for a few dollars a week whereas big-time Manhattan exhibitors were charged as much as $3,000 a week.

As for original productions, the Division of Films began by working with Signal Corps and navy footage, fashioning ten- or twenty-minute short subjects out of whatever was available. Gradually, civilian cameramen were sent to shoot material to augment that footage. The result was such films as *The 1917 Recruit; Submarines; Army and Navy Sports; Labor's Part in Democracy's War; Making of Big Guns; Woman's Part in the War; The Conquest of the Air;* and many others. Short subjects such as these were in great demand and were shown in the nation's movie houses on bills that included regular commercial features. By mid-1918, Creel and Hart decided to further increase the CPI's penetration of the movie market by producing feature-length films of their own, and Division of Film writers, directors, and cameramen increasingly took over from Signal Corps and navy personnel. The first CPI feature, the seven-reel (seventy-minute) *Pershing's Crusaders,* was followed by *America's Answer* and *Under Four Flags* (both fifty-minute films) and a four-part set of two-reel films called the *U.S.A. Series.* The Division of Films also produced a short feature intended for distribution in the so-called race market, the theaters patronized mainly by African American audiences, called *Our Colored Fighters.*

Even as CPI personnel worked on these films, Creel and Hart realized that it would be more productive, professional, commercially appealing, and cost-efficient to enlist the cooperation of the major film studios. On June 1, 1918, a Scenario Department was created within the Division of Films to write documentary screenplays that would be produced and directed by major motion picture studios. Studio heads were reluctant, protesting that government propaganda films could never be made commercially successful, but Rufus Steele, the writer who was put in charge of the Scenario Department, argued that he could turn out scripts that would put the government's message across while also holding the interest of moviegoers. Reluctantly, the producers agreed to dip a toe; for the sake of the war effort, they would finance a series of one-reelers for which the CPI would furnish scripts as well as all necessary permits to give cameramen access to government and military facilities. Moreover, the resulting films would be the property of the studios, and no income would be shared with the government. Under this arrangement, eighteen one-reel shorts were created. Paramount-Bray Pictograph produced *Keep 'Em Singing and Nothing Can Lick 'Em; I Run the Biggest Life Insurance Company on Earth; A Girl's a Man for a' That;* and *I'll Help Every Willing Worker Find a Job.* Pathé turned out *Solving the Farm Problem of the Nation* (a documentary about the U.S. Boys' Working Reserve) and *Feeding the Fighter.* Universal produced *Reclaiming the Soldiers' Duds* and *The American Indian Gets into the War Game.* C. L. Chester, a small studio, produced the most films: *Schooling Our Fighting Mechanics; There Shall Be No Cripples; Colored Americans; It's an Engineer's War; Finding and Fixing the*

Enemy; Waging War in Washington; All the Comforts of Home; Masters for the Merchant Marine; The College for Camp Cooks; and *Railless Railroads.* The Scenario Department proved to be a great success, and private producers soon agreed to make longer pictures using the department's scripts. Production on most of these had not begun by the time of the armistice, however, and many projects were abandoned. Nevertheless, encouraged by studio interest, Creel authorized the Division of Films to produce six two-reelers entirely on its own, using original Scenario Department scripts: *If Your Soldier's Hit; Our Wings of Victory; Our Horses of War; Making the Nation Fit; The Storm of Steel;* and *The Bath of Bullets.*

While scripting and production became an increasingly important Division of Film function, distribution and promotion remained its primary mission. Creel and Hart knew that they could use the force of law to compel—or at least coerce—movie exhibitors to show CPI films, but they believed it would be far more effective to market the films to exhibitors as genuinely desirable merchandise. Film was a marvelous medium for propaganda, Creel knew, but the effect of a film increased in direct proportion to the extent to which it was perceived as genuine entertainment rather than federally required viewing. Thus the CPI employed seventeen sales reps in major cities to support the efforts of the CPI's commercial distributors. The films were heavily promoted in newspaper publicity and ads, subway cards, and window displays, and in a number of magnificent posters produced by the CPI's own Division of Pictorial Publicity. In accordance with the pioneering practices of the public relations industry, George Bowles, manager of the Division of Films feature film unit, sent in advance of the St. Louis opening of *Pershing's Crusaders* in May 1918 personal telegrams to thirty men he identified as the city's most prominent community leaders. In these messages, he asked for their "personal cooperation and influence" to make the movie a popular success. Bowles had taken a somewhat different approach for the film's opening in Cincinnati a few days earlier, sending personal letters to every theater critic in the city and telegrams to the editors of the *Enquirer, Tribune, Times-Star,* and *Post.* As always, the objective of public relations was not to advertise to the masses but to create mass opinion by appealing to the small minority of tastemakers to whom the masses looked for guidance.

The combination of PR and advertising made popular successes of *Pershing's Crusaders* and *America's Answer* (also called *America's Answer to the Hun*), each of which was booked in more than four thousand theaters. Indeed, costs for the Division of Films from its inception in September 1917 to the armistice on November 11, 1918 amounted to $1,066,730.59. Gross receipts for the division's films totaled $852,744.39, which meant that the U.S. government's major movie propaganda effort for the entire period of the war cost the taxpayers just $213,986.20.

From the beginning of movies as a major entertainment medium just a few years before the war broke out, the United States had been the center of the global industry, its films and its stars in greatest demand throughout much of the world. Creel and Hart knew they had, in American cinema, powerful leverage for getting their own message out to the Allied and neutral countries. The Division of Films cooperated with the Foreign Film Division of the CPI's Foreign Section to distribute American war and propaganda films abroad. The export operation was put under the direction of U.S. Army lieutenant John Tuerk and movie industry pioneer Jules E. Brulatour. One of the organizers of Universal Film Company and its first president, Brulatour also had extensive experience with the European film industry, having served as chief of Lumière North American Company, which was headquartered in France.

In all, the Foreign Film Division distributed about 6,200 reels worldwide. To achieve this impressive figure, Tuerk and Brulatour made intensive use of the Trading-with-the-Enemy Act, which included a provision that no American film could be exported without a license from the War Trade Board. Since the War Trade Board worked closely with the CPI, this really meant that no film could be exported without the Creel Committee's approval. Tuerk and Brulatour arranged with Creel to condition export of each entertainment film on the exporter's agreement to send along with it a certain number of CPI reels. As Creel himself put it, "Charlie Chaplin and Mary Pickford led *Pershing's Crusade* and *America's Answer* into the enemy's territory and smashed another Hindenburg line."[15]

Not all of the most important propaganda films sent to foreign countries were devoted to military subjects. Many portrayed the "good life" enjoyed by free citizens of America's democracy. Moreover, the CPI influenced the content of the entertainment features themselves by granting export licenses only for commercial fare that conveyed "wholesome views of American life."[16]

Rarely did the CPI refuse a license strictly on censorship grounds. In large part, doubtless, this was because the American film industry, generally enthusiastic about the war from the beginning, produced very little that was objectionable. There were a few exceptions, however. In January 1917, a fifteen-episode serial titled *Patria* was released by Hearst-Pathé and was heavily promoted as a patriotic story with a strong preparedness theme. As it turned out, however, the preparedness advocated was not against Germany but Japan—a friendly Allied nation. Episode 14 of the serial depicted nothing less than a full-scale Japanese invasion of the United States, masterminded by the evil Baron Huroki (played by a young Warner Oland, the Caucasian actor who would later earn modest fame for his portrayal onscreen of Chinese American detective Charlie Chan), a plot ultimately foiled through the efforts of a plucky American woman named Patria Channing (played by Irene Castle, more famous as the ballroom dancing partner of her British husband Vernon Castle, who perished as a Royal Flying Corps pilot in February 1918). The CPI intervened not only to prevent export of the serial but to halt its domestic distribution, and rumors abounded that the film had actually been influenced by German spies in the U.S. film industry. In truth, the anti-Japanese slant of *Patria* seems to have been the product of William Randolph Hearst's own intensely anti-Japanese bias. The CPI was instrumental in blocking the film, although Hearst managed to recoup his investment by introducing new title cards—as silent film captions were called—in which the Japanese agents and troops were given

Mexican names and the story became a tale about an invasion of the United States by renegade Mexicans.

Stranger than the case of *Patria* was that of *The Spirit of '76*, a patriotic retelling of episodes from the American Revolution produced by Robert Goldstein, who had been instrumental in the production of no less a masterpiece than D. W. Griffith's 1915 *Birth of a Nation*. *The Spirit of '76* was finished just before U.S. entry into the war—an instance, it would seem, of most fortunate timing. After all, what could be better than a movie about the triumphant struggle for America's liberty released at the very moment of America's entry into a war to make the world safe for democracy?

But federal officers working with the CPI objected to the treatment in this film of Great Britain as the enemy, despite the indisputable historical fact that the objective of the American Revolution had been to win independence from England. Censors took particular exception to the depiction of the Wyoming Massacre (July 1778) in the Pennsylvania backwoods, which showed British redcoats killing women and children and abducting young girls. The film was seized by federal agents, and Goldstein was summarily charged with having violated Title XI of the Espionage Act. It was not just that the depiction of the British was objectionable but that the Wyoming Massacre had been deleted from the version of the film shown to censors, only to be restored to the print when it was commercially released; moreover, Goldstein was further accused of having appealed to German American anti-English elements to obtain financing. In the end, he was indicted, tried, convicted, and sentenced to ten years in the federal penitentiary for having attempted "to incite to mutiny U.S. Armed Forces." At sentencing, the judge declared that "history is history and fact is fact . . . the United States is confronted with . . . the greatest emergency . . . [in its] history. There is now required . . . the greatest devotion to a common cause . . . this is no time . . . for sowing dissension among [the] people, and of creating animosity . . . [with the] allies." Goldstein appealed to the Ninth Circuit Court of Appeals, which upheld the conviction on the grounds that the content of the film was sufficient proof of intent to incite to mutiny, even though the prosecution had failed to offer evidence that a single soldier or sailor had even seen the film, let alone had been adversely influenced by it.[17]

As effective as posters and movies were in creating and disseminating propaganda, Creel believed that there was no substitute for a live presentation, whether it was a speech by a Four-Minute Man or a CPI extravaganza called the United States War Exposition.

Committee on Public Information sponsorship of major exhibitions in twenty-one cities, shows (Creel wrote) that "had all the attraction of a circus and all the seriousness of a sermon," drew more than 10 million people and earned an income of $1,438,004, representing a profit of some $400,000 over the $1,006,142.80 required to mount and tour the exhibitions. The public exposure, logistics, and money involved made the War Expositions one of the biggest of the CPI's endeavors. The Departments of War, the Navy, Agriculture, Commerce, the Interior, and the U.S. Food Administration all contributed exhibits, including an array of guns, grenades, gas masks, depth charges, and a host of captured war souvenirs. Soldiers and sailors served as lecturers. Always, the greatest draw was the "big torpedo, captured by the British navy, and known to be a mate to the one with which the Germans sank the *Lusitania*."[18]

Straightforward in their appeal, the War Expositions gave the American people a feeling of immediate participation in the great crusade. Admission was 25 cents for adults and 2½ cents for children. That alone brought in more than $1.4 million, and Creel could not calculate how many additional dollars were generated from the purchases of Liberty Bonds and War Savings Stamps the traveling shows stimulated. As sophisticated and forward-looking as most of the CPI's operations were, drawing on artists and experts in all fields, partaking heavily of the emerging art and science of public relations, the War Expositions, which had all the homespun familiarity of a state fair, were at the simple heart of the committee's propaganda effort, bridging idealism and passion, giving the distant conflict a thrilling presence, by allowing people to see, touch, and learn about the weapons of war.

CHAPTER 9

COMBAT COMES TO CLASSROOM AND FACTORY

George Creel and the Committee on Public Information not only had a monopoly on the news, they controlled virtually every channel of information, expression, and thought concerning America in the Great War. As it was created and managed by the Creel Committee, propaganda reached into every aspect of American life. Indeed, Creel and his staff thought of themselves as the troops who manned the "inner lines" of the war while General Pershing and the doughboys of the American Expeditionary Force manned the "outer lines," the trenches of France.[1] It was all one vast campaign. Journalists, advertising men, PR pioneers, amateur speechmakers, artists, photographers, movie moguls, and filmmakers were all "soldiers," and some recruits came to the CPI not from the hard-driving fields of news, commerce, and entertainment but from the tranquil groves of academe. The most important among these was Guy Stanton Ford.

Born in 1873, Ford left the faculty of the University of Illinois in 1913 to join that of the University of Minnesota as professor of European history and dean of the Graduate School. His special interest was Germany—he had studied at Wisconsin, Columbia, *and* Berlin—although he

was most interested in the German nation not as it existed in the twentieth century but the disjointed Germany of the late eighteenth and early
nineteenth centuries. He titled his Columbia University Ph.D. disserta-
tion, which he completed in 1903, "Hanover and Prussia, 1795–1803: A
Study in Neutrality." His work since then and up to America's entry into
the war had been drably diligent journeyman scholarship, a collaboration
on something called *Syllabus of Continental European History from the Fall
of Rome to 1870* (1904) and editorship of *Essays in American History, Dedicated to Frederick Jackson Turner* (1910), a collection of essays by an as-
semblage of Turner's "Former Pupils at the University of Wisconsin." A
slight, slender, ascetic-looking man, quiet, modest, and retiring even by
scholarly standards, when President Wilson called for war, Ford boldly
took up his pen and, as he explained years later, "wrote an open letter to
school principals about the possibility of using the coming high school
commencements for patriotic purposes. I wrote it for the signature of the
[U.S.] Commissioner of Education, but he modestly declined to sign it
and sent it out, however, over my name." With this, another one of Creel's
happy accidents occurred: A copy of the letter "fell into" the CPI chairman's hands, and he fired off a telegram to Minneapolis. Ford boarded the
next train to Washington.[2]

Named to direct what Creel christened the Division of Civil and Educational Cooperation, Dean Ford took a leave of absence from the University of Minnesota and set up offices at 8 Jackson Place (the division
would move to number 10 and then number 6 on that street before finally settling in at 1621 H Street, N.W.). Joining him was a two-man
staff—Samuel B. Harding, professor of history at Indiana University,
served as Ford's chief assistant, and James W. Searson, a Kansas State University professor of English and journalism, took up editorial duties—
and a handful of stenographers. Together, Ford, Harding, and Searson
would recruit and coordinate the work of scores of scholars from all over
the United States—but especially from the University of Illinois, the
University of Chicago, Columbia, Princeton, Minnesota, and Wisconsin—to publish, between June 10, 1917, and the armistice on November
11, 1918, 105 historical and political works, which circulated in a cumulative print run of more than 75 million, ranging from four-page leaflets

to the *War Cyclopedia: A Handbook for Ready Reference on the Great War,* coming in at 321 pages as published in 1918.

This phenomenon of academic publishing was instigated and managed by just three men and a few stenographers. Their achievement goes to the heart of what the CPI was all about: to create, transform, shape, and mobilize the feelings, attitude, morale, and *war-will* of a nation. Through these professors, Creel came to commandeer academia at every level, from the elementary grades through college. As with operations in the other units of the CPI, Creel revealed himself with the Division of Civic and Educational Cooperation a master of intellectual leverage. Recruit the most influential people, the people at the top of the pyramid, and you gain control of the entire pyramid, no matter how enormously broad its base.

The maiden mission in this scheme was the first assignment Creel handed Ford. Woodrow Wilson's "War Message" of April 2, 1917, by which he had requested of Congress a declaration of war, was already widely read. A document pregnant with Wilson's idealism, Creel regarded it as the chief intellectual, spiritual, and emotional justification for U.S. entry into the war. Eager to educate America to the full meaning of the speech, he asked Ford to commission a pamphlet titled "The War Message and the Facts Behind It." Ford gave the work to a University of Minnesota colleague, William Stearns Davis, who was not a student of modern history, as one might have expected, but head of Minnesota's Department of Ancient History. Davis was not only a historical scholar, he was a historical novelist, whose most popular works of fiction included *Friend of Caesar,* set in ancient Rome, and *"God Wills It!" A Tale of the First Crusade.* He had also earned success as a nonfiction popularizer of history with his *Day in Old Athens.* As a student of ancient Greek and Roman history and culture, Davis, Ford knew, would be amply capable of appreciating the timeless principles of government embodied in the president's "War Message," a concept of democracy as old as the Greeks. Furthermore, as a novelist and popular historical writer, he would be able to communicate these principles vividly to a mass audience. The pamphlet appeared on June 10, 1917, and consisted of the text of the speech annotated with more than forty extensive footnotes that made America's case against Germany and that outlined the foreign policy of the United States.

The Government Printing Office distributed 2,499,903 copies of "The War Message and the Facts Behind It," which was also reprinted in its entirety by many magazines and newspapers. "Probably no man in American history had ever before put to press a scholarly work destined for a larger printing," James R. Mock and Cedric Larson wrote in their account of the CPI.[3] Based on its reception, Creel and Ford launched the vast CPI publication program that issued 75 million items in the space of one and a half years.

Ford did not see himself as the director of some great history factory, churning out books and pamphlets willy-nilly in the hope and expectation that people would read them. As Creel used public relations, the professor exploited another profession newly emerging from American commerce: marketing. He did not call it that, but marketing was precisely what he practiced. On May 25, 1917, Ford wrote to Howard M. Strong, one of the leaders of the Minneapolis Civic and Commerce Association: "We must depend upon the activities of local groups who know the needs of their section and can more promptly and adequately meet them than can a temporary organization in Washington." Ford wanted leaders of local civic groups to tell him what information the people needed and wanted. In effect, he was asking for market research in an attempt to provide the intellectual merchandise that would satisfy each local as well as national market for information.[4]

Ford's bottom-up, democratic marketing approach soon began to work *too* well, as professors, teachers, and citizens routinely flooded him with unsolicited "essays on every subject from Plato's *Republic* to the insidious influence of Bach and Beethoven."[5] Very little of the unsolicited material was usable, of course, and Ford, working with other CPI units and in consultation with other departments of government, increasingly took over the planning of material. Once he had a requirement for a pamphlet or leaflet drawn up, he would send a telegram to the scholar he considered best suited to the job.

Well over a hundred separate titles were produced in this manner, the most important of which were grouped into two series, the "War Information Series" and the "Red, White, and Blue Series." Twenty-one pamphlets were issued in the first series, which began with "The War Message and the Facts Behind It," then continued with pamphlets by members of Wilson's cabinet and by prominent academics. They ranged from immediate issues—"The Nation in Arms," by Secretary of the Interior Franklin K. Lane and Secretary of War Newton Baker, explained in layman's terms the problems of wartime finance and supply—to the historical and ideological background of the war. Among the most inventive of the publications was "American Loyalty by Citizens of German Descent" (700,000+ copies) and its German translation, *"Bürgertreue von Bürgern deutscher Abkunft"* (564,787 copies), which presented a collection of essays by prominent German American citizens, including one that linked the German democratic uprising of 1848 to the crusade to make the world safe for democracy in 1917, thereby defining America's war *against* the kaiser as a war *on behalf of* Germany. This was typical of the appeal the CPI made to German Americans. The admonition was *not* "You are no longer a German but an American, therefore you must be loyal to America" but rather a plea to look beyond parochial nationalism altogether and toward the larger issue of ideology, to support the ideology of democracy against the ideology of imperialist autocracy. German, American, or German American—democracy was a benefit to all.[6]

The series took a sharply practical turn with "Home Reading Course for Citizen-Soldiers," written by "The War Department," which offered sixty-two pages of advice and instruction designed to ease the transition from civilian to military life. This was followed by a pamphlet simply titled "First Session of the War Congress," which summarized the ninety-one acts passed by the first session of the 65th Congress. But it was not until the twelfth pamphlet in the series, "The German War Code," by George Winfield Scott, professor of international law and diplomacy at Columbia, and James Wilford Garner, professor of political science at the University of Illinois, that the division issued what most people would commonly understand by the term *propaganda*. The pamphlet summarized the principal war-fighting manual of the German army, *Kriegsbrauch im Landkriege* (Customs of war in wars fought on land, 1902) and compared it to summaries of U.S. and other Allied manuals in order to contrast the ruthless immorality of the German approach to war with the honorable and compassionate approach taken by the Allies.

German ideology was targeted again in "German Militarism and Its German Critics," which drew heavily on the German Socialist press. Even peace advocates were appealed to in "The War for Peace: The Present War as Viewed by Friends of Peace," by Arthur D. Call, secretary of the American Peace Society. No less a figure than William Jennings Bryan, who had resigned as Wilson's secretary of state on June 9, 1915, in protest of what he deemed Wilson's provocative response to the sinking of the *Lusitania,* contributed to the pamphlet.

Historian John S. P. Tatlock of Stanford University wrote "Why America Fights Germany," published in March 1918. This pamphlet once again took a more baldly propagandistic approach, arguing that the "net of German intrigue has encompassed the world" and that it was therefore necessary to "fight Germany in Europe with help, that we may not have to fight her in America without help." *Facts,* George Creel repeatedly asserted, were the basis of effective propaganda. Tatlock took what he claimed to be the documented "facts" of German conduct in Belgium and France and extrapolated them to create a lurid imaginary vision of a German invasion of the United States:

> Now let us picture what a sudden invasion of the United States by these Germans would mean; sudden, because their settled way is always to attack suddenly. First they set themselves to capture New York City. While their fleet blockades the harbor and shells the city and the forts from far at sea, their troops land somewhere near and advance toward the city in order to cut its rail communications, starve it into surrender and then plunder it. One body of from 50,000 to 100,000 men lands, let us suppose, at Barnegat Bay, New Jersey, and advances without meeting resistance, for the brave but small American army is scattered elsewhere. They pass through Lakewood, a station on the Central Railroad of New Jersey. They first demand wine for the officers and beer for the men. Angered to find that an American town does not contain large quantities of either, they pillage and burn the postoffice and most of the hotels and stores. Then they demand $1,000,000 from the residents. One feeble old woman tries to conceal $20 which she has been hoarding in her desk drawer; she is taken out and hanged (to save a car-

tridge). Some of the teachers in two district schools meet a fate which makes them envy her. The Catholic priest and Methodist minister are thrown into a pig-sty, while the German soldiers look on and laugh. Some of the officers quarter themselves in a handsome house on the edge of the town, insult the ladies of the family, and destroy and defile the contents of the house. By this time some of the soldiers have managed to get drunk; one of them discharges his gun accidentally, the cry goes up that the residents are firing on the troops, and then hell breaks loose. Robbery, murder and outrage run riot. Fifty leading citizens are lined up against the First National Bank building, and shot. Most of the town and the beautiful pinewoods are burned, and then the troops move on to treat New Brunswick in the same way—if they get there.

This is not just a snappy story. It is not fancy. The general plan of campaign against America has been announced repeatedly by German military men. And every horrible detail is just what the German troops have done in Belgium and France.[7]

Tatlock's emotionally compelling fantasy was a sensationalist exception in the vast output of the CPI, yet it was, of all CPI publications, probably the single most-often cited passage. Praised by the war's staunchest supporters, it was also condemned by critics of the Creel Committee, who accused the CPI of circulating hysterical and unfounded stories of atrocity.

Evarts B. Greene of the University of Illinois addressed the German American population with a biography, "Lieber and Schurz: Two Loyal Americans of German Birth." Francis (Franz) Lieber was a German American political scientist who wrote, during the Civil War, *Code for the Government of Armies in the Field,* popularly called the "Lieber Code," which set out ethical and humane conventions governing the conduct of troops during wartime. Even better known than Lieber was Carl Schurz, a leader of the German democratic revolution of 1848 and subsequently, in the United States, a politician, statesman, reform advocate, Union army general, journalist, cabinet secretary, and the first German-born American elected to the Senate.

The twentieth pamphlet, "The German-Bolshevik Conspiracy," presented the so-called Sisson Documents, which were covertly obtained in 1918 by Edgar Sisson while he was serving in revolution-wracked Russia as the Petrograd representative of the CPI. The documents purported to offer irrefutable evidence that Trotsky and Lenin, along with other top Bolsheviks, had been in the pay of the German General Staff, which employed them as agents to bring about the collapse of czarist Russia and thereby Russian withdrawal from the war. Even before the CPI published the documents, their authenticity was called into question, but Creel and others managed to persuade themselves that at least most of the sixty-eight documents were authentic, and the pamphlet containing them was published in an edition of 137,000. Publication touched off an intense controversy, which did not end until 1956, when George F. Kennan (the same American diplomat whose "Long Telegram" sent from the U.S. Embassy in Moscow in February 1946 had outlined what became America's cold war strategy for a half-century) definitively showed that the documents were forgeries.[8]

Less controversial was the final pamphlet of the "War Information Series," Professor Carl L. Becker's "America's War Aids and Peace Program," published just before the armistice and intended to demonstrate that the impending peace would conform "to the better thought of all those who have paid by sacrifice and suffering the price of the world's redemption from the imminent threat of military medievalism."

The publications of the "Red, White, and Blue Series" appeared simultaneously with those of the "War Information Series" but were generally longer, more elaborate, more ambitious, and often more colorful. "How the War Came to America"—note the syntactical order of the nouns—was printed in an edition of 6,227,912 copies in eight languages. Another highlight of the series was "Conquest and Kultur: Aims of the Germans in Their Own Words," issued on November 15, 1917. At 160 pages, this compilation by University of Minnesota faculty members Wallace Notestein and Elmer Stoll presented a host of quotations ranging from contemporary German politicians and military men to Friedrich Nietzsche. Selling 1,203,607 copies, the publication was especially popular with speakers who were looking for convenient petards on which to hoist anyone tagged as an apologist for Germany. This was followed by "German War Practices," edited by professors from the University of Minnesota and Princeton, which drew German atrocity stories from Belgium, France, and Poland, all counterpointed to German pronouncements on the glories of combat. Critics charged that few of the atrocity accounts had been definitively documented; many even had been entirely discredited. That did not prevent nearly 1.6 million copies from being sold. Later, a second volume, "German War Practices II: German Treatment of Conquered Territory," was issued in a quantity of about 700,000.

The magnum opus of the "Red, White, and Blue Series" was the impressive 321-page *War Cyclopedia,* which sold nearly 200,000 copies at a quarter apiece. Editors Frederic L. Paxson (Wisconsin), Edward S. Corwin (Princeton), and Samuel B. Harding (Indiana) presided over some fifty contributors, including the distinguished historians Charles A. Beard and Carl L. Becker. Coverage was A to Z, from "Acts of Congress" to "Zimmermann Note."

The penultimate volume in the series, *War, Labor, and Peace,* was a collection of writings by President Wilson, mostly on the subject of reaching a peace settlement. The volume was published in March 1918 and sold about half a million copies. It was followed by the final publication in the series, *German Plots and Intrigues in the United States during the Period of Our Neutrality,* by E. E. Sperry (Syracuse University) and Willis Mason West (Minnesota), detailing German espionage and agitation on American soil from 1914 to 1917. A total of 127,153 copies were issued.

As impressive as the output of the Division of Civic and Educational Cooperation was, a handful of influential critics complained that the professors, try as they might, had failed to reach the proverbial man and woman on the street. Harold L. Ickes, at the time chairman of the executive committee of the Illinois Council of Defense, wrote to Ford on October 24, 1917, that he had not "seen anything yet that will appeal to the farmers, to the laboring men, or to the average run of citizens who do not do profound reading." Ford responded by authorizing a new series of publications consisting entirely of four- and eight-page "Loyalty Leaflets," seven in all, presenting what today would be euphemistically called "executive summaries" of the topics addressed in the works of the "War Information Series" and the "Red, White, and Blue Series." More bluntly, they might be characterized as dumbed-down versions of these.[9]

Perhaps the strangest—yet most innovative—approach to those Americans who were not given to "profound reading" was "The Kaiserite in America," a thirty-nine page collection of 101 German lies and rumors purportedly circulating throughout the United States, each lie printed together with a statement of the truth specifically intended to counter it. The lies ranged from rumors that public schools in towns located near planned U.S. Army training camps were to be closed for fear that female students "are about to become mothers," to a rumor that a German-born doctor at Camp Bowie, Texas, had injected soldiers with "spinal meningitis serum instead of typhoid serum sending 1,400 men to the hospital," to a tale that U.S. Food administrator Herbert Hoover had wolfed down a seven-dollar banquet meal then delivered a speech on the vital importance of food conservation.[10] What was innovative about "The Kaiserite" was its having been printed expressly for distribution to traveling salesmen ("commercial travelers"), who were addressed in the pamphlet's preface:

> Here is an opportunity for the Commercial Travellers of America to do a great work toward winning the war.
>
> You are summoned as specifically as if you were enlisted in the army or navy to aid the national cause.
>
> Our troops will meet the enemy abroad. You can meet him at home.
>
> Throughout the land the Kaiser's paid agents and unpaid sympathizers are spreading by word of mouth rumors, criticisms and lies that aim to disrupt our national unity and to weaken the will of our people. . . .
>
> It is your immediate task to "swat the lie." Whenever you hear one of these rumors or criticisms, pin the tale-bearer down. Ask him for proof. Don't be satisfied with hearsay or rumor.[11]

In September 1918 the Division of Civil and Educational Cooperation decided to penetrate America's public, private, and parochial schools by creating and distributing the *National School Service,* a sixteen-page news-paper, liberally illustrated with war photographs, distributed to school-children of all ages and intended for them to share with their parents. By this means, it was estimated that the Creel Committee reached directly into 20 million homes on a monthly basis by the end of the war.

American wars of questionable motivation have often been branded with the name of the chief executive who presided over them. Thus the War of 1812 has been called "Mr. Madison's War"; the U.S.-Mexican War, "Mr. Polk's War"; and the Iraq War, "Bush's War"(in this day and age, the po-lite manner of address having been dropped). A number of recent histori-ans have referred to U.S. entry into World War I as "Wilson's War." Yet Woodrow Wilson himself had always taken great pains to portray it as a "People's War," which he sharply contrasted with the "Junkers' War" being waged to preserve the medieval autocracy of imperial Germany. The key to the Wilsonian vision of America's participation was that the war had to be seen not as the fiat of statesmen and politicians in Wash-ington but as an expression of the will of the people, and it was always the principal work of the Creel Committee to shape the perception of the war accordingly.

Nowhere was the challenge of creating this perception more difficult or more important than among labor. The Ludlow massacre during the Colorado mine strikes in 1914 had given George Creel bitter firsthand experience of relations between capital and labor. The early twentieth century was an era of vigorous and radical labor movements in opposi-tion to the often-naked rapacity of management. Woodrow Wilson wanted labor to see itself as participating in a People's War, but many workingmen were far more inclined to regard the conflict in Europe as "Capital's War," a scheme for the rich to become richer feeding the unap-peasable hunger of a ravenous war machine while demanding, in the name of patriotism, more and more of labor: more productivity and more hours, both for the usual bad pay. Gustavus Myers, a pro-labor muckraking journalist (his books included *History of Public Franchises in New York City,* 1900; *The History of Tammany Hall,* 1901; a three-volume

History of the Great American Fortunes, 1909–1910; *Beyond the Borderline of Life,* 1910; and a groundbreaking "Study of the Causes of Industrial Accidents," published in *Journal of the American Statistical Association,* 1915), wrote to President Wilson in 1917 that the "real reason why certain sections of our working and farming populations are either apathetic to our part in the war, or antagonistic to it, is the widespread conviction that the German government has done more for its working people than any other government," including, of course, that of the United States. Myers went on to explain that this "conviction is the result of more than twenty-five years of astute German propaganda in this country." Ironically, Myers's own condemnation of the inequality of American society, *History of the Great American Fortunes,* was translated as *Geschichte der grossen amerikanischen Vermögen* and published in the war year of 1916 by the Berlin firm of S. Fischer. The CPI published in serial form a series of essays by Myers aimed at exploding what he called the "myth" of Germany's social progress claims. The series included "Germany's Sinister Propaganda," "Oppression of the Farmers," "The Hard-driven Underpaid Workers," "Industrial Enslavement of Women and Children," "Wretched Housing Conditions," "Chronic Underfeeding and Great Infant Mortality," "The Large Extent of Pauperism," "Counterfeit Social Insurance," and "Teaching Mental and Social Servitude," all of which were later collected in a single volume commercially published in 1918.[12]

But Creel and many others in government came to believe that getting labor behind the war would take more than articles attacking German lies. The facts were that the antagonism of labor and capitalism was deeply ingrained, that many American workingmen were first-generation immigrants with little reason for loyalty to the United States, and that many laborers, regardless of ideological orientation or national origin, were genuinely fearful that employers would use the war as a convenient excuse to suppress unions and to demand more hours and more work without fair compensation. For their part, employers were afraid that union leaders would take advantage of the "national emergency" to threaten crippling strikes unless outrageous wage demands were met. Most of all, those who ran the wartime government feared any major interruption in productivity. A big strike, they believed, could lose the war.

Employers, government officials, and even many workers began to talk about passing legislation to suspend the right to strike. A Mr. A. C. Hetherlin of the American Woodworking Machinery Company in Rochester, New York, forwarded to the Creel Committee on April 30, 1918, a letter he had received from Henry A. Wise Wood, chairman of an industry organization called the Conference Committee on National Preparedness. "The weakest point in our war work today," Wood warned, "is the attitude of labor. . . . Labor must be shown the necessity for rising above its *technical rights,* and that instead of doing its duty in a merely perfunctory manner, it must put all of its might into the work of producing."[13]

Rights, of course, are either rights or they are not, and although George Creel had created the CPI on the basis of a concept very close to "rising above . . . *technical rights,*" the convenient fiction of *voluntary* censorship of the press, he was clearly uncomfortable with what he himself criticized as the government's "continued emphasis on the responsibilities of labor while never a word is said concerning the employer." In a letter to the National Americanization Committee on January 14, 1918, Creel found himself defending the government, which, he wrote, "is doing everything in its power to prevent strikes, but . . . avoids very carefully any suggestion that it denies the right of labor to protest against conditions." His ambivalence is evident in the ambiguity of his language. Instead of simply declaring that the government upholds the right of labor to protest against conditions, he asserted only that it very carefully *avoids any suggestion that it denies* the right. Creel subsequently endorsed a letter he received from University of Chicago professor S. H. Clark, who pointed out that his two sons fighting in France were paid $33 each per month. Why, then, should captains of industry and barons of high finance "be paid more? . . . Unless we conscript wealth to the justifiable limit, all appeals whether by the Four-Minute Men or a letter from the President . . . all appeals will fall eventually on deaf ears: and we shall have a sullen, scowling, half-hearted cooperation, instead of a wholehearted, inspiring to-the-last-ditch, united democracy." Creel himself wrote that "the most important task we have before us today in the fight for unity is that of convincing the great mass of workers that our interest in democracy and justice begins at home." When F. L. Collins, editor of *McClure's Magazine,* asked Creel if he favored "conscription of labor" and implored the chairman of the CPI to "tell all the rest of us how to act," adding that it would "not be an impossible task to make every industrial slacker in the United States ashamed to be seen in the company of his own dinner pail," Creel replied that American workers "feel that if they are to surrender their demands in the matter of hours and overtime, that employers, manufacturers, wholesalers, retailers, and others, should make like concessions in the matter of profits. The fact that there are so many employers who put greed before patriotism makes it very difficult to level any blanket attack against workers, who are likewise guilty of thinking of themselves before their country." The fight, Creel advised Collins, "should be made against both kinds of 'slacker,' so that the class line would be wiped out entirely, and suspicion removed that one side or the other was attempting to use a national emergency for its own selfish purpose."[14] As with every other aspect of the CPI, then, the approach to labor would be positive rather than negative, an effort to unite rather than to scold.

Creel exercised great care to avoid obviously connecting the CPI— and, therefore, the government—too closely to a movement to rally labor to the cause of war. Accordingly, soon after U.S. entry into the war, the American Alliance for Labor and Democracy (AALD) was set up as an independent organization, although it was, in fact, a CPI proxy. As for the CPI's own Division of Industrial Relations, it was transferred to the U.S. Department of Labor shortly after it had been established. Nevertheless, much of the propaganda, news, and educational materials other CPI divisions produced were directed at labor, and the CPI itself soon became the wartime publicity arm of the Department of Labor.

Samuel Gompers, the most prominent labor leader in the United States, served as president of the AALD, and Robert Maisel, the AALD's director-organizer, also headed the CPI's Division of Labor Publications, which shared a New York City office with the AALD. The Division of Labor Publications included a publicity director, Chester M. Wright, a newspaper editor and Socialist leader who had broken with the party over its refusal to support the war, and a special "Jewish organizer," Joseph

Chykin. The well-known investigative journalist George Seldes served as the director of speakers. Not so secretly wedded to the CPI, the AALD functioned, in effect, as the Creel Committee's field office for labor affairs. Its three main departments—Organization, Literature (which worked closely with the CPI's Division of Labor Publications), and Public Speaking—were charged with rallying labor behind the war effort, keeping workers at work, and ensuring that they were productive. The AALD established 150 branch offices in forty states and distributed nearly 2 million pamphlets, convened some two hundred mass rallies, and claimed space in more than ten thousand newspaper columns.

While the AALD organized, published, and rallied, the CPI's Division of Industrial Relations (entirely separate from the already established Division of Labor Publications) came into being in February 1918 under the directorship of Roger W. Babson, president of Wellesley Associates, a consulting firm specializing in industrial relations. The most important propaganda innovation Babson introduced was a series of "Pay-Envelope Stories," which were miniature pamphlets (measuring 2¾ by 2¼ inches) designed for insertion into employee pay envelopes. Each pamphlet contained a story intended to spur productivity and increase patriotic commitment to the war. The stories were often lurid. "Human Bait," for instance, told how German troops had tied a captured doughboy to the barbed wire of no-man's land in an effort to draw his comrades out of the trenches and into the sights of their guns.

Babson, along with the entire Division of Industrial Relations, left the CPI for the Department of Labor after only a few months, but the AALD, the Division of Labor Publications, and other CPI units continued to work in labor relations, publishing and distributing literature, posters, and conducting meetings while also serving as the publicity arm for the Department of Labor.

Although the CPI took a positive approach to labor, endeavoring to educate workers about the war and why it was being fought, and despite Creel's own feelings that labor *and* capital should be made to shoulder equal burdens, the CPI also served to coordinate efforts to detect and suppress labor unrest. No CPI or other government agents were officially dispatched to factories, but the Creel Committee corresponded with factory owners and managers all across the nation, each of whom had set up in-house intelligence operations to monitor, encourage, and even coerce worker "loyalty." Typical of this micro-level of propaganda and loyalty enforcement was the Winchester Repeating Arms Company plant in New Haven, Connecticut. Its personnel superintendent proudly wrote to Creel that the company gave each employee a "service flag for display in the window of the home" and a "war medal" to wear. It also maintained a "factory Intelligence Bureau to which are reported disloyal utterances or actions." Additionally, the plant presented "daily at noon and periodically during working hours, talks by prominent persons and veterans of the war to keep the matter clearly in the minds of all." The superintendent reported that employee purchase of Liberty Bonds "has been very good," but he made abundantly clear the reason for this: "the spirit has developed to the point where co-workers of any slacker use the necessary moral (or physical) suasion upon those declining to participate. You will note from the bracket clause that we have had to exercise care to see that the spirit developed did not get beyond reasonable bounds."[15]

No one can doubt that George Creel believed labor would always fare better under Wilson's democracy than under the kaiser's autocracy, and he strove to guide the CPI on a positive course where industrial propaganda was concerned. Yet he was not above suspending so-called technical rights in the interest of maintaining uninterrupted industrial production. If he perceived this as a distinctly undemocratic compromise in defense of democracy, he never acknowledged—let alone apologized for—it.

CHAPTER 10

HYPHENATED AMERICA

R obert Paul Prager was a native of Dresden, Germany, who came to the United States in 1905 at the age of nineteen. His was not a bright story of immigrant success. Never married, he drifted, often jobless, through the Midwest and spent a year in an Indiana jail for theft. In April 1917, when the United States declared war on Germany, he was living hand to mouth in St. Louis. America had given him little enough, but the declaration nevertheless aroused in him sufficient patriotic passion to prompt his taking out his first citizenship papers and then sent him to the navy recruiting office, where he tried to enlist. Rejected for medical reasons, he drifted again, winding up in the grim Illinois coal town of Collinsville, where he went to work for a baker, who, finding him intolerably obstinate, soon fired him. Prager next applied to the United Mine Workers for union membership and, during his probationary period, found work in a mine at Maryville, not far from Collinsville.[1]

His career as a miner did not last long, either. Union officials rejected his UMW membership application because, first and foremost, they considered him an enemy alien. In addition, he was a bachelor, abrasive, stubborn, argumentative, harbored Socialist sympathies, and was blind in one eye. If all this were not bad enough, the other miners thought he looked like a spy. In fact, on the night of April 3, 1918, a gang of miners ambushed him, roughed him up, and warned him to get out of Maryville—now.

There was still an element of sanity left in town. UMW leaders Moses Johnson and James Fornero, fearing that Prager would be lynched, appealed to the nearby Collinsville police to put him under protective custody. The Collinsville chief wanted nothing to do with the German, so Johnson and Fornero personally escorted him to his home in Collinsville. The rest of the night passed quietly, but, come morning, Prager proved that the baker and the miners had been right about one thing. He *was* pig headed. He went back to Maryville and drew up a proclamation of protest declaring that he was "heart and soul for the good old U.S.A." and accusing Fornero (one of the men who had tried to protect him) of branding him as a German spy and inciting "an angry mob [to] deal with me." He appealed to the people of Maryville "in the name of humanity to examine me to find out what is the reason I am kept out of work." Prager made carbon copies of the document and posted them around town. Then he lay low until nightfall, when he stalked back to Collinsville.

The main street of that town was lined with dingy saloons, in one of which some of the miners who had attacked Prager in Maryville were getting drunk. Deep in their cups, they resolved to pay the German another visit, this time in his home. They trooped out of the bar, walked to his house, and burst in on him. Robert Paul Prager soon found himself pleading for his life. *Yes,* the stubborn man pleaded. *Yes, he would leave town, he would even leave the state.*

But it had gone too far for that now. The men dragged him into the street. It is unclear whether he was dressed for bed at the time, barefoot and in his underclothes, or whether the mob stripped him of shoes and outer garments, but witnesses agree that he was dragged into the street, shoeless and seminude, and that someone draped an American flag over him as they marched him toward the center of town.

Once again, an agent of sanity intervened. Patrol officer Fred Frost intercepted the mob, grabbed Prager, and hauled him off in protective custody to the jail inside city hall. By this time, Collinsville mayor John H. Siegel appeared and appealed for calm. Someone—perhaps it was

Mayor Siegel—ordered the town's saloons to be shut down early. The police officer who was dispatched to make the rounds of the taverns with the closing order took it upon himself to explain the purpose of his mission. He told the crowd in each barroom that he was shutting them down because a "German spy was in jail."

Drawn from one closing saloon after another, a swelling mob coagulated in front of city hall by 11 P.M. Standing before the door, the mayor yelled to the crowd, three hundred strong and liquored up, that Prager had already been taken away. Joe Riegel, an ex-soldier who now made his living as a miner and part-time cobbler—a man who lived alone because his wife had left him on account of his heavy drinking—demanded that the mayor let him into the jail to have a look for himself. Doubtless with an eye toward the seething throng, Mayor Siegel stepped aside. Riegel threw open the door—and the mob swarmed in after him.

The jail cell was vacant, as the mayor said it would be, but saloon porter Wesley Beaver kept looking and in short order found Prager cowering under a pile of spare tiling in the city hall basement. At Beaver's shout of discovery, as many men as possibly could jammed themselves into the basement, rushing in as if irresistibly drawn by a vacuum. They laid rough hands on Prager, dragged him upstairs, and the four-man night patrol of the Collinsville police force stood aside as the mob shoved their prisoner toward the city limits.

"All reports indicate that at this time there was no intention to hang Prager," the *New York Times* reported in its June 2 account of the trial of those accused of lynching the man. "It was planned to tar and feather him, but tar and feathers were not to be obtained, and a passing automobile in which was a rope suggested hanging. The rope was knotted around the man's neck and he was secured a mile down the road."

They took him to a tree on Mauer Heights, along the St. Louis Road, a mile west of town. The first attempt at hanging Prager failed. The rope was thrown around a sufficiently lofty limb, and the crowd eagerly pulled him up, but they had neglected to tie his hands behind him, and he instinctively grabbed the rope. He was lowered and, the *St. Louis Globe-Democrat* (April 5, 1918) reported, "was asked if he had anything to say. 'Yes,' he replied in broken English. 'I would like to pray.' He then fell to his knees, clasped his hands to his breast and prayed for three minutes in German. . . . Before praying, Prager wrote a letter to his parents, Mr. and Mrs. Carl Henry Prager, Preston, Germany. It follows: 'Dear Parents—I must this day, the 5th of April, 1918, die. Please pray for me, my dear parents. This is my last letter. Your dear son. ROBERT PAUL PRAGER.'"

It was 12:30 A.M. While some two hundred looked on, the "enemy alien" (as several newspapers described him) was jerked into the air at least ten feet. This time, they had remembered to tie his hands.

On June 1, eleven men, including Riegel and Beaver, were tried for Prager's lynching. In his closing argument, their attorney, Thomas Williamson, declared that the "present war situation had developed a now 'unwritten law,' which had been invoked by the men who hanged Prager. . . ." The presiding judge, reported the *New York Times,* instructed the jury that the "war should have no bearing on the case, which, he said, was one in which a helpless prisoner was taken from a jail and murdered."

After closing arguments and the judge's admonition, the jury retired, only to return forty-five minutes later with its verdict: not guilty. The announcement of the verdict "was attended by a wild demonstration in the courtroom in which the accused men were overwhelmed with congratulations." As for Prager, he had been buried in St. Louis by fellow members of the local Oddfellows lodge. The *New York Times* noted: "In answer to a request said to have been made by the dying man, an American flag was draped over his coffin."

George Creel feared the America that lynched Robert Paul Prager. Yes, he was in the propaganda business, and, yes, he knew that, of a U.S. population of about 100 million, 14.5 million had been born in foreign countries and another 17.5 million were first-generation natives. "Hyphenated Americans" they were called during the war years, and Creel understood that "deleting the hyphen" was a top priority for the Wilson government. A big part of the CPI's job was to create and ensure loyalty among the immigrants. But Creel saw what few in the administration and even fewer in the American public saw: that the threat of disloyalty came not so much from the immigrant community itself as from the fearful and intolerant nativist community that surrounded it. Writing after the war, Creel commented on the "loyalty of 'our aliens,'" which, "splendid as it was, had in it nothing of the spontaneous or accidental. Results were obtained only by hard, driving work. The bitterness bred by years of neglect and injustice were not to be dissipated by any mere war-call but had to be burned away by a continuous educational campaign."[2]

Long before the war, immigrants had been the target of suspicion, prejudice, and outright hatred. With the outbreak of the war, however, these passions were intensified—at their worst, leading to violence of the kind that befell Prager. "In all of us," Creel wrote, "there is a certain savage something that thrills to the man-hunt." Throughout the war, he observed, people and, even worse, the press "were keyed up to a high pitch, an excited distrust of our foreign population, and a percentage of editors and politicians were eager for a campaign of 'hate' at home."[3] The last thing Creel wanted was for CPI propaganda to feed that hate. That kind of collateral damage was the greatest risk of his mission, the worst-case scenario. But even if a campaign of crude jingoism did not result in an epidemic of hate crimes, such clumsy and hollow propaganda was simply ineffective in creating loyalty among the foreign born.

Native-born Americans often held "a firm conviction that our declaration of war carried an instant knowledge of English with it, and that all who persisted in speaking any other tongue after April 6, 1917, were either actual or potential 'disloyalists,' objects of merited suspicion and distrust." For their part, "the overwhelming majority of aliens [had] an almost passionate desire to serve America that was impeded at every turn by the meannesses of chauvinism and the brutalities of prejudice, as well as the short-sightedness of ignorance." The nation was swept by "fears of 'wholesale disloyalty'" and "armed uprisings" of entire immigrant communities. "No imagination was too meager to paint a picture of America's adopted children turning faces of hatred to the motherland."[4]

To counter the nativist combination of intolerance, self-righteousness, and hysteria, which made it almost impossible to win the loyalty of the immigrant community—a community that was actually inclined to be loyal—Creel believed that the "foreign-born" had to be shielded from the jingoist "Americanizers" and shown instead the "*real* America . . . its drama of hope and struggle, success and blunders." To achieve this education by propaganda, Creel was determined to studiously avoid "the professional 'Americanizers'" and steer clear of "the accepted forms of 'Americanization.'" Instead, the CPI would work "from the *inside,* not from the outside, aiding each group to develop its own loyalty league, and utilizing the natural and existing leaders, institutions, and machinery." The CPI would offer "cooperation and supervision," and it would give "counsel, not commands."[5]

The obstacles to this campaign were formidable. Difficult as it would be to design appeals to the foreign-born from the *inside* of their communities, persuading the nonimmigrant population out of its intolerant suspicion, fear, and hatred of "aliens" presented an even greater propaganda challenge. Not only were German-Americans suspected and feared as potential internal enemies in a time of war, the burgeoning temperance movement, which had assumed enormous political and cultural importance on what was virtually the eve of ratification of a prohibition amendment, joined in the attack on German-Americans for what was perceived as their intimate connection with the brewing industry. Ordinary citizens wrote Creel daily with recommendations of how to carry out Americanization. L. B. Foley of the Merritt and Chapman Derrick Company, New York, for example, suggested that shooting or hanging those who spread "anti-American propaganda" was the only effective means of clearing the way "for more immigrants to become [loyal] citizens of our country. The writer is convinced that the apathy and dilatory methods of our government, in regard to traitorous enemies within our midst, are responsible for much of the hard work in connection with Americanizing foreigners who come to our shores."[6]

Shooting and hanging were often suggested—though rarely employed—but, more commonly, it was through language that the Americanizers sought to extort loyalty not only from German-Americans but from all of the foreign-born. It seemed that anyone living in the United States who spoke a foreign tongue, whatever it was, fell under suspicion. In some parts of the nation, especially in the Midwest, state laws, proclamations, decrees, and local ordinances were enacted to curb or prohibit the use of German and other foreign languages in public, whether in spoken, written, or published form. In many places, German-language courses were summarily stricken from school curricula, and the U.S. Treasury Department fielded suggestions from many Americans that any bank containing the phrase "German-American" in its name should be compelled rename itself or be closed down forthwith. All across the United States, sauerkraut was instantly renamed "liberty cabbage" (much as, in 2003, anti-Gallic sentiment compelled some to dub French fries *freedom fries* early in Operation Iraqi Freedom[7]). Even the German measles became "liberty measles" and dachshunds "liberty hounds." In St. Louis, which had a large German population, the city fathers responded to a newspaper editor's demand for "wiping out everything German in this city" by renaming Berlin Avenue *Pershing Avenue,* Bismarck Street *Fourth Street,* and Kaiser Street *Gresham.*

The federal Espionage Act and Trading-with-the-Enemy Act gave the government authority to require all foreign-language newspapers to operate under license, the licenses to be issued only after the applicant paper had been thoroughly investigated. Licensing was administered by the U.S. Post Office Department, whose solicitor general, W. H. Lamar, wrote to Julius Koettgen, assistant secretary of the Friends of German Democracy (an ostensibly independent immigrant loyalty organization that was actually a CPI surrogate) on January 29, 1918, that America's German-language newspapers had been almost universally "sympathetic with Germany before this country entered the war" and that many later professed loyalty to the United States yet "continued to publish matter which not only showed sympathy with Germany, but intense hostility to the Allies." Nevertheless, the government managed to bring a good many publishers to a realization of "what their duty to their adopted country means now," and, Lamar reported, the Post Office Department was therefore able "to grant quite a number of permits . . . and I think many others still will ultimately be able to hold permits."[8]

Nowhere was language subject to more sweeping and draconian regulation than in Iowa, whose governor, William L. Harding, issued the so-called Babel Proclamation on May 23, 1918, which summarily outlawed the public use of *all* foreign languages. The proclamation was the culmination of a statewide movement that had begun on November 23, 1917, when the Iowa State Council of Defense resolved that the teaching of German in public schools would be discontinued. Immediately, all German-language instructors on the state payroll were fired, and all German textbooks were burned. The renaming of Iowa towns and streets proceeded apace. Berlin Township became Hughes Township; Muscatine's Bismarck Street became Bond Street, Hanover Avenue, Liberty Avenue; the village of Germania in Kossuth County was rechristened Lakota. As for the Babel Proclamation, Harding announced that it would have the full force and effect of law, and he dismissed protests that it blatantly violated the First Amendment to the U.S. Constitution. "The official language of the United States and the State of Iowa is the English language," he wrote. "Freedom of speech is guaranteed by federal and state constitutions, but this is not a guarantee of the right to use a language other than the language of this country—the English language." English—which the governor often called "American"—was to be the only language of instruction in public as well as private schools; moreover, all conversation in public places, on public conveyances, and over the telephone was required to be conducted in English. (Most arrests under the Babel Proclamation resulted from telephone operators eavesdropping on party-line conversations and reporting to the authorities those conducted in a foreign language.) English and English only was to be spoken in churches (the proclamation was silent on the subject of Latin in the Catholic liturgy and made no mention at all of worship in synagogues), and those who could not speak or understand English were required to confine their worship to the privacy of their homes.[9]

The Iowa situation was extreme—the public use of German was banned in many parts of the country, but only Nebraska followed Iowa's lead by forbidding the use of other non-English languages—but it was more representative than exceptional. Apologists for English-only laws argued that they were not manifestations of xenophobic prejudice but were necessary to foil the communications of foreign agents among us. More sophisticated Americans, including George Creel, rejected this argument. The language laws had nothing to do with security, they said, and everything to do with ignorant misunderstanding at best and, at worst, government-sanctioned hate. It was the dark side of the populism Creel himself had long embraced.

For Creel the journalist and freelance writer, language was the medium in which he lived his life and made his living. It was also the principal vehicle of propaganda—the most effective way to enter and to move the hearts and minds of the masses. Like any good writer, Creel appreciated the need to speak the language of one's audience. If your goal was to educate and persuade a factory worker, for example, you did not appeal to him in the language of a college professor. If your aim was to reveal to a German-born immigrant the "real" America, the America of democracy and freedom, you did not try to appeal to him in any language other than his own. Creel had to overcome the laws of the government as well as the suspicions of the public to allow CPI publications to be issued in German and other languages and to use the CPI to sponsor a large number of local and national immigrant loyalty societies.

At first, Creel personally worked with prominent immigrant leaders to form quasi-independent patriotic groups, which would conduct their business in immigrant neighborhoods and largely in the language of their constituents. Understandably, the first to receive CPI attention were the German-Americans, and in October 1917 the American Friends of the German Republic was organized. The name made some in government nervous, as if the United States were promising to support a revolution in Germany, so it was soon changed to Friends of German Democracy, which took the specific emphasis off of American and German nationalism and shifted it onto the ideology, democracy, advocated by President Wilson.

The Friends of German Democracy was officially founded and organized by private German-American citizens and was run by a group of prominent German professors, teachers, writers, and businessmen. Julius Koettgen, assistant secretary of the Friends, was the key liaison with the CPI, in which he served as director of the German Bureau of the CPI's Division of Work with the Foreign Born.[10] Thus the Friends of German Democracy was actually a CPI surrogate, a government propaganda pipeline into the German-American community. Financial support, however, came not from the CPI but from membership dues and individual donors.

In its strictly domestic guise, the Friends of German Democracy coordinated the patriotic education of its members and also reached out to the larger German-American community. It distributed translations of CPI publications, it held meetings and rallies, and it conducted celebrations of American national holidays, most notably the Fourth of July. But it also played a role on the world stage, aiming to create a bond of brotherhood with Germans everywhere, including those in Germany itself. Its manifesto of December 8, 1917, announced as its purpose "to unify the people of America in the common cause as well as to arouse the people of Germany to a sense of their duty and their opportunity."[11] The United States was home to the world's second-largest German population, and Creel wanted Germany—and the rest of the world—to know that America's Germans lived under democracy and that they were convinced that their brothers—in many cases, family members—who were still in Germany would be far better off under a democratic government as well.

The Friends extended the CPI's reach abroad even more directly. Dr. Frank Bohn, a prominent member of the Socialist Party who also held the title of secretary of the Friends of German Democracy, was sent to neutral Switzerland, ostensibly to represent the organization among the German-speaking community there. In fact, he worked with German refugees in Switzerland to smuggle CPI propaganda into Germany itself, including material communicated directly from the German-American community. Despite Creel's frequent denials to Congress and other officials of the U.S. government that the CPI was involved in any radical or revolutionary agitation abroad, Bohn and others were dedicated to encouraging and even fomenting separatist movements in enemy lands, including Germany.

Although the German Bureau, along with its Friends of German Democracy surrogate, was the single most important foreign working group within the CPI, it was only the first of many that came into being before the Armistice. All were organized under the auspices of the Division of

Work with the Foreign Born, which was directed by Josephine Roche, the Vassar and Columbia graduate who, from 1910 to 1912, had earned a national reputation for her investigations of conditions of working children and immigrants and whom George Creel, when he was Denver's police commissioner, had hired as the city's first policewoman, in charge of rehabilitating the youthful prostitutes of Denver's infamous red-light district. "Under Miss Roche," Creel wrote, "the government frankly established direct and continuous contact with fourteen racial groups through the following bureaus: the Italian, Hungarian, Lithuanian, Russian, Jugoslav, Czechoslovak, Polish, German, Ukrainian, Danish, Swedish, Norwegian, Finnish, and Dutch."[12] In fact, the number of bureaus was at least twenty-three, and included, in addition to those Creel enumerated, Croatian, Jewish (Yiddish-language), Spanish, Chinese, and others.

Each bureau was headed by a chief of the appropriate nationality, who was fluent in the culture and the language. For each nationality, the CPI worked vigorously to provide a steady stream of speakers, news stories, and translations of CPI pamphlets and other publications, including posters, advertisements, and Liberty Loan appeals. Roche was at pains to avoid blanketing the groups with a single pro-American message and instead enlisted the various bureau chiefs to help her deliver to each group individual, customized messages that demonstrated President Wilson's special interest in that group's homeland.

Of all the activities each loyalty group engaged in, two were most effective as propaganda.

The first was providing news relevant to the nationality. This included war news relating to the homeland as well as to the immigrant community in America, with emphasis on reports of the heroism of, for example, Norwegian-American or Italian-American doughboys. CPI agents stationed abroad, especially in neutral nations bordering Germany and Austria-Hungary, worked to secure news from the enemy popular press to send back to the foreign-language newspapers in the United States. This material ranged from human-interest stories to news of staggering losses in the Austro-Hungarian army, devastating hunger in Germany, and so on. Not only was this a means of showing Austrian-Americans, Hungarian-Americans, and German-Americans how much

better off they were in democratic America than in their autocratic an-
cestral lands, it also secured the wholehearted cooperation of the American foreign-language press in supporting the CPI's propaganda and
loyalty efforts. As William Churchill, director of the Division of Foreign
Language Newspapers, explained to Creel: "For three years the German-
American papers have been cut off from their foreign exchanges, always
the most important part of the papers. If we undertook to let them have
this look-in they will feed out of our hands on all the propaganda that
we supply."[13]

Of particular value was the pipeline to the homeland established by
the American-Hungarian Loyalty League (like the Friends of German
Democracy, a CPI surrogate) established by the end of February 1918.
Not only did Hungarian-Americans get a shocking look at the oppression
and poverty the war had brought their native land, and not only did they
learn of the routine abuse of Hungarian troops at the hands of their Austrian officers, U.S. military intelligence obtained an unprecedented window onto conditions in one of the major Central Powers. As for raising
the *war-will* of the Hungarian-American community, this was especially
important, because so many men of this immigrant group worked in key
war-production plants.

The second most effective exercise of propaganda among the foreign
groups was public meetings and rallies. These events created a sense of
national and ethnic community bonded to a feeling of American community. For example, a program sponsored by the American-Hungarian
Loyalty League in the industrial war-production town of Bridgeport,
Connecticut, on March 10, 1918, deftly mingled American and Hungarian cultural and national streams. The program opened with the "Star-
Spangled Banner" performed by the choir of the First Reformed Church
and then was followed by a torrent of speeches—from the chairman of
the local League chapter; from Alexander Konta, president of the national League; from C. B. Wilson, lieutenant governor of Connecticut
and mayor of Bridgeport; from the postmaster of Bridgeport; from the
pastor of the First Reformed Church; from a prominent local Hungarian-
American attorney; from the pastor of Holy Trinity Greek Catholic
Church; from a Roman Catholic priest (speaking in English and Hun-

garian); and from the vice-chairman of the local League chapter. All of this was interspersed with Hungarian and American patriotic songs and war songs, and the entire program concluded with a rousing sing-along of "America."

As with the Four-Minute Men, Creel's propaganda strategy for America's immigrant community blended carefully guided grassroots organizing with at least the appearance of a grassroots message, then cast over these the aura of a beneficent central government authority. It was CPI propaganda at its most effective. its message never became divisively individualistic or parochial yet it always seemed to rise from the individuals of the local community, even as it contributed to a sense of national unity and of unity in a great crusade. The object of the crusade was something far more important than nationhood. It was a crusade for the *idea* of democracy, which Wilson held aloft as a timeless ideal that was, beyond all question, worth fighting for, no matter the historical accident of one's place of birth.

CHAPTER 11

EXPORTING THE MESSAGE

The Committee on Public Information had been created as an alternative to outright, government-imposed censorship. Its primary mission was to control the news and to create propaganda that would ensure the transformation of an ambivalent and traditionally isolationist America into a nation of ideologically motivated warriors. It also had a secondary mission, which, paraphrasing President Wilson, Creel said was to "fight for the mind of mankind."[1]

This was to be the chief work of the CPI's Foreign Section, initially helmed by Creel himself, who soon appointed as his own successor Arthur Woods, former police commissioner of New York City. After serving for a few months, he in turn yielded his place to Will Irwin, a journalist and foreign correspondent whom Creel credited with having had "one of the great ideas of the war" when he masterminded a nationwide program in 1918 of Fourth of July celebrations entirely planned and conducted by immigrant groups affiliated with the CPI.[2] Late in July 1918, Irwin, having directed the Foreign Section for six months, was replaced by former *Cosmopolitan* editor Edgar Sisson, who had just returned from revolution-wracked Russia as the CPI's "Petrograd representative." Harry N. Rickey then replaced Sisson at the very end of the war. Rickey had formerly headed the Newspaper Enterprise Association and had served as the CPI's representative in London.

Creel and his succession of Foreign Section directors were responsible for bringing the ideas of Woodrow Wilson to every corner of the world. In this, they were remarkably successful. By the armistice, Wilson was a universally admired figure, greeted with great enthusiasm by the people of all the Allied nations. In an age before electronically broadcast sound bites, the Creel apparatus transformed Wilson into what today would be called a political "brand," fully identified with democracy as the leading idea of the twentieth century.

Subordinated to the mission of providing high-level public relations for the president, were five more specific yet equally ambitious international missions.

1. CPI units produced and the Foreign Section disseminated propaganda for covert as well as overt distribution to Germany and the other Central Powers. This mission also involved a campaign of disinformation, intended to disrupt and mislead enemy civilian and military planners, and outright espionage, designed to gauge the true state of the enemy's civilian and military morale.

2. The committee distributed propaganda, including many CPI movies, to the neutral nations of Europe in a successful effort to keep them out of the German camp and win a measure of positive moral, financial, and even strategic support for the Allies.

3. Closer to home, the committee sent propaganda materials and agents into Mexico and other Latin American nations. U.S.-Mexican relations had deteriorated precipitously by the eve of America's entry into the war, and the Foreign Section played both a positive propaganda role and a counter-propaganda role, attempting to prevent Mexico from being exploited by German propagandists. Throughout much of the rest of Latin America, the mission consisted mostly of straightforward news management.

4.   Creel gave special committee envoys the task of wading into the chaos of revolutionary Russia in the hope of salvaging that nation for the Allies. It was a mission at once hazardous, desperate, heroic, and hopeless.

5.   Perhaps the Creel Committee's most controversial international mission was a public relations campaign among the *Allied* nations, especially Italy, France, and Britain. The campaign was aimed at shaping public opinion among the Allies to ensure that the people of these nations would be receptive to President Wilson's war aims and his idealistic program for the postwar world.

At the time of its entry into the war, the United States did not possess what modern military intelligence professionals would call a psychological warfare capability. Called on to address the deficiency as best and as quickly as it could, the Foreign Section took two approaches to disseminating propaganda among the enemy.

1.   Working in close cooperation with the U.S. Army's rather primitive Military Intelligence Branch (MIB), CPI agents prepared material that was used as "trench propaganda," directed immediately at enemy soldiers.

2.   On their own, CPI operatives worked from bases in neutral nations bordering Germany and Austria to infiltrate the Central Powers with propaganda.

The first approach, trench propaganda, began with efforts to discover the vulnerabilities in the enemy's morale. MIB personnel would interview prisoners of war, deserters, civilian refugees, and travelers in order to develop a picture of current conditions in Germany and Austria. MIB and CPI operatives also combed German, Swiss, Scandinavian, and Dutch newspapers for information on daily life in the lands of the enemy, and, whenever possible, they intercepted and read international mail. Based on findings from analysis of all these sources, CPI and MIB agents engineered propaganda materials. For example, when fears of critical manpower shortages dominated the enemy press or were reported by POWs and deserters, the American propagandists collected CPI documentary photographs showing tens of thousands of crisply uniformed U.S. doughboys emerging from training camps or boarding troop ships. When food shortages and bad military rations appeared as especially pressing issues among the Central Powers, the CPI prepared a leaflet enumerating, in German, the food ration of a doughboy, including alongside each item the weight or quantity supplied daily. The message was clear: You are starving while we enjoy abundance. In contrast to the ideological propaganda the CPI customarily dealt in, this trench propaganda was largely documentary, focusing on concrete issues. It did not preach democracy, but it did show photographs of tens of thousands of well-equipped, clean, well-fed, fresh, and eager American troops en route to *fight for* democracy. Instead of making bellicose threats, it exhibited the doughboy's daily menu. The object of most trench propaganda was to grind away at enemy morale and exacerbate defeatism.

The MIB was in charge of actually distributing the trench propaganda. It dropped leaflets—"paper bullets," the CPI called them—over enemy territory from airplanes and balloons, or it lobbed them across enemy lines with trench mortars, rockets, rifle grenades, and even in special artillery shells delivered by the fabled French 75-mm guns. Each leaflet had to be carefully designed so that it was clear, vivid, and persuasive yet readily concealed by anyone who picked it up. The Allies were well aware that a standing order had been issued throughout the German army to shoot on sight any soldier seen reading an Allied leaflet. The leaflets designed to be carried in ammunition or rockets also had to be compact enough to be packed in sufficient numbers to gain wide distribution—typically, several thousand per shell or rocket.

Aircraft were highly effective for distributing leaflets, but commanders were reluctant to risk the valuable machines and the even more valuable pilots in flights over enemy lines for the purpose of dropping mere paper. Pilots also hated leaflet missions, considering them dangerous. Often they dumped their loads overboard as soon as they had flown far enough from their own lines to escape observation.

Unmanned balloons carrying leaflets were designed to drift over enemy lines and either float down to earth, spilling their contents, or "sow" the leaflets from the air by means of various mechanical devices. The balloons were much cheaper and safer than aircraft, but they were unreliable. As U.S. diplomat Hugh Gibson complained, "No system has been devised for controlling the flight of the balloons." He continued: "They say the winds on the Western Front have been arranged for the benefit of the Germans," and he pointed out that many of the propaganda balloons "float down into Switzerland and some of them even to Italy and Spain, while the French peasant in the Midi is frequently enraged by picking up in his fields what he believes is Boche propaganda." By the closing months of the war, more reliable balloons were developed, including one, nine feet in diameter, capable of carrying ten thousand leaflets, which would be automatically released at the rate of twelve to twenty per minute. After all of the leaflets had been dropped, an onboard explosive would detonate, destroying the balloon. The cost of this method of distribution was a mere dollar per thousand leaflets released.[3]

The army never thought much of the balloons, even the most sophisticated models, and it was up to the CPI to persuade President Wilson himself to foot the bill for the first five hundred using the National Security and Defense Fund he personally controlled.

If army brass was reluctant to risk aircraft and largely contemptuous of balloons, the doughboy in the trench hated the alternative to these: the use of rifle grenades, trench mortars, rockets, or larger artillery pieces to shoot leaflets into the enemy lines. The problem was that as soon as fire commenced from the American trenches, the Germans would sight on the powder flash, which gave them the location and range of the gunners. And when the Germans started firing back, it was certainly not with "paper bullets."

To reach German civilians, who, of course, lived behind the front lines, leaflets were customarily dropped during air raids, but CPI agents were convinced that smuggling the material into Germany was a far more effective method of distribution. The Bolshevik provisional government had taken Russia out of the war with the Treaty of Brest-Litovsk, concluded on March 3, 1918, and had assumed nonbelligerent status. This hardly meant that the Russian people entertained friendly feelings toward Germany, however, and, while he was stationed in Petrograd (present-day St. Petersburg), Edgar Sisson recruited disaffected Russians who had access to the German border to smuggle large quantities of CPI documents and other propaganda into the country.

Always a champion of women's rights and an admirer of many in the feminist movement, Creel appointed the prominent New York suffrage leader Vira B. (Mrs. Norman de R.) Whitehouse to head CPI operations in Switzerland. She worked with the American military attaché in Berne to recruit sympathetic Swiss businessmen and others who regularly crossed into Germany to smuggle propaganda. Under Whitehouse's direction as well, German soldiers interned in Switzerland were provided with CPI material in the hope that at least some of it would get back to the German homeland, either in letters or as a result of internee exchanges. This practice was extended to German, Austrian, and Turkish internees in other neutral countries too.

The CPI had no way of determining how much of its propaganda actually penetrated into enemy territory, much less a method for measuring its effect. The MIB believed its joint efforts with the CPI were at least making a dent, and intelligence officers cited the report of a Romanian officer who had returned from German captivity as the result of a POW exchange. He assured the U.S. military attaché stationed in Iaşi (Jassy) that "American propaganda in both interior and front has excellent effect, and German soldiers and civilians are getting our ideas."[4]

Will Irwin, the CPI's agent in London, had high hopes for a cooperative propaganda effort with the French, British, and Italians; however, the great obstacle to inter-Allied cooperation proved to be the unwillingness of the four principal Allies to yield even the least potential postwar influence to one another. Moreover, the three European Allies were especially suspicious of American propaganda motives, since it was already quite clear that Woodrow Wilson intended to play a dominant role in creating the terms of peace. The only ground on which Allied propaganda managers could find any room for meaningful collaboration was in mounting an effort to encourage discontent and social revolution in the countries of the Central Powers. The so-called Padua Board—representatives of France, Britain, Italy, and the United States as well as Romania, Poland, Bohemia, and Yugoslavia, who convened regularly in Padua, Italy—agreed that inciting revolution among the Central Powers was a good idea, but they had a great deal of difficulty deciding precisely what they should do to bring it about. Ultimately, Yugoslavs, Bohemians, Poles, and irredentist Italians (earlier captured as POWs) were trained as political agitators and sent to the Italian-Austrian front, where they attempted to subvert Hungarian and other "Slav" troops in the Austrian army. Their efforts met with little or no success.

Of probably greater effect were the direct CPI efforts, which took two tracks. The first was an initiative of the CPI's domestic Division of Work with the Foreign-Born. Its director, Josephine Roche, persuaded a number of the quasi-independent national loyalty groups affiliated with the division to pass resolutions of nationalistic support for their country-men "enslaved" by Germany. The resolutions were widely distributed in Europe and smuggled to underground resistance groups in Hungary, Bohemia, and the territory of the Yugoslavs as well as to exiled resistance workers operating in neutral countries. The second track was an amplification of U.S. diplomacy at the highest levels. The CPI carried deep into enemy-controlled territory the announcement on May 30, 1918, of Secretary of State Robert Lansing's official "interest" in the Congress of Oppressed Peoples of Austria-Hungary, which was meeting in Rome. The announcement included an official expression of U.S. "sympathy" for the national aspirations of Czechoslovakia and Yugoslavia.

The announcement created great international excitement, gave a boost to CPI propaganda efforts abroad, and offered renewed hope for genuinely effective inter-Allied cooperation in propaganda matters on a large scale. In July 1918, Chicago publisher James Keeley was put in charge of all CPI propaganda directed against the enemy. G. H. Edgell, a Harvard University architecture professor, was appointed Keeley's deputy and was assigned to serve as U.S. commissioner to the Padua Board. He, in turn, was assisted by U.S. Army lieutenant Walter F. Wanger, an expert in aerial propaganda. (In later life, Wanger would produce Hollywood films ranging from *The Cocoanuts* of 1929, starring the Marx Brothers, to *Invasion of the Body Snatchers* in 1956, only to end his long career on a sour note when he was fired from the massively overbudget 1963 epic *Cleopatra*.) Despite bright predictions, the spirit of inter-Allied cooperation quickly died, and Keeley reported to Creel on August 18, 1918, that the French and British were working fitfully, but independently of one another, and that while there was "considerable stirring of the ground [there was] no clear and scientific ploughing and not an American machine on the whole farm."[5]

———

More important and certainly more extensive than trench operations and attempts at inter-Allied cooperation was the CPI's work in the neutral countries, projects that were carried on independently of the other Allies. Operations from Switzerland, the Netherlands, and Denmark, all bordering Germany, included propaganda smuggling and outright espionage. While these countries were regarded as geographically convenient bases of operation, other, more distant neutrals were propaganda prizes in themselves. The location of Sweden, for example, meant that it could either augment the effectiveness of the British naval blockade of Germany—a major strategic factor in the war—or help Germany circumvent it. CPI propaganda was aimed at winning the hearts and minds of the Swedes to Wilsonian idealism. Spain, although geographically distant from Germany and the other Central Powers, nevertheless was in a position to menace Britain's important base at Gibraltar and, even more critically, to serve as a second front *against* France—a backdoor, as it were, to a second invasion. In both Sweden and Spain, German agents—spies as well as disseminators of propaganda—were hard at work, and CPI personnel were tasked with opposing them.

Latin America was remote from Europe but within the geographical sphere of American interest, and Mexico in particular shared a long border with the United States. Motives of commerce, politics, and security dictated a strong American propaganda presence in these countries.

Finally, there was Russia. The 1917 Bolshevik Revolution that had removed this massive Allied force from the war failed to transform the nation into an unambiguous enemy, ally, or even neutral. The Treaty of Brest-Litovsk rendered it at best a nonbelligerent, a status by which Germany enjoyed more of an advantage than if Russia were clearly neutral. Yet the treaty, which imposed heavy economic, political, and territorial costs on Russia, created great bitterness and a willingness among many Russians to continue to oppose Germany, regardless of what the Bolsheviks wanted. The combination of war and revolution made Russia a bewildering chaos in 1918, but the CPI struggled to maintain an effective intelligence and propaganda presence there.

Chronologically, Spain was the first neutral on which the CPI focused its attention. Creel appointed Frank J. Marion, president of the Kalem Motion Picture Company, to distribute CPI films in Spain and Italy.

German agents had been at work in Spain even before the outbreak of the war and had been disseminating propaganda to continually remind Spaniards that the British "stole" Gibraltar and still held it, that France's Napoleon had ravaged northern Spain, and that, most recently (no more than twenty years earlier), the United States had stripped Spain of the last vestiges of its empire in the Caribbean and the Philippines. Against this, Marion threw his CPI films. By the end of February 1918, he was also put in charge of arranging for American news dispatches to enter Spain via the wireless service operated by the U.S. Navy. Marion hired journalist Irene Wright to serve as business manager and editor of what he dubbed the *American News,* a daily compilation of the translated dispatches. Wright set up her offices in Madrid, opposite the U.S. Embassy and near the Fabra news agency, to which each *American News* dispatch was hand carried.

Wright was typical of the CPI at its best. Like George Creel himself, she was an enthusiastic and imaginative improviser. Hired to put out the news, she did not confine herself to the *American News,* but on March 9, 1918, persuaded Marion to approach the major American companies doing business in Spain—chief among them were Singer Sewing Machine and a number of automobile firms—to display CPI photographs in their office and shop windows. Singer jumped at the chance, the company's Spanish representative, C. P. Adcock, instantly ordering two hundred sets of CPI photographs for "display in the shops of the Singer Company in Madrid and the Provinces." He even volunteered to foot the bill for transportation and distribution.[6]

Still, countering the long-established and deeply entrenched German propaganda machine in Spain was an uphill struggle. To give American goodwill and Wilsonian idealism a boost, Marion recommended coercing pro-German Spanish newspaper editors by gaining control of the supply of newsprint. "I believe," Marion wrote to Creel, "that at this moment I could alter the complexion of the most influential journal in the country (*ABC*) if I could assure its owners of a supply, or lack of supply, of print paper, depending on their attitude toward the United States."[7] The surviving records of the CPI do not reveal whether this economic warfare was actually waged, but that it was even suggested is a vivid indication of the extent to which the CPI's agents were willing to go.

Doubtless, American propaganda had a salutary effect in Spain, although the Spanish attitude shifted most decidedly away from Germany only late in the war, as it became increasingly clear that the Central Powers would lose. By the final phase of the conflict, the two most powerful CPI propaganda streams flowing into Spain illustrated American (and Allied) military success and the ideas and idealism of Woodrow Wilson. By October 11, 1918—one month before the armistice—Marion was able to report that "Wilson's speeches are the biggest [news] features of the day. . . . Anything and everything about Wilson goes [in Spain]."[8]

And that presented a brand-new difficulty. On October 25, 1918, Marion wrote to Edgar Sisson: "Daily evidence is accumulating in my office that the British and French are trying in many ways to offset the growing influence of President Wilson. It is reliably reported to me that a member of the French Embassy said to a prominent Spaniard yesterday, 'President Wilson may think he is going to be the arbiter of this war but he is fooling himself. When the time comes, the French and the British will settle it as they please.'"[9] Woodrow Wilson was becoming too powerful a propaganda presence—not just for America's enemies, but for its allies as well.

The CPI effort in Scandinavia did not get under way until early in 1918, but it generally proceeded more smoothly than that in Spain. Agents exploited the natural connection between the Scandinavian countries and the United States, which was home to many Swedes, Norwegians, and Danes, by directing a steady stream of news stories highlighting the lives and activities of Scandinavian immigrants. Eric H. Palmer, CPI commissioner in Stockholm, cabled Creel on May 7, 1918, with a request for statistics on the number of Scandinavians in the U.S. Army and Navy and the names of Swedes holding prominent public and political offices in national, state, and local governments. Edwin Bjorkman, prominent in the Swedish-American community as a newspaperman, literary critic, translator, and author, was associated with the Division of Work with the Foreign Born. Shortly before the armistice, he wrote to Palmer in Stockholm to tell him that he had been working with U.S. businesses to direct a large amount of advertising into the "Scandinavian countries, not for the sake of bribing or buying up the press [which was often flooded with German material], but to show that we are interested in them and the markets they offer us."[10]

To an appeal compounded of fraternal fellow feeling and economic imperative, the CPI added movies. Guy Croswell Smith, who had brought CPI films into Russia during 1917, was put in charge of distributing movies in the Scandinavian countries. On August 16, 1918, he was able to write to Edgar Sisson from Stockholm, "We now absolutely control Scandinavia, 90 per cent of the films shown being American." He had achieved this degree of cultural penetration *despite* the British, who were apparently blind to "the propaganda value which nearly every film carries . . . and insist[ed] upon regarding them as flour, cotton or other commercial commodities. Instead of aiding the circulation of the Allies' films they constantly put restrictions in the way."[11] Smith may well have mistaken for stupidity what was a deliberate effort to block Wilsonian influence. Regarding propaganda, the British had hardly shown themselves to be stupid. British propaganda, after all, was instrumental in pulling the United States into the war.

It was one thing for American propaganda to encounter the obstacle of Allied resistance, but quite another for the Wilson message of democracy, including the right of peoples to determine their own national destiny, to confront the far more formidable obstacle represented by the United States' long and troubled history with the peoples of Latin

America. Promoting Wilsonian idealism to nations living under the long shadow cast by a U.S. economic imperialism repeatedly enforced by soldiers, sailors, and marines was a tall order indeed. As recently as 1914, President Wilson had ordered the invasion of Mexico at Veracruz, and in 1916–1917, he had sent General Pershing—now commanding the American Expeditionary Force in Europe—to invade Mexico in pursuit of Pancho Villa and his army.

The CPI's Foreign Press Bureau, led by muckraking journalist Ernest Poole, sent Lieutenant F. E. Ackerman to all of the major cities in South America early in 1918, where he set up a host of press bureau offices. The CPI also dispatched Edward Bernays, soon to emerge as the dean of American public relations professionals, to direct the entire Latin American news service. Bernays enlisted the aid of American firms doing business there to create a pervasive propaganda network. Instead of relying on official CPI offices to distribute pamphlets, books, posters, and the like, he appealed to Ford, Studebaker, Swift, Remington Typewriter, International Harvester, and many other marquee American firms to distribute CPI materials from their offices and to use those offices to display posters and photographs. He also persuaded American companies to make a point of directing their advertising business to local papers friendly to the American cause and to withhold it from those that proved less compliant.

Nowhere in all of Latin America was the propaganda situation more critical or more delicate than in Mexico, where German agents had been active since the beginning of the war in 1914. But, of course, German agents did not create the hostility between Mexico and the United States. They exploited a long-standing situation, and they did so to convey the idea that America in the trenches of France was sharpening a bayonet that it would soon turn against Mexico. As Robert H. Murray, *New York World* correspondent and director of the CPI's Mexico City office, reported to Creel on February 27, 1918, committee operatives were faced with "a fanciful revolutionary government which conservatively may be assumed to be at least passively anti-American and pro-German."[12]

Given widespread illiteracy in Mexico, it was decided to make the first big propaganda assault with CPI films. There was some thought of showing them for free in public squares, but this, it was feared, would give too heavy-handed an appearance of propaganda. The films were shown instead in Mexican movie theaters, together with regular commercial features. Short subjects came across the border initially, but when the first CPI feature film arrived, Murray was aghast at the title: *Pershing's Crusaders.* Mexicans still seethed with outrage over the "Punitive Expedition"—the crusade against Villa—Pershing himself had led into their country just a year earlier. Murray quietly changed the title of the film to *America at War,* but German agents leaked word of the picture's original title, and many movie house owners balked at showing the film. Murray persuaded them by offering a stark choice: either show *America at War* or suffer blacklisting and receive not a single movie made in the U.S.A.— not Chaplin, not Pickford, not Fairbanks or Valentino.

Through efficient distribution, the irresistible allure of American commercial movies, and an unabashed willingness to apply economic extortion, CPI films reached 4.5 million Mexicans by the armistice. This meant that German film propaganda did not have a chance in Mexican theaters. Although agents provocateurs in the German employ worked vigorously to set off demonstrations and even riots in and near many theaters, Murray wrote to Creel that "the demonstrations in the cinés lessened, and finally ceased. The pictures won their way. The attitude of the public altered until after a few months we were repaid for our persistence by reports from our agents, telling of cheering and applause in place of hoots and yells, and even of 'Vivas!' being given for the flag, the President, American war vessels, and American soldiers."[13]

To the motion picture campaign, posters and so-called news pictorials were added—again with a nod toward widespread illiteracy. CPI-supplied photographs were liberally displayed on curbside billboards and in American-owned or American-affiliated shop windows. CPI pamphlets were selectively translated, including "How the War Came to America" and anything that portrayed German atrocities in Belgium. Some 100,000 leaflets—similar to the "Loyalty Leaflets" created for domestic distribution—were printed for insertion in patent-medicine packages.

Following sound public relations as practiced so masterfully by the likes of Bernays, CPI operatives compiled a list of the most influential

Mexicans and Americans living in Mexico. To them, the CPI sent personally addressed propaganda letters in the hope that they would be disseminated by the molders of popular opinion who received them. The
messages were invariably positive, intended to make common cause between the interests of the United States and those of Mexico yet, at the
bottom of each letter was this footer: "THE WAR. REMEMBER: THE
UNITED STATES *CANNOT* LOSE!" It was a small masterpiece of ambiguity, at once implying the United States was so mighty a power that
defeat was simply impossible yet also suggesting that the United States
would spare no nation—and no one—to ensure victory. It was a threat of
force veiled in the thinnest of gossamer.

Despite the dim view CPI personnel had of the intelligence of the
Mexican people, ultimately the most powerful propaganda wielded in
that country was the very same that the CPI used in the United States
and elsewhere: the news. Cable and telegraph service streamed daily, to
the tune of 4.4 million printed words by the armistice. The Mexican
postal service agreed to carry—at no charge—daily and weekly news
bulletins, which found their way into virtually every Mexican newspaper, urban and rural. George F. Weeks, the California newspaperman
who directed the CPI's Mexican News Bureau, was sufficiently imaginative and innovative to include among the publications of his unit an
English-language newsletter published for distribution in the United
States and intended to correct American-held anti-Mexican prejudices
and misunderstandings. Issued from October 3, 1918, to January 30,
1919, the newsletter translated official statements from the Mexican
government, ensuring that these reached American readers—mostly
newspaper editors—without having been filtered or interpreted by the
American media.

The army of Nicholas II, czar of all the Russias, had mustered 1.4 million
men on the eve of the Great War in July 1914. Immediate mobilization
more than doubled this, to 3.1 million by August. During the war some
12 million Russians wore the uniform. These staggering numbers are the
reason why the western Allies invested so much of their hope of victory

in what they called the "Russian steamroller." But there was another number, even more overwhelming. Of the 12 million Russians who fought in World War I, nearly 7 million were killed or wounded. Catastrophic Russian losses led to mass mutinies and helped ignite the general revolution that had long threatened to explode. Still, the western Allies had some reason for hope. The provisional government of Alexander Kerensky, prominent leader of the February (1917) Revolution that had dethroned the czar, pledged to remain in the war. Even though the Russian army had faltered as an offensive force, its continued presence meant that the Germans would have to keep many divisions in the East—and away from the Western Front—to stave off the threat of invasion. Even more hopeful, especially for the government of Woodrow Wilson, was Kerensky's politics. In the spring of 1917, it appeared as if czarism had given way to democracy in Europe's most populous nation, and the CPI was called on to lend support to this emerging brother in democratic ideology. Creel dispatched Ernest Poole and journalist-statesman Arthur Bullard to Petrograd. Their letter of introduction signed by Creel was dated June 18, 1917: "It is our belief that the free exchange of news for the informing of the public, made possible by the printing press and the newspapers, is the foundation stone of Democracy. And I am sure that I speak for all American newspapermen in expressing the most hearty good wishes to the Press of Russia."[14] In October, President Wilson decided to put into CPI hands all U.S. publicity in Russia, and Edgar Sisson, Creel's own associate CPI chairman, was sent there to join Poole and Bullard.

Getting to Russia in 1917 was a long journey, especially during wartime. While Sisson was en route, the Bolshevik Revolution unfolded, hurling against Kerensky's faltering democracy a far more aggressively militant communism. Creel could not reach Sisson, but he cabled Bullard in Petrograd, admonishing him to "Handle Russian situation firmly," whatever that meant. He continued: "United States hoping Petrograd local disturbance unaffecting great freedom-loving Russian people stop Trusting nation to understand that the Bolsheviki success menaces revolution and invites return autocracy." *Hoping, trusting*—these were telling words, and they were hardly a sufficient foundation on which to build a foreign policy. Creel continued: "America at war for certain great

fundamental principles and neither reverse nor desertion will cause surrender stop Only possible peace based on justice with guarantees of per-
manence stop. Give this as coming from high official sources."[15]

But, at the moment, the CPI's Russian bureaus were unable to give
anybody anything. Bullard cabled Creel from Moscow: "For a week we
have been marooned in the consulate, most of the time without any tele-
phonic communication. The only [news]papers issued are the revolutionary ones. They do not have any general news."[16]

Creel understood, but he continued to insist that the CPI get out its
material by whatever means it could find. Sisson arrived in Petrograd on
November 25, 1917, and Creel cabled him on December 2 with orders
to "Drive ahead full speed regardless of expense stop Coordinate all
American agencies in Petrograd and Moscow and start aggressive campaign stop Use press billboards placards and every possible medium to
answer lies against America stop Make plain our high motives and absolute devotion to democratic ideals. . . . Engage speakers and halls. . . .
Cable if send motion pictures."[17] Creel decided not even to await Sisson's
reply. He immediately ordered a half-million feet of film to be sent to
Russia through Sweden.

Although Creel had acted quickly, it was too late. The Bolsheviks
had already closed the border with Sweden. On December 22, Sisson
managed to cable Creel that no news was coming in or going out, not via
cable and not via wireless; nevertheless, he had managed to print a million Russian-language copies of Wilson's war message to Congress, and
CPI offices in Petrograd and Moscow were busy distributing these. A few
days later, on December 30, Bullard cabled the bad news that 300,000
CPI posters and handbills had vanished in transit, but he was about to
issue the first number of the CPI's *Russian News-Letter,* and he wanted
authorization to open offices in Rostov-on-the-Don and Kiev as well as
one or two in Siberia. Creel agreed, but ultimately these plans were foiled
by the closure of Russia's banks. "If the banks are closed," Bullard subsequently cabled Creel, "no one can cash checks and no one can draw
money to meet his payroll."[18]

The displacement of a democratic government by a communist
regime inherently hostile to the capitalist western powers, especially the

United States, was a hard blow. The Treaty of Brest-Litovsk, concluded in March 1918, was worse. The treaty did not mean that Russia had become a German ally, but it did take the nation out of the war, and it gave Russia a nebulous status that was not enemy, ally, or even officially neutral. There was the very real prospect that diplomatic relations between the United States and Russia would be severed, and there was a great fear that all CPI personnel in the country would be held hostage. Remarkably, the CPI did manage to keep some news circulating. It also distributed various pamphlets, posted billboards bearing Wilson's speeches, and even managed to show a small number of films. Astoundingly, too, CPI operatives penetrated the remotest reaches of Siberia (where enthusiasm for the Bolshevik Revolution was weak) in collaboration with the U.S. Military Intelligence Bureau. The CPI continued to operate in Russia for months after the armistice, until February 4, 1919, when the Petrograd office received a cable from Henry N. Rickey, then in charge of the Foreign Section, ordering the commencement of demobilization.

The CPI's efforts in Russia were determined, even heroic, but they were doomed. The collapse of the regular communications networks, the complete takeover of the press by the Bolsheviks, the ideological absolutism of Lenin and the other communist leaders all conspired to squash any competing propaganda effort. Edgar Sisson did believe he had come away from Russia with one great propaganda coup in the so-called Sisson Documents, which he acquired in Petrograd in the spring of 1918 and which he believed were conclusive proof that (as he put it) "the present Bolshevik government is not a Russian government at all but a German government acting solely in the interests of Germany and betraying the Russian people, as it betrays Russia's allies, for the benefit of the Imperial German Government alone."[19]

Sisson's report on the documents was delivered to President Wilson on May 9, 1918, and the papers were released to the American press on September 15. Most of the press took them at face value, declaring that Lenin and Trotsky had been hired by the German General Staff. A few newspapers, however, reported that some authorities were calling the documents forgeries. Had the CPI been able to convince the American public and the world that the revelations of the Sisson Documents were absolutely authentic, a significant propaganda victory would have been scored, and it is even possible that the anti-Bolshevik movement in Russia would have garnered more support both internally and from abroad. But the doubts about the documents grew quickly, and their propaganda value dissolved in controversy.[20]

Publication of the Sisson Documents created international controversy and also exacerbated the endemic hostility Congress directed against George Creel. He had vouched for the authenticity of the documents, and now he was widely criticized as reckless and self-serving for having done so. Yet perhaps the most controversial aspect of Foreign Section activities was its work to "educate" America's allies.

President Woodrow Wilson was an idealist, but, contrary to the opinion of many of his Republican opponents, that did not make him naive. He understood that the leaders of America's chief allies, Britain, France, and Italy, would want to end the war with a conventional victory, a victory in which the losing side is shamed, punished, beaten, and conquered. It was precisely the victory Wilson wanted to avoid, believing, as he did, that it would serve only to ensure the eruption of a retaliatory war sooner or later. His intention was to build a new kind of peace, one that would make war unnecessary, undesirable, and all but impossible. He knew that he would be opposed in this plan, but he believed that, backed by the kind of propaganda that had won his own nation to his idea of war, he would prevail over his opponents and achieve peace as he wanted it.

Along with schooling the Allies in the practical wisdom of Wilsonian idealism, the CPI was tasked with elevating Allied morale, which was being battered by the final, desperate, all-out offensives Germany launched on the Western Front during 1917–1918. Except for Russia, a lost cause, no ally wallowed in a more dismal morass of depressed morale than Italy, which was suffering catastrophic losses in a bitter stalemate against Austria along its northern border lands. On October 29, 1917, Charles Edward Russell, writing from the CPI's London office, told Creel that Italy had "collapsed. . . . It is of no use to try to fool ourselves." He warned that the Germans could now easily overrun northern Italy, which would give the enemy a means of breaking the deadlock of the Western Front: Germany "can strike France in the back and have both France and England practically licked before we can get ready to do any real fighting."[21]

Having committed everything to its all-out offensives on the Western Front, the German high command was not, in fact, prepared to overrun Italy at this time. But the kaiser's government did devote a staggering amount of money—$5 million annually, according to the U.S. MIB—to propagandize within Italy, steadily working to further erode that nation's rapidly dissolving will to continue the fight. On March 15, 1918, the CPI sent to Thomas Nelson Page, United States ambassador to Italy, a cable informing him that Captain Charles E. Merriam, former professor of political science at the University of Chicago, was being dispatched to Rome to take charge of U.S. propaganda. A fellow Chicago professor, Rudolph Altrocchi, would assist him, mainly to organize speakers.

What Merriam and Altrocchi had on their side was the widespread affection of the Italian people for all things American. Italian Americans formed a huge immigrant community, of course, and most kept in close contact with friends and relatives in the old country. This had created a largely favorable image of the United States in the Italian popular mind. The CPI's agents built on this with translations of CPI pamphlets, photographs of famous Italian Americans, and films—plenty of films, CPI fare as well as enormously popular commercial movies. On May 24, 1918, Merriam and Altrocchi were able to circulate a special message from Woodrow Wilson himself, who conveyed from "the people of the United States . . . warm fraternal greetings . . . to the Italian people" on the anniversary of Italy's entry into the war. Wilson spoke of the "profound interest and sympathy" of the American people with regard to "the efforts and sacrifices of the Italian people," and he cited "many personal and intimate ties" between the two peoples "in a struggle whose object is liberation, freedom, the rights of men and nations to live their own lives and determine their own fortunes."[22] This personal appeal proving highly effective, John H. Hearley, Merriam's assistant, sought to amplify it by orchestrating the visit of twenty-three wounded American doughboys of Italian descent to receive honors in the hometowns of their immigrant parents and grandparents.

CPI propaganda was not directed at France until late in the war, beginning in the winter of 1918. Creel sent a good friend, James Kerney, publisher of the *Trenton* (New Jersey) *Times,* to serve as CPI commissioner in Paris. He drew heavily on the navy-run wireless and the CPI-managed news cables for dispatches to feed to the French papers, which, however, were often indifferent to American news. (Creel's critics blamed this on his choice of Kerney, pointing out that Trenton was a very, very different place from Paris.) The French people were far more responsive to CPI films, however, and the second CPI feature-length production, *America's Answer* (also called *America's Answer to the Hun*) was a huge popular success, especially when it was shown to munitions workers in their own plants. Louis Renault, whose automobile factories had been converted to war production, believed that the film staved off for at least six months the labor unrest and general strikes that were a way of life in France and that chronically posed a grave threat in time of war.[23]

Wilson's idealism played well among the French people, but propaganda dramatizing the sheer, irresistible might of American productivity proved a double-edged sword. A. M. Brace, who headed the Paris office of the CPI's Wireless-Cable Service, cautioned that "news regarding the American steam roller, the tremendous gathering of the great industrial and military machine set in motion by an aroused and powerful people—it all has been invaluable, whether viewed from the standpoint of weakening enemy morale or bolstering the morale of the Allies. But we must watch out for the kick-back. I know that there is the belief in some quarters in France that the American industrial machine (and military machine) are a power that may some day wish to dictate terms." Accordingly, Wilson's insistence that America sought no material gain from the war, but was sacrificing only to achieve an enduring, meaningful peace, was emphasized in pamphlets and broadside posters. As Brace put it, victory would bring the "golden hour . . . to hammer home American ideals and America's will to see them through." Now, he advised, was the time to prepare for it with unceasing press and film propaganda.[24]

Everywhere the Foreign Section of the Creel Committee set up propaganda operations—to some extent even in the chaos of Russia—there was a measurable degree of success. At the very least, two American exports always proved popular: movies (including those created by the CPI) and the ideals of Woodrow Wilson. Yet in Britain, the ally closest to the United States in shared language, culture, and history, the CPI was never able to establish even a marginally effective propaganda program. Directors and personnel passed ineffectually through the London office, and British military intelligence and propaganda officers cooperated little with their American counterparts.

The problem was largely a conflict of interest between the conservative Tory circles that controlled Britain's military high command and the democratic idealism of Wilson and his followers. The Tories saw the Great War as a threat to the British Empire, and, what is more, they judged that Woodrow Wilson's war aim of self-determination for every nation and people would surely transform that threat into reality. It is ironic that the nation with the deepest fraternal, historical, cultural, political, and linguistic ties to America should offer, at least at the level of the military, the greatest degree of resistance to American propaganda. But so it was. If any CPI foreign propaganda effort can be judged to have been halfhearted, even a nonstarter, it was the operation that struggled into feeble existence in Great Britain. Unfortunately, failure here heralded a more consequential failure of propaganda to come, after November 11, 1918—at Versailles, in the halls of the United States Congress, and even among the American people.

CHAPTER 12

LEGACY

The Great War ended on the eleventh hour of the eleventh day of the eleventh month of 1918. Within twenty-four hours of the armistice, Creel issued orders for the "immediate cessation of every domestic activity of the Committee on Public Information." In his estimation, many of the CPI's divisions had a "continuing value," but he believed even more strongly that the CPI was "a *war organization* only, and that it was without proper place in the national life in time of peace." War was simple, "with victory as its one objective," Creel wrote, whereas "Peace is far from simple, and has as many objectives as there are parties and political aims and prejudices." On November 14, the government announced the discontinuance of the "volunteer censorship agreement," and on the very next day the CPI issued a formal statement announcing an end to the censorship of cables and mails.[1]

Creel's tidy declaration that war is simple and peace is not was either disingenuous or just plain wrong. Victory may have been the one objective of Clemenceau's war, Lloyd George's war, Orlando's war, but it was never the one objective of Woodrow Wilson's war. CPI propaganda was always aimed at shaping popular opinion to support Wilson's ideological objectives, central to which was the concept of what the president once called "war without victory," war that ended with no nation the winner and no nation the loser but with democracy enabled and the conditions thereby established that would make war forever after an undesirable alternative, perhaps even an impossible one. Rallying support behind a war for abstract ideological ends, in which hate, fear, and nationalism should play no part, was far from simple. For the battles in Wilson's war did not end on November 11. The president knew he would have to fight for peace on his terms, to persuade the badly battered victors—France's Premier Georges Clemenceau, Britain's Prime Minister David Lloyd-George, and Italy's Prime Minister Vittorio Orlando—to renounce victory in the conventional sense. It was widely recognized throughout the Wilson administration and among Democratic lawmakers that the need for propaganda had not ended with the stillness that had come to the many fronts of the war. What is astounding is that George Creel, of all people, failed to recognize this fact.

In a meeting with President Wilson, Creel "insisted upon . . . the government's compete surrender"—the word is most telling—"of every supervisory function as far as news was concerned and the restoration to the press of every power, liberty, and independence." The press, understandably, clamored for total freedom, but so did the Republican majority in Congress. Republican senators and representatives were already raising objections to the idea of American participation in the planned "League of Nations," and they did not want to give the Wilson administration the apparatus to propagandize in favor of the league as it had propagandized in support of its war policies. This partisan opposition should have alerted both Creel and Wilson that now was no time to end the propaganda program, but Creel held Wilson to the very letter of his idealism by urging "the lifting of every barrier."[2] Wilson agreed. The news would no longer be managed.

This matter—apparently—settled, and the domestic activities of the Creel Committee summarily ended, Creel turned to the dismantling of the CPI's Foreign Section. Here motives become cloudier. In his 1920 account of the Committee on Public Information, *How We Advertised America,* Creel wrote that Wilson believed demobilizing the Foreign Section required Creel's "personal attention," So he asked Creel "to be his guest on the *George Washington* if I could make my plans coincide with his sailing date. This, then, was why I went to Paris, and how I happened to be on the *George Washington*." Twenty-seven years later, in his memoir *Rebel at Large,* Creel told a different story, reporting that Wilson asked him to attend the peace conference "in a personal capacity."[3]

As far as most of the press and all of the congressional Republicans were concerned, there was nothing at all vague about Creel's mission: It was to sell America on Wilson's peace and on Wilson's League of Nations.

Even if George Creel really did not see himself as a "press agent" for Wilson and the League, his intensive experience as a master propagandist should have dissuaded him from sailing *with* the president on the president's ship. He of all people should have understood the deep distrust, even revulsion, with which Americans regarded both a standing army and a standing propaganda apparatus. With the end of the war came one great rush to demobilize, to demobilize the army of 4.5 million and the propaganda apparatus that had helped to create it. A "return to normalcy," Wilson's successor Warren G. Harding would call this, "normalcy" in large measure defined as the absence of a standing army and the absence of a ministry of propaganda.

But now here was George "Censor" Creel, wartime propaganda czar, sailing off to Europe in company with Woodrow Wilson. And even as he and the president set sail, Postmaster General Albert S. Burleson suddenly announced that the Post Office Department was taking over control of trans-Atlantic cable communication to and from the peace conference. A new cry of censorship rose up from the press and Senate Republicans. Creel protested that Burleson's action was "as remote as the moon from my authority and duties," but newspaper editorials and Senate speeches flowed in a torrent, accusing Wilson and Creel of conspiring to muzzle the press.

Even now, we cannot say whether a "conspiracy" existed. All that is certain is that George Creel had blundered badly. The man who had built the first and biggest American ministry of propaganda and who had run it imaginatively and successfully throughout a terrible war became party to a public relations catastrophe. At precisely the moment in history when keeping the faith between the Wilson administration and the American people was more critically important than ever, Creel let his guard down, and sinister perception combined with destructive rumor to undercut the peace process in Paris and Versailles.

In an effort to counteract the rising tide of protest from the press and Congress, Wilson ordered the Departments of State and War to expedite passport arrangements for all members of the press, and Creel himself was tasked with signing credentials requesting foreign governments to extend courtesy and access to a long line of correspondents. Wilson also took the extraordinary step of commandeering the passenger ship *Orizaba* to carry the American press to Paris. But the damage had already been done, and Creel, it seemed, could do no right. On arriving in Paris, he noted that only four transatlantic cables were available for correspondents, "a totally inadequate service, and the men who had been most hysterical in demanding that I get out were loudest in insisting that I stay on." In an effort to expedite the transmission of news by reducing the demands on the cable, Creel asked the U.S. Navy to maintain its wireless operations to transmit all official speeches and statements to all three press associations in New York. He also allotted correspondents 3,500 words of original text to be transmitted daily over the navy radio. Remarkably, this gesture, intended to free up cable availability, was twisted by hostile correspondents into an attempt by Creel to censor the news by "rationing" it.[4]

If Wilson and Creel intended to create a propaganda effort in support of the president's positions on the peace treaty and the League of Nations, they faltered and failed. If they never intended to mount such a campaign but had decided to trust a free press to report the story of the peace conference in a way that would promote the treaty and the League, they failed in this, too. In place of either positive propaganda or the confidence that news was flowing free and unfettered were rumors of arm twisting, information control, and outright censorship. Amid a firestorm of negative publicity, Wilson and Creel agreed that he should leave Paris. Accordingly, the president sent him on a tour to inspect conditions in the newly created Czechoslovakia and in Poland and Hungary. Creel distributed CPI pamphlets in the three nations and, on his return to Paris, reported to the Food Commission on the appalling conditions of semistarvation throughout much of the region. He salved himself with the knowledge that his report "won quick and effective relief for Czecho-slovakia and Poland," but his journey had taken him away from the peace conference and had left entirely in the hands of free, unfettered, and unguided correspondents the task of reporting the progress toward a treaty and the creation of the League of Nations.

Creel later wrote that the reception the American people gave the peace conference and the League of Nations depended "upon the spirit in which the correspondents reported and interpreted the activities of the conference." And that spirit, he believed, had been "bad." Creel ascribed the failure of America to endorse the Treaty of Versailles and the League of Nations to the failure of an American press that "interested itself only in the personal and obvious, not in the educational and interpretative."[5] In short, as Creel saw it, propaganda had helped win the war; then, absent propaganda, the *free* American press contributed to losing the peace.

After Creel returned to Paris from his tour of devastated central Europe, Wilson hastily bundled him off to England and Ireland "for a look at the Irish situation."[6] Locked in a desperate and bloody struggle to win independence from Britain, the Irish had appealed for aid to President Wilson as the world's great champion of national self-determination. The president could not deny that, in accordance with his own internationally proclaimed principles, Ireland deserved self-determination, but he was caught in the difficult position of having been the boon ally of Britain in the war just ended, and he did not want to alienate British leadership during the critical peace process. As a less-than-official emissary of the president, Creel had the delicate and ultimately thankless mission of meeting with all sides in an effort to propose some solution that might satisfy all parties. Not surprisingly, Creel's experience in Ireland proved dismally frustrating, and he ultimately confessed his mission a failure. In his 1947 memoir, he even expressed his belief that the question of Irish independence, left unaddressed by President Wilson and the Treaty of Versailles, created among Irish-Americans sufficient hostility to ensure the ultimate rejection of both the treaty and the League.

Creel returned from Europe in March 1919 and, back in Washington, oversaw the dismantling of the Committee on Public Information. He was eager to collect and preserve CPI records for what he judged to be their great historical importance. On June 30, however, Congress peremptorily "wiped the Committee out of existence, leaving no one with authority to indorse checks, transfer bank balances, sign a pay roll, or rent quarters." On his own, Creel borrowed trucks from the U.S. Army to move the committee's records to vacant space he had found in the Fuel Administration Building, personally riding with each load of papers "to see that nothing was spilled," and because the offices into which he deposited the records were completely vacant, he hired a watchman out of his own pocket to keep an eye on things while he searched for an agency—*any* agency—willing to take over the job of liquidation.[7]

Everyone in Washington knew that Congress, always resentful of Creel, intended to humiliate him. In fact, Congress tried to do worse. The CPI chairman was publicly accused of incompetence, of leaving everything "in grossest disorder, premeditatedly designed to cover reckless waste and probable corruption." For many months, Creel was plagued by accusations of having wallowed in an "orgy of corruption." Fortunately, his efforts to save the committee's records allowed him to produce, quite literally, a paper voucher for every dollar spent, and, eventually, he was exonerated.[8]

Yet, except for a personal letter from President Wilson, George Creel was never honored or even officially recognized for the work he had done. He remained in public life after the war, though he was little in the public eye. During FDR's New Deal, he served with the San Francisco Regional Labor Board in 1933, was chief of the Western Division of the National Recovery Administration (NRA), and chairman of the National Advisory Board of the Works Progress Administration (WPA). In 1934, he lost the Democratic nomination as governor of California to the muckraking novelist Upton Sinclair. At the close of his working life, he was a successful writer of popular nonfiction. His best-known book, published in 1944 while World War II raged, advocated the identification, exposure, and punishment of Axis war criminals. Dramatized for the radio, *War Criminals and Punishment* was instrumental in motivating the postwar tribunals in Nuremberg and Tokyo. It was his last great effort to create public opinion and, having created it, to push it into action. George Creel died in 1953.

James R. Mock and Cedric Larson's *Words That Won the War: The Story of the Committee on Public Information 1917–1919* was published in 1939, somewhat more than two years before Pearl Harbor hurled the United States into World War II. It has long been out of print, and when I opened the well-worn copy I had acquired from a used bookseller, a faded and yellowed onion-skin sheet slid out from between the pages. It was a carbon of a memorandum dated June 4, 1942, addressed to "Staff Members of the Bureau of Intelligence and Consultants" from Cornelius DuBois (an authority on public opinion research who, before the war, had been promotion manager for *Time* magazine) on the subject of "Coming Surveys of Intelligence Materials." The memorandum specified due dates for surveys on "Susceptibility to the Axis Line," "Public Attitudes Before and After the President's Speech of April 28," "The Alien Problem," "Influences That Mold Attitudes—Media, Thought Leaders, the Pressure Groups, etc.," "The Labor Problem," "The Negro Situation," and so on.

Clearly, the people in charge of propaganda in the *second* world war were at least reading about the people who had run propaganda in the *first,* although we do not know precisely how much they learned from George Creel. What we do know is that nothing as centralized or as comprehensive as the Committee on Public Information was established during World War II. Intelligence and propaganda efforts were divided up among various agencies, and Creel, writing in 1947, even offered his opinion that the latter-day propaganda was not nearly as effective as the work he and his colleagues had done.[9] In some ways, it did not have to be. The fiery fact of Pearl Harbor and the demonic rapacity of Adolf Hitler were more potent motivators than any propaganda could possibly have been.

If Congress had had its way, Creel and his committee would have left barely any trace of ever having existed, let alone a legacy of national information management. On June 30, 1919, the Creel Committee simply ceased to exist, and when it came time to build a propaganda apparatus for World War II, everyone started virtually from scratch to create a series of essentially ad hoc agencies and operations.

Yet if the United States Congress scrambled to erase all trace of propaganda operations after the Great War, the lessons of the Creel Committee were not lost on the private sector, America's captains of industry. In his 1928 tract titled *Propaganda,* Edward Bernays observed that "it was, of course, the astounding success of propaganda during the war that opened the eyes of the intelligent few in all departments of life to the possibilities of regimenting the public mind. . . . It was only natural, after the war ended, that intelligent persons should ask themselves whether it was not possible to apply a similar technique to the problems of peace." For the most part, those "problems" went something like this: How can my business gain an overwhelming competitive advantage in the American marketplace over every other business? With his fellow "public relations counselors," Bernays made a fortune applying the principles of propaganda to those problems and, mostly, to those problems only.[10]

During the years between the two world wars, however, certain other "intelligent persons" also paid attention to the achievement of the Creel Committee. Among these was a political agitator serving a term for treason in Landsberg Prison, where he wrote the manuscript of a book he intended to call *Four Years of Struggle against Lies, Stupidity, and Cowardice* but ended up publishing in 1925 as *Mein Kampf.* "It was not until the [First World] War that it became evident what immense results could be obtained by a correct application of propaganda," Adolf Hitler wrote. "Here again, unfortunately, all our studying had to be done on the enemy side."[11]

What was "done on the enemy side" had been done largely by George Creel and the CPI. Over the years, various commentators have observed that Hitler's propaganda minister, Joseph Goebbels, used the CPI as a model for guiding his propaganda efforts before and during World War II. There is no surviving statement from Goebbels crediting Creel, no "smoking gun," but it is almost certain that his research had taken in the CPI, the most important propaganda organization of

World War I. We do know that, in 1933, CPI alumnus Edward Bernays hosted a dinner at which Karl von Weigand, foreign correspondent of the Hearst newspapers, having just returned from Germany, entertained the other guests with stories of how Goebbels boasted of his plans to consolidate Nazi power. Goebbels showed Weigand his extensive library of works relating to propaganda—the most impressive collection of such material Weigand had ever seen. Weigand then turned to Bernays and told him that Goebbels was specifically using his 1923 book, *Crystallizing Public Opinion,* "as a basis for his destructive campaign against the Jews of Germany." Bernays, an Austrian-born Jew, nephew of Sigmund Freud, expressed his reaction to this news with dumbfounding understatement—"This shocked me"—then went on to observe that "obviously the attack on the Jews of Germany was no emotional outburst of the Nazis, but a deliberate, planned campaign," one made possible, in fact, by the very techniques Bernays had honed while working on the Creel Committee.[12]

Propaganda, both Bernays and Creel believed, was a tool, morally neutral in itself. It could be used to further the most evil of purposes but was also indispensable to reinforcing public opinion for the best and noblest of ends. Although the great apparatus of World War I had been dismantled, "psychological operations"—PSYOPS—did figure importantly in Allied efforts during World War II. That did not mean everyone liked it. American airmen sent on missions to drop propaganda leaflets over German cities disparaged their aircraft as "bullshit bombers" and referred to the operations themselves as "controlled littering."[13] It is not that the Allies denied using propaganda, but that, for the most part, during "the Good War," propaganda was thought of as the lowdown province of Japan's "Tokyo Rose" and Germany's "Axis Sally" and "Lord Hawhaw," not the work of good old honest Uncle Sam.

During the Cold War that followed World War II, the concept of propaganda became even more pervasive and took on more sinister implications as mass mind control practiced by "godless" Communists. This view culminated during the Korean War in the concept of "brainwashing," the idea (dramatized so chillingly in the 1959 novel and 1962 film *The Manchurian Candidate*) that adept practitioners of PSYOPS could not only shape public opinion but actually seize complete control of the human mind and the human will, regardless of existing beliefs and loyalties.[14]

In the climate of the Cold War and since the Korean War and the era of discredited red-baiting senator Joseph McCarthy, U.S. government propaganda was eyed with as much suspicion as propaganda generated by other governments and other sources. Since the celebrated televised duel between CBS news broadcaster Edward R. Murrow and Senator Mc-Carthy in 1954, Americans have tended to rely on a "free" and "unbiased" press to counteract the "spin" of agenda-driven sources, whether located in the U.S. government or elsewhere. During much of the Vietnam era, from 1965 to 1975, a large segment of the American population did not even dignify government-supplied information, assessments, and pronouncements about the war with the term *propaganda* but simply dismissed it all as lies.

The situation that prevailed when President George W. Bush decided to wage war against Saddam Hussein's Iraq in 2003 more closely resembled the climate of fear and hysteria that characterized the Red Scare of the early 1950s than it did the cynical national mood that developed during the Vietnam era. The terrorist attacks of September 11, 2001, had not been carried out by "godless Communists" but by "religious extremists" who believed in a different god from the God of most Americans. This apparently made them willing not only to kill indiscriminately but to kill themselves in the process of killing others. Fearful, confused, and outraged, many Americans were in a frame of mind and emotion that was highly receptive to the Bush administration's neoconservative identification of Saddam Hussein and Iraq—a *secular* dictator presiding over a *secular* government that had played no direct role in the religiously motivated attacks of 9/11—as the fountainhead of *Islamic* extremism and terror. George Creel, when he was authorized to create the CPI in April 1917, believed that his principal task would be to forge a unified American *war-will* out of a diverse, reluctant, and even skeptical American population. He quickly discovered that the cumulative effects of such events as German atrocities (both real and reported), the U-boat attack on the

Lusitania and other passenger vessels, and the Zimmermann Telegram had already created a high degree of receptiveness to U.S. entry into the war. Similarly, those who managed information in the Bush White House eighty-six years later were gratified to find a public largely receptive to military action. What is more, in 2003, the "free and unbiased press" turned out to be neither. For whatever reasons—overweening fear of "Islamic terror" shared with the average American, a distorted sense of patriotism, a desire for access to government sources (to be "embedded" with the troops), corporate conflicts of interest, or a simple absence of curiosity—the professional skepticism of the epoch of Edward R. Murrow was rarely in evidence among the media of 2003.

What Happened: Inside the Bush White House and Washington's Culture of Deception, written in 2008 by President Bush's former press secretary, Scott McClellan, was stunning not so much because the presidential press secretary accused his former employer of perpetrating deception and disseminating propaganda in a "permanent campaign"—by 2008, a majority of the American people already assumed this was the case—but because McClellan revealed the extent to which the media had been complicit in ratifying the deception and in broadcasting the propaganda by failing to challenge the administration with "the hard questions."[15]

On February 7, 2003, a month before the United States attacked Baghdad and began the Iraq War, Secretary of Defense Donald Rumsfeld held a photo-op "town hall meeting" with an assembly of troops. When one soldier asked him how long a war with Iraq was likely to last, the secretary replied that it "could last, you know, six days, six weeks. I doubt six months." On May 1, 2003, President Bush seemingly validated Rumsfeld's prediction when, in another elaborately orchestrated propaganda event, he landed on the aircraft carrier USS *Abraham Lincoln* in a roaring Lockheed S–3 Viking, as the ship lay off San Diego, having returned from operations in the Persian Gulf. Emerging from the jet in full flight suit, he posed on deck for photographs with pilots and crew members, then, a few hours later, standing before a colorful banner festooning the *Lincoln's* superstructure and proclaiming "Mission Accomplished," he spoke: "Major combat operations in Iraq have ended. In the Battle of Iraq, the United States and our allies have prevailed."

Fast forward more than two years, to the summer of 2005. The Iraq War was still being fought, with no end in sight. By this time, the phrase "mission accomplished" had entered the American popular lexicon as a sarcasm applied to any hopelessly botched endeavor, and every day brought new criticism of a war that more and more Americans believed to have been both unwise and unnecessary. The gulf between evident facts and administration propaganda—the current euphemism for the latter was *spin*—had grown increasingly wider. That season, however, the latest, most pressing criticism directed at the White House did not directly concern Iraq but another fixture of what the president called the "war on terror," the detention center at Guantánamo Bay, Cuba. After Amnesty International had condemned it as "the gulag of our times," a cascade of negative reports issued from a media establishment that was no longer so complacent.

In a *New York Times* story published on April 20, 2008, correspondent David Barstow reported on how the "administration's communications experts [had] responded swiftly" to the negative press in the summer of 2005. "Early one Friday morning, they put a group of retired military officers on one of the jets normally used by Vice President Dick Cheney and flew them to Cuba for a carefully choreographed tour of Guantánamo." As far as the American public was concerned, these men were "'military analysts' . . . whose long service . . . equipped them to give authoritative and unfettered judgments about the most pressing issues of the post-Sept. 11 world." And so they were presented on network radio and television news and issues programs as objective experts "decrying Amnesty International, criticizing calls to close the facility and asserting that all detainees were treated humanely." One analyst, a retired air force general, told CNN that the "impressions that you're getting from the media and from . . . people who have not been here . . . are totally false," and a retired army general working for NBC News as an analyst pointed out on the *Today* show that "There's been over $100 million of new construction. The place is very professionally run."[16]

Barstow's investigative reporting revealed that "hidden behind that appearance of objectivity . . . is a Pentagon information apparatus that has used those analysts in a campaign to generate favorable news coverage of the administration's wartime performance." Moreover, the "effort, which began with the buildup to the Iraq war and continues to this day, has sought to exploit ideological and military allegiances, and also a powerful financial dynamic: Most of the analysts have ties to military contractors vested in the very war policies they are asked to assess on air." Barstow wrote that the Bush administration made "an effort to transform the analysts into a kind of media Trojan horse—an instrument intended to shape terrorism coverage from inside the major TV and radio networks."

The use of prepared or biased "authorities" to shape public perception, sentiment, and opinion may have been especially egregious as practiced by the Bush-era Pentagon, but we know that it was nothing new. Edward L. Bernays would have instantly recognized it as the working of what he had called in 1928 the "invisible government which is the true ruling power of our country."[17]

It is certainly tempting to draw a straight line from Creel and the nation's first ministry of propaganda, the Committee on Public Information, to the administration of George W. Bush (especially to his "spinmeister," presidential advisor Karl Rove) and to the tainted "military analysts" David Barstow exposed. Was George Creel really the father of what Scott McClellan called "Washington's Culture of Deception"? At least one noted scholar, Christopher Sharrett, professor of communications at Seton Hall University, has argued that the work of the Creel Committee constituted a "legacy" that influenced the remarkable transformation of 9/11 by the Bush administration into what he called a "useful incident," a credible pretext for war.[18]

But a "legacy" is not the same as a "straight line." The connection between the Creel Committee and propaganda in the Bush era is at once less direct than a simple line but also far more pervasive. The alumni of the committee, men like the advertising giant James Webb Young of the J. Walter Thompson agency and public relations pioneers Carl Byoir and Edward Bernays, went on to make their professions central to modern American life: the very mechanisms of Bernays's invisible government. The work of the committee not only created and applied the techniques of propaganda to promote and manage a war, it also demonstrated that these techniques could be applied to *any* project of creating, shaping, and managing public opinion, whether to support a war or, on behalf of the American Tobacco Company, to encourage women to smoke cigarettes. The CPI converted the commercial instruments of public relations and advertising into weapons of war, and when the war was over, it returned them to the realm of commerce substantially hardened and keenly sharpened. The apparatus Creel had built was torn down and would not be rebuilt in any substantial form until World War II. When that happened, when propaganda was reenlisted in the government service, it was not built directly on the foundation Creel had laid—Congress demolished that in 1919—but in a cultural, commercial, and political environment he and his operatives had forever transformed. George Creel had made the world safe for propaganda.

If it is an oversimplification to draw a straight line from Creel to Bush, so it is a gross distortion to say that he fathered Washington's "culture of deception." Yet he was certainly an ancestor. Call him, then, the first of a breed rather than the father of that breed.

But even this may do him a grave injustice. George W. Bush's motive for waging war in Iraq has often been compared to Woodrow Wilson's motive for entering World War I. The spur in both cases was ideological rather than existential. Neither Germany nor Iraq attacked the United States; instead, both presidents brought the war to the other nation for the purpose of "making the world safe for democracy" by fighting an enemy "over there" so that we would not be obliged to fight him "over here." For the propagandists of both presidents, the mission was similar: to sell the American people on the urgent necessity of what was—again, in both cases—a war of choice rather than necessity, a war fought from ideological motives on the mere theory that fighting now and in a foreign land would preclude the necessity of fighting later at home.

Where, then, is the difference between "Wilson's man" and the men and women who have served President Bush?

George Creel was a self-admitted "Wilson man." He believed in the president and in the president's war. But he saw his mission as far more than selling the president or his war. He saw his task as creating unity by managing information in a manner that was consistent with Wilson's own idealistic war aims. That is, Creel believed he had to control information to shape popular sentiment without destroying democracy in the process. This made his work especially difficult and demanding, and I freely admit my hope that this book has convincingly shown that, to a remarkable degree, he succeeded. The Committee on Public Information was often controversial. Members of the press were suspicious of it. Republicans in Congress took frequent aim at it. But its existence was never secret, nor was its mission covert or its methods deceptive.

The same cannot be said of an administration that passed off paid political operatives, often in the employ of both the Pentagon and major defense contractors, as unbiased consultants to network news organizations or that lied to its own press secretary so that he could speak those lies to a gullible press. It may or may not be valid to label George Creel and the Creel Committee a necessary evil, but it would be both an error as well as an injustice to call him and what he did simply evil. And it would be even less accurate and more unjust to identify an earnest and honorable, if flawed, believer in democracy as the source of the current "culture of deception." George Creel was better than that. The question is, are we?

The genie of propaganda has been out of the bottle at least since 1917. There is no question of putting it back in now. Our world is mediated by a technology Creel could not have imagined. The Internet and the continually evolving software tools associated with it—aimed at discovering and tracking individual habits of thought, sentiment, belief, opinion, desire, fear, and purchase—have exponentially expanded the potential, the power, and the reach of "managed" information. There is no going back. The issue now is how propaganda, as leveraged by these ever-evolving vehicles, will be used in the years to come. A democratic nation lives and dies by the information its people possess and the beliefs they embrace. Propaganda can be crafted for partisan and other selfish purposes to perpetuate a culture of deception, or it can be employed selflessly for the ethical stewardship of the nation. In great part, the choice between these courses will always depend on the leaders we choose. That choice, in turn, is strongly influenced by what can only be called propaganda, and we are therefore left to contemplate whether self-government is only an illusion and democracy, in any real sense, actually impossible.

Yet if propaganda were truly doomed to a future in which it would always be nothing more than a technologically enhanced amplification of what the Creel Committee produced, information developed and disseminated by a central source, the future of democracy would be bleak indeed. However, the technology that has enhanced both the nature and dissemination of propaganda has also put its tools in many more rather than in fewer hands. If George Creel was the first of a breed, he was also quite possibly the last—the last propagandist who could actually own a monopoly on information. The new tools of technology are powerful indeed, but they are available to us all. In Creel's time and place, the culture of information was a pyramid, with propaganda originating at the top and flowing down in a widening cascade from a single source. At least since the proliferation of the Internet and all that is associated with it beginning in the early 1990s, the culture of information has been collapsing, the pyramid flattening out. In the future, it will increasingly approach the intellectual geometry of a perfect plane, as theorists like Thomas L. Friedman, author of *The World Is Flat,* have argued, and in a flat world, propaganda, as Creel, Bernays, Goebbels, Rove, and George W. Bush have understood it, will finally become impossible because all available information will be available to everyone at all times. In this way, technology, not great thinkers and their great ideas, may create the apotheosis of democracy.

What a gain! And yet we—or, at any rate, the generation that follows us—will also be left to contemplate a substantial loss: How will the masses be moved in a civilization without propaganda? By what means will the leaders lead?

NOTES

PREFACE

1. Edward L. Bernays, *Propaganda* (New York: Horace Liveright, 1928), p. 9.
2. Ibid., p. 27.
3. George Creel, *How We Advertised America* (New York: Harper & Brothers, 1920), p.4.

CHAPTER 1

1. George Creel, *Rebel at Large: Recollections of Fifty Crowded Years* (New York: G. P. Putnam's Sons, 1947), p. 3.
2. Ibid., p. 15.
3. Ibid., p. 10.
4. Ibid., pp. 10, 11.
5. Ibid., p. 17.
6. Ibid., pp. 11–12.
7. Ibid., p. 18.
8. Ibid., pp. 19–20.
9. Ibid., pp. 35–36.
10. Ibid., p. 36.
11. Ibid., pp. 40–41.
12. Ibid., p. 44.
13. Ibid., p. 47.
14. Ibid., pp. 47–48.

CHAPTER 2

1. George Creel, *Rebel at Large: Recollections of Fifty Crowded Years* (New York: G. P. Putnam's Sons, 1947), pp. 61–62.
2. Ibid., p. 71.
3. Ibid., p. 72.
4. Ibid., pp. 72–73.
5. Ibid., p. 74.
6. Charles Ferguson, quoted in ibid., pp. 75–76.

7. Ibid., p. 76.
8. Ibid.
9. Ibid., p. 77.
10. Ibid.
11. Ibid.
12. Ibid. p. 78.
13. Ibid., p. 85.
14. Ibid.
15. Ibid., p. 86.
16. Ibid.
17. Ibid.
18. Ibid., p. 92.
19. *Democratic Central,* "March 17, 1906—Teddy Roosevelt gives 'Muckraker' speech," at www
   .democraticcentral.com/showDiary.do?diaryId=1732. Accessed June 9, 2008.
20. Creel, *Rebel at Large,* p. 95.
21. Ibid., p. 96.
22. Ibid., p. 104.
23. Ibid., pp.104, 105, 106.
24. Ibid., pp. 110–111.
25. Ibid., pp. 116–117, 111.
26. Ibid., p. 113.

CHAPTER 3

1. George Creel, *Rebel at Large: Recollections of Fifty Crowded Years* (New York: G. P. Putnam's
   Sons, 1947), p. 148; Woodrow Wilson, "Address Supporting the League of Nations, Sioux
   Falls, SD, September 8, 1919," in Albert Shaw, ed., *The Messages and Papers of Woodrow Wilson*
   (New York: Review of Reviews Corporation, 1924), vol. 2, p. 822.
2. Creel, *Rebel at Large,* pp. 141, 142.
3. Ibid., p. 142.
4. Ibid., pp. 128, 129–130.
5. For a discussion of the quotation, see "Ivy Lee," *Wikipedia,* http://en.wikipedia.org/wiki/
   Ivy_Lee.
6. Shortly before Ivy's death, the U.S. Congress investigated his public relations work in Nazi
   Germany on behalf of the I. G. Farben conglomerate of chemical firms. I. G. Farben had produced synthetic nitrate for explosives and munitions during World War I, and its subsidiary,
   Degesch, had made Zyklon B, the infamous cyanide compound used in the extermination
   camps. Ivy was charged with no crime, but his reputation was irretrievably tarnished.
7. Sullivan's observation is quoted—and Creel comments on it—in Creel, Rebel at Large, p. 143.
8. Ibid., p. 145–146.
9. Ibid., pp. 146–147.
10. Ibid., p. 147.
11. Quoted in William Roscoe Thayer, *Theodore Roosevelt* (1919), online version published by
    Bartleby.Com, at www.bartleby.com/170/24.html. Accessed June 9, 2008.
12. Alan Axelrod, *Political History of America's Wars* (Washington, D.C.: CQ Press, 2007), p. 358.
13. Creel, *Rebel at Large,* p. 149.
14. Ibid., p. 150.

15. Ibid., p. 151.
16. George Creel, *Wilson and the Issues* (New York: Century Co., 1916), p. 1.
17. Ibid., p. 3.
18. Ibid., pp. 19, 23.
19. Ibid., p. 23.
20. Ibid., pp. 25, 27, 36.
21. Ibid., pp. 63–64.
22. Ibid., p. 64.
23. Ibid., pp. 70–71.

CHAPTER 4

1. *Literary Digest,* 50 (May 22, 1915). pp. 1200–1201.
2. Lane quoted in Byron Farwell, *Over There: The United States in the Great War,* 1917—1918 (New York: W. W. Norton, 1999), p. 34.
3. Quoted in Farwell, *Over There,* p. 34.
4. Ibid., p. 35.
5. Ibid.
6. Woodrow Wilson, "War Message," April 2, 1917, *Historical Documents in United States History,* at www.historicaldocuments.com/WoodrowWilsonsWarMessage.htm. Accessed June 3, 2008.
7. George Creel, *How We Advertised America* (New York: Harper & Brothers, 1920), p. 5.
8. Ibid., pp. 5–6.
9. George Creel, *Rebel at Large: Recollections of Fifty Crowded Years* (New York: G. P. Putnam's Sons, 1947), p. 156.
10. Ibid., p. 157; Creel, *How We Advertised America,* p. 17.
11. Creel, *How We Advertised America,* p. 17.
12. Ibid., p. 18; Creel, *Rebel at Large,* p. 157.
13. Creel, *Rebel at Large,* p. 157.
14. Ibid., p. 158.
15. Ibid.
16. Woodrow Wilson, "Executive Order 2594—Creating Committee on Public Information, April 13th, 1917," at The American Presidency Project, http://www.presidency.ucsb.edu/ws/index.php?pid=75409. Accessed June 9, 2008.
17. FirstWorldWar.com, "Primary Documents: U.S. Espionage Act, 15 June 1917," at www.firstworldwar.com/source/espionageact.htmwords. Accessed June 3, 2008; James R. Mock and Frederic Larson, *Words That Won the War: The Story of the Committee on Public Information 1917–1919* (Princeton, NJ: Princeton University Press, 1939), p. 23.
18. Mock and Larson, *Words That Won the War,* p. 27.
19. *Philadelphia Public Ledger,* Hartford Courant, and The Rocky Mountain News quoted in ibid., p. 32.
20. "Spy Bill Passes," *New York Times,* May 15, 1917, front page.
21. "House Defeats Censorship Law by 184 to 144," *New York Times,* June 1, 1917, front page.
22. FirstWorldWar.com, "Primary Documents: U.S. Espionage Act, 15 June 1917, at www.firstworldwar.com/source/espionageact.htmwords. Accessed June 9, 2008.
23. FirstWorldWar.com, "Primary Documents: U.S. Espionage Act, 7 May 1918, at www.firstworldwar.com/source/espionageact1918.htm. Accessed June 9, 2008.

CHAPTER 5

1. George Creel, *Rebel at Large: Recollections of Fifty Crowded Years* (New York: G. P. Putnam's Sons, 1947), pp. 164, 163.

2. Josephus Daniels, letter to Mock and Larson, quoted in James R. Mock and Frederic Larson, *Words That Won the War: The Story of the Committee on Public Information 1917–1919* (Princeton, NJ: Princeton University Press, 1939), pp. 49–50.

3. Creel, *Rebel at Large*, p. 158; Mock and Larson, *Words That Won the War*, p. 50. Lansing lost "no opportunity to hound me with the petty complaints of a humorless man," Creel later wrote in *Rebel at Large*, p. 158.

4. Robert Lansing, *War Memoirs* (Indianapolis: Bobbs-Merrill, 1935), pp. 322–324; Creel, *Rebel at Large*, p. 160.

5. Josephus Daniels, letter, quoted in Mock and Larson, *Words That Won the War*, p. 50.

6. Mock and Larson, *Words That Won the War*, pp. 49, 48, 49. Although no one—not Daniels, Baker, Wilson, or Lansing—would have denied that the Creel Committee was run by George Creel, Daniels at least wanted to give the impression—whether it was based on fact or not—that the government was out in front of the CPI idea. We do know that Lansing, Baker, and Daniels jointly addressed a letter to President Wilson on April 13, 1917:

   Dear Mr. President:
   Even though the cooperation of the press has been generous and patriotic, there is a steadily developing need for some authoritative agency to assure the publication of all the vital facts of national defense. Premature or ill-advised announcements of policies, plans, and specific activities, whether innocent or otherwise, would constitute a source of danger.
   While there is much that is properly secret in connection with the departments of the government, the total is small compared to the vast amount of information that it is right and proper for the people to have.
   America's great present needs are confidence, enthusiasm, and service, and these needs will not be met completely unless every citizen is given the feeling of partnership that comes with full, frank statements concerning the conduct of the public business.
   It is our opinion that the two functions—censorship and publicity—can be joined in honesty and with profit, and we recommend the creation of a Committee on Public Information. The chairman should be a civilian, preferably some writer of proved courage, ability, and vision, able to gain the understanding cooperation of the press and at the same time rally the authors of the country to a work of service. Other members should be the Secretary of State, the Secretary of War, the Secretary of the Navy, or an officer or officers detailed to the work by them.
   We believe you have undoubted authority to create this Committee on Public Information without waiting for further legislation, and because of the importance of the task, and its pressing necessity, we trust that you will see fit to do so.
   The committee, upon appointment, can proceed to the framing of regulations and the creation of machinery that will safeguard all information of value to an enemy, and at the same time open every department of government to the inspection of the people as far as possible. Such regulations and such machinery will, of course, be submitted for your approval before becoming effective. (Lansing et al., letter to Wilson, quoted in David Culbert, ed., *Film and Propaganda in America: A Documentary History*, vol. 1. *World War I* [Westport, CT: Greenwood Press, 1990], p. 127.)

7. See John Marks, *The Search for the "Manchurian Candidate": The CIA and Mind Control* (New York: McGraw-Hill, 1980).

8. Mock and Larson, *Words That Won the War,* p. 6.

9. Ibid.

10. Creel, *Rebel at Large,* p. 160.

11. George Creel, *How We Advertised America* (New York: Harper & Brothers, 1920), p. 79; Creel, *Rebel at Large,* p. 160; Mock and Larson, *Words That Won the War,* p. 65.

12. Lansing, *War Memoirs,* p. 323.

13. Mock and Larson, *Words That Won the War,* p. 66.

14. Creel, *Rebel at Large,* p. 160; Creel, *How We Advertised America,* p. 19.

15. Creel, *How We Advertised America,* pp. 19, 20.

16. Ibid., p. 21.

17. Ibid., pp. 21–23.

18. Creel, *Rebel at Large,* p. 161.

19. Ibid., p. 162.

20. Mock and Larson, *Words That Won the War,* p. 68.

21. Woodrow Wilson, executive order, quoted in ibid., p. 71.

CHAPTER 6

1. General J. C. Koons, quoted in James R. Mock and Frederic Larson, *Words That Won the War: The Story of the Committee on Public Information 1917–1919* (Princeton, NJ: Princeton University Press, 1939), p. 78.

2. CPI *Official Bulletin,* quoted in ibid., pp. 80–81.

3. "Censor Creel Gives Out Rules For Newspapers," *New York Times,* May 27, 1917.

4. Ibid.

5. Ibid.

6. *New York Times* and *Washington Herald* quoted in Mock and Larson, *Words That Won the War,* p. 79.

7. Josephus Daniels's statement quoted in ibid.

8. "Censor Creel Gives Out Rules For Newspapers."

9. Ibid.; Creel's "Preliminary Statement" is quoted in Mock and Larson, *Words That Won the War,* pp. 82–83.

10. Creel's "regulations" quoted in ibid., p. 84.

11. George Creel, *How We Advertised America* (New York: Harper & Brothers, 1920), p. 71.

12. Ibid., pp. 71–72.

13. Ibid., p. 72.

14. Ibid.

15. Ibid.

16. Ibid.

17. Ibid., pp. 72–73.

18. Ibid. p. 73.

19. Ibid.

20. Ibid., p. 74.

21. Ibid., p. 75.

22. Creel, letter to Hughes, quoted in Mock and Larson, *Words That Won the War,* p. 85.

23. Creel, telegram to editor, *San Francisco Examiner,* quoted in ibid., p. 86.

24. Creel, *How We Advertised America,* pp. 77, 76.

25. Ibid., p. 79.

26. Ibid., p. 78.

27. Mock and Larson, *Words That Won the War,* p. 92.

CHAPTER 7

1. George Creel, *How We Advertised America* (New York: Harper & Brothers, 1920), p. 84.

2. Edward L. Bernays, *Biography of an Idea: Memoirs of Public Relations Counsel Edward L. Bernays* (New York: Simon & Schuster, 1965), p. 54.

3. The critical response to *Damaged Goods* is discussed in Larry Tye, *The Father of Spin: Edward L. Bernays and the Birth of Public Relations* (New York: Owl Books, 1998), p. 8.

4. Reviews and testimonials are quoted in Upton Sinclair, "Press Comments on the Play," in Eugene Brieux, *Damaged Goods: The Great Play "Les Avaries," Novelized with the approval of the author by Upton Sinclair* (reprint ed., Charleston, SC: Bibliobazaar, 2008), pp. 12–16.

5. Ibid.

6. Tye, *Father of Spin,* p. 8. Edward L. Bernays, *Propaganda* (New York: Horace Liveright, 1928), p. 25.

7. Bernays, *Propaganda,* 27.

8. James R. Mock and Frederic Larson, *Words That Won the War: The Story of the Committee on Public Information 1917–1919* (Princeton, NJ: Princeton University Press, 1939), p. 117; Livingston County (Michigan), *Honor Roll of Livingston County, Michigan, U.S.A. 1917, 1918, 1919,* at www.memoriallibrary.com/MI/Livingston/WWI/Home/Four/. Accessed June 9, 2008.

9. Creel quoted in Mock and Larson, *Words That Won the War,* pp. 117–118.

10. Committee on Public Information, *Four-Minute Men Bulletin,* May 22, 1917, n. pg.

11. Ibid.

12. The lantern slide is reproduced in Mock and Larson, *Words That Won the War,* p. 114.

13. Committee on Public Information, *Four-Minute Men Bulletin,* n. pg.

14. Livingston County, *Honor Roll.*

15. Creel quoted in Mock and Larson, *Words That Won the War,* pp. 117–118.

16. Ibid., p. 118.

17. "Full-Blooded Sioux Acts as Four-Minute Man," Committee on Public Information, *Four Minute Men Bulletin,* May 22, 1917, n. pg.

18. "Yiddish-Speaking Four Minute Men Reach Jewish Section of New York/Organized Under Rabbi Robinson to Carry Government Messages Into Jewish Theaters and Playhouses/Now Planning to Send Yiddish Speakers Into Shops Where Jewish People Are Largely Employed," Committee on Public Information, *Four-Minute Men Bulletin,* May 22, 1917, n. pg.

19. Mock and Larson, *Words That Won the War,* p. 118.

20. Creel's account of the attacks leveled against him is given in George Creel, *Rebel at Large: Recollections of Fifty Crowded Years* (New York: G. P. Putnam's Sons, 1947), pp. 186–192.

21. Ibid., p. 187.

22. Ibid., p. 193.

23. Creel, *How We Advertised America,* pp. 7, 13.

24. *Four-Minute Men Bulletin,* November 3, 1917, and *Four-Minute Men Bulletin,* January 2, 1918, quoted in Mock and Larson, *Words That Won the War,* pp. 122–123; "Exponent of Violence Not a Four-Minute Man," Committee on Public Information, *Four-Minute Men Bulletin,* May 22, 1917, n. pg.

25. Mock and Larson, *Words That Won the War,* pp. 120–121.

26. *Four Minute Men Bulletin,* January 2, 1918, quoted in ibid., pp. 123–124.

27. Liberty Loan statistics cited in Walton Rawls, *Wake Up, America! World War I and the American Poster* (New York: Abbeville Press, 1917), pp. 195–234.

CHAPTER 8

1. George Creel, *How We Advertised America* (New York: Harper & Brothers, 1920), p. 139.

2. Fairfax Davis Downey, *Portrait of an Era as Drawn by C. D. Gibson: A Biography* (New York: Charles Scribner's Sons, 1936), p. 156.

3. "C. D. Gibson's Committee for Patriotic Posters," *New York Times,* January 20, 1918. The complete list of Division of Pictorial Publicity senior personnel is given in Creel, *How We Advertised America,* p. 134: associate chairmen—Herbert Adams, E. H. Blashfield, Ralph Clarkson, Cass Gilbert, Oliver D. Grover, Francis Jones, Arthur F. Matthews, Joseph Pennell, Edmond Tarbell, and Douglas Volk; executive committee—F. G. Cooper, N. Pousette-Dart, I. Doskow, F. E. Dayton, C. B. Falls, Albert E. Gallatin, Ray Greenleaf, Malvina Hoffman, W. A. Rogers, Henry Reuterdahl, H. Scott Train, H. D. Welsh, J. Thompson Willing, H. T. Webster, Walter Whitehead, and Jack Sheridan; departmental captains—C. B. Falls, H. T. Webster, Walter Whitehead, Ray Greenleaf, I. Doskow, N. Pousette-Dart, and H. Scott Train. Cass Gilbert is quoted in Walton Rawls, *Wake Up, America! World War I and the American Poster* (New York: Abbeville Press, 1988), p. 150.

4. Creel, *How We Advertised America,* p. 133.

5. Pennell quoted in Rawls, *Wake Up, America!* p. 14.

6. Pennell quoted in ibid; Creel, *How We Advertised America,* pp. 133–134.

7. Creel, *How We Advertised America,* p. 135.

8. Ibid.; "C. D. Gibson's Committee for Patriotic Posters," *New York Times,* January 20, 1918.

9. "C. D. Gibson's Committee for Patriotic Posters," *New York Times,* January 20, 1918.

10. Reproduced in Rawls, *Wake Up, America!* p. 197.

11. "New York Shelled on 'Movie' Screen," *New York Times,* August 7, 1915.

12. *Exhibitor's Trade Review* interview quoted in James R. Mock and Frederick Larson, *Words That Won the War: The Story of the Committee on Public Information, 1917–1919* (Princeton, N.J.: Princeton University Press, 1939), p. 132.

13. Ibid., p. 134.

14. Creel quoted in ibid., p. 136.

15. Creel quoted in ibid., p. 142.

16. Ibid., p. 142.

17. See John Davis Collins, "The Tragic Odyssey of Robert Goldstein," at www.angelfire.com /bc/RPPS/revolution_movies/golstn.htm. Accessed June 9, 2008. In the end, Goldstein's sentence was commuted after he had served three years. With his company having folded in bankruptcy, he went to Europe and tried, without success, to restart his career as a producer. Stranded in Germany in 1935, penniless, unable even to scrape together the nine-dollar fee required to renew his U.S. passport, Goldstein, a Jew, vanished—whether from history or the face of the earth is uncertain. Some believe he perished in the Holocaust. Others hold that he was deported by the German government before World War II and died in complete obscurity in New York City.

18. Creel, *How We Advertised America,* p. 142.

CHAPTER 9

1. See George Creel, *How We Advertised America* (New York: Harper & Brothers, 1920), pp. 3–15; and James R. Mock and Frederic Larson, *Words That Won the War: The Story of the Committee on Public Information 1917–1919* (Princeton, NJ: Princeton University Press, 1939), p. 159.
2. Guy Stanton Ford, *Essays in American History, Dedicated to Frederick Jackson Turner* (New York: Henry Holt, 1910); Ford's account of his recruitment into the CPI is quoted in Mock and Larson, *Words That Won the War,* pp. 158–159.
3. Mock and Larson, *Words That Won the War,* p. 160.
4. Ibid., p. 161.
5. Ibid., pp. 161–162.
6. The survey of the division's publications in this and the next several paragraphs is based on ibid., pp. 163–164. A nearly complete list of CPI publications is found in Creel, *How We Advertised America,* pp. 455–459.
7. John S. P. Tatlock, *Why America Fights Germany,* War Information Series, no.15 (Washington, DC: CPI, 1918), excerpted in Mock and Larson, *Words That Won the War,* pp. 166–167.
8. George F. Kennan, "The Sisson Documents," *Journal of Modern History* 28 (June 1956): 130–154.
9. The Loyalty Leaflets are described in Mock and Larson, *Words That Won the War,* p. 168.
10. Committee on Public Information, *The Kaiserite in America: One Hundred and One German Lies* (Washington, DC: Government Printing Office, 1918), excerpted in Mock and Larson, *Words That Won the War,* p. 173.
11. Ibid., pp. 176–177.
12. Gustavus Myers, *The German Myth: The Falsity of Germany's "Social Progress" Claims* (New York: Boni and Liveright, 1918).
13. The Henry A. Wise Wood, letter of April 30, 1918, reproduced in Mock and Larson, *Words That Won the War,* pp. 197–198.
14. Creel is quoted in ibid., p. 210; Creel, letter to the National Americanization Committee, January 14, 1918, reproduced in ibid., pp. 210–211; Creel's exchanges with Professor Clark and with F. L. Collins are reported and quoted in ibid., pp. 211–212.
15. The letter is excerpted in ibid., p. 203.

CHAPTER 10

1. The account of the Prager affair given here is drawn from Frederick C. Luebke, *Bonds of Loyalty: German-Americans and World War I* (DeKalb: Northern Illinois University Press, 1974), and from: "Extra—Illinoisan Lynched for Disloyalty," *Chicago Daily Tribune,* April 5, 1918; "German Enemy of U.S. Hanged by Mob/St. Louis Collinsville Man Killed for Abusing Wilson," *St. Louis Globe-Democrat,* April 5, 1918; "German Is Lynched by an Illinois Mob," *New York Times,* April 5, 1918; "Jury Finds Prager Defendants Not Guilty and Others Are Free," *Edwardsville Intelligenser,* June 18, 1918; "Prager Lynchers Quickly Acquitted," *New York Times,* June 2, 1918. For a discussion of the United Mine Workers' role in the lynching, see E. A. Schwartz, "The Lynching of Robert Prager, the United Mine Workers, and the Problems of Patriotism in 1918," *Journal of the Illinois State Historical Society* (Winter 2003), online at http://findarticles.com/p/articles/mi_qa3945/is_200301/ai_n9170046. Accessed June 8, 2008.
2. George Creel, *How We Advertised America* (New York: Harper & Brothers, 1920), p. 184.

3. Ibid., p. 169.

4. Ibid., p. 167.

5. Ibid., p. 184.

6. L. B. Foley, letter to Creel quoted in James R. Mock and Frederic Larson, *Words That Won the War: The Story of the Committee on Public Information 1917–1919* (Princeton, NJ: Princeton University Press, 1939), p. 214.

7. On March 11, 2003, Representatives Robert W. Ney (Republican, Ohio) and Walter B. Jones, Jr. (Republican, North Carolina) proposed on the floor of the House that all references to French fries and French toast on the menus of the cafeterias and snack bars serving the House of Representatives should be removed. As chairman of the Committee on House Administration, Ney had the authority to order House restaurants to rename French fries "freedom fries" and French toast "freedom toast." This administrative action did not require a House resolution. While the action was widely mocked, many eating establishments across the country followed the example of the House.

8. W. H. Lamar, letter to Julius Koettgen (January 29, 1918), quoted in ibid., pp. 215–216.

9. Stephen J. Frese, "Divided by a Common Language: The Babel Proclamation and Its Influence in Iowa History," *The History Teacher* 39:1 (November 2005), pp. 59–88. Also see Nancy Derr, "The Babel Proclamation," *The Palimpsest* 60, no. 4 (July/August 1979), pp. 98–115. The "Babel Proclamation" is officially "Governor's Proclamation, 23 May 1918," and is filed in the Council of Defense Collection, Box 46, "File: State Organizations. Gov. Harding, Personal. Feb. 1918–July 1918. File 13," State Historical Library, Des Moines, Iowa.

10. Like the Austrian-born, American-raised Edward L. Bernays, Koettgen had to fight to prove his loyalty before government officials would accept his offer of service to the CPI. Koettgen was a British subject—a citizen of an Allied nation—but he had been born in Germany and he had even translated one of the books that ended up on the War Department's "Index Expurgatorius." The Department of Justice required Koettgen to register as an alien enemy. "The registration, however, should not be taken as a reflection upon your good intentions or your loyalty to the United States," the department's official letter offered. (Mock and Larson, *Words That Won the War,* p. 217.)

11. Mock and Larson, *Words That Won the War,* p. 218.

12. Creel, *How We Advertised America,* pp. 191–192.

13. Mock and Larson, *Words That Won the War,* p. 228.

CHAPTER 11

1. See George Creel, *How We Advertised America* (New York: Harper & Brothers, 1920), p. 3, and James R. Mock and Frederic Larson, *Words That Won the War: The Story of the Committee on Public Information 1917–1919* (Princeton, NJ: Princeton University Press, 1939), p. 235.

2. Creel, *How We Advertised America,* p. 200.

3. Hugh Gibson quoted in Mock and Larson, *Words That Won the War,* p. 253.

4. Mock and Larson, *Words That Won the War,* pp. 255–256.

5. James Keeley, report to Creel (July 1918), quoted in ibid., pp. 258–259.

6. Mock and Larson, *Words That Won the War,* p. 267.

7. Frank J. Marion, letter to Creel (March 18, 1918), quoted in ibid., pp. 267–268.

8. Frank J. Marion, letter to Creel (October 11, 1918), quoted in ibid., p. 274.

9. Frank J. Marion, letter to Edgar Sisson (October 25, 1918), quoted in ibid., p. 274.

10. Edwin Bjorkman, letter to Eric H. Palmer (November 9, 1918), quoted in ibid., p. 280.

11. Guy Croswell Smith, letter to Edgar Sisson (August 16, 1918), quoted in ibid.

12. Robert H. Murray, letter to Creel (February 27, 1918), quoted in ibid., pp. 323–324.

13. Robert H. Murray, "final report" to Creel, quoted in ibid., p. 327.

14. Creel, letter of introduction to Russian press (June 18, 1917), quoted in ibid., pp. 301–302.

15. Creel, cable to Arthur Bullard (November 9, 1917), quoted in ibid., pp. 303–304.

16. Arthur Bullard, cable to Creel (November 16, 1917), quoted in ibid., p. 304.

17. Creel, cable to Edgar Sisson (December 2, 1917), quoted in ibid.

18. Arthur Bullard, cable to Creel (December 30, 1917), quoted in ibid., p. 305.

19. Edgar Sisson, *One Hundred Red Days: A Personal Chronicle of the Bolshevik Revolution* (New Haven, CT: Yale University Press,1931), p. 65.

20. A *New York Times* story ("Historians Pass on Sisson Documents") published on November 12, 1918—the day after the armistice—announced that a "Special Committee on the Genuine-ness of the Documents of the National Board for Historical Service" had not vouched for the authenticity of the Sisson Documents but "finds no internal evidence of forgery in the main bulk of them." The special committee concluded that "we have no hesitation in declaring that we see no reason to doubt the genuineness or authenticity of these fifty-three documents." Still, critics noted that most of the so-called "Sisson Documents" had actually been in Allied or American hands "long before they reached Mr. Sisson, but that no use had been made of them because of doubt of their genuineness." Critics asserted that they had been released to the British press before Sisson brought them to the CPI, and all of the British newspapers had re-fused to publish them. Also see "Documents Prove Lenine and Trotzky Hired by Germans" *New York Times,* September 15, 1918; "Sisson Book Says Germans Paid Reds," *New York Times,* April 17, 1931; and George F. Kennan, "The Sisson Documents," *Journal of Modern History* 28 (June 1956): 130–154. Sisson's full report on the documents is reproduced in the appendix to his *One Hundred Red Days.*

21. Charles Edward Russell, letter to Creel (October 29, 1917), quoted in Mock and Larson, *Words That Won the War,* p. 286.

22. Wilson's remarks are quoted in ibid., pp. 295–296; also see "Wilson to be Patron," *New York Times,* May 13, 1918.

23. A. M. Brace quoted in Mock and Larson, *Words That Won the War,* p. 296.

24. Ibid., p. 288.

CHAPTER 12

1. George Creel, *How We Advertised America* (New York: Harper & Brothers, 1920), pp. 401–402.

2. Ibid., pp. 402–403.

3. Ibid., p. 404; George Creel, *Rebel at Large: Recollections of Fifty Crowded Years* (New York: G. P. Putnam's Sons, 1947), p. 205.

4. Creel, *How We Advertised America,* p. 409.

5. Creel, *Rebel at Large,* pp. 205, 209; Creel, *How We Advertised America,* pp. 426, 415–416.

6. Creel, *Rebel at Large,* p. 214.

7. Creel, *How We Advertised America,* pp. 427–434.

8. Ibid., pp. 51–69, 433–434.

9. George Creel, *Rebel at Large,* p. 160.

10. Edward L. Bernays, *Propaganda* (New York: Horace Liveright, 1928), pp. 27–28. Unquestion-ably, the most controversial campaign Bernays mounted came after World War I, when he was

hired by the president of the American Tobacco Company to persuade American women to take up smoking cigarettes. The story is told in Alan Axelrod, *Profiles in Folly: History's Worst Decisions and Why They Went Wrong* (New York: Sterling, 2008), pp. 88–100.

11. Adolf Hitler, *Mein Kampf* (1925), vol. 1., ch. 6 in Project Gutenberg online edition, http://gutenberg.net.au/ebooks02/0200601.txt. Accessed June 9, 2008.

12. Larry Tye, *The Father of Spin: Edward L. Bernays and the Birth of Public Relations* (New York: Owl Books, 1998), p. 111. Also see "CPI," *Time,* October 16, 1939, a review of Mock and Larson's *Words That Won the War:*

> George Creel, the genius of the CPI . . . was no Goebbels, but a Wilsonian from way back. . . . Like Wilson, he discovered the basic dilemma of a democracy at war: how to suppress democracy in the name of democracy. . . . If the U.S. gets into World War II, would the CPI be revived? Authors Mock & Larson's answer: Yes. Better the CPI, say they, "as buffer between military dictatorship and civil life," than censorship of the British and French variety. "If another war should come to this country," say the authors, "no American would need to read the story of the CPI. He would relive it."

And see too: "We Need No Goebbels," *Time,* June 15, 1942:

> Harvard's Professor of Government Carl Joachim Friedrich . . . in *Common Sense* last week ripped into the whole idea of "indoctrinating" people with hatred or anything else. Wrote Dr. Friedrich, developing a theme he expressed last year as "losing the war by propaganda": "We need no Goebbels. . . . Can the methods of a Goebbels fashion the mind of a new democracy? One consideration that suggests a ministry of propaganda to its proponents is the fact that we had a Committee on Public Information in the last war. . . . The Creel Committee, as it was known, has been studied thoroughly. But from the learned battle emerges only one conclusion: this country would have won the war, anyhow. . . . The great formulae of the Creel Committee, like 'making the world safe for Democracy,' became a mockery soon after the armistice. The man at the breakfast table felt that he had been duped. . . . It was then that the little man began to shout, 'Back to normalcy.' The violence of the reaction was stunning; it lost us the peace."

13. S. F. Tomajczyk, "Psychological Operations (PSYOP)," in *Dictionary of the Modern United States Military* (Jefferson, N.C.: McFarland, 1996), p. 444.

14. The 1959 novel by Richard Condon was twice adapted for the screen, faithfully in 1962 and much more loosely in 2004. In its original novel form, *The Manchurian Candidate* garnered the distinction of being banned throughout the Communist bloc and also condemned by the American Legion.

15. See Scott McClellan, *What Happened: Inside the Bush White House and Washington's Culture of Deception* (New York: Public Affairs, 2008). Although McClellan's most explosive charges concerning White House propaganda relate to the rationale for going to war with Iraq, his most penetrating insight is his discussion of the "permanent campaign," a term borrowed from Norman J. Ornstein and Thomas E. Mann (*The Permanent Campaign,* Washington, DC: American Enterprise Institute Press, 2000) to describe government as an "offshoot of campaigning rather than the other way around." In the permanent campaign, the "sources of public approval" are "manipulated . . . using such tools as the news media, political blogs, popular web

sites, paid advertising, talk radio, local organizations, and propaganda disseminated by interest groups to shape narratives to one's advantage" (McClellan, p. 64). The "permanent campaign," effectively Creel-style propaganda on steroids, both recruits and engulfs what should be a disinterested press. The deceptive use of paid—as it were, tainted—military analysts exposed by David Barstow ("Behind TV Analysts, Pentagon's Hidden Hand," *New York Times*, April 20, 2008) is a case in point of the "permanent campaign" and the co-option of the media.

16.   The quoted material here and in the next two paragraphs is from Barstow, "Behind TV Analysts, Pentagon's Hidden Hand."

17.   Edward L. Bernays, *Propaganda* (New York: Horace Liveright, 1928), p. 9.

18.   Christopher Sharrett, "9/11, The Useful Incident, and the Legacy of the Creel Committee," *Cinema Journal* 43, no. 4 (Summer 2004): 125–131.

INDEX